MINNESOTA

MAINE

WISCONSIN

VT. N.H.

MICHIGAN

NEW YORK

MASS.

CONN. RI.

Birthplace of Donna Reed

Birthplace of Mamie Eisenhower

Marshalltown

Henry Ostermann Fatal Crash

HEAD-QUARTERS L

Franklin Grove

AURORA L SHELTER

Notre Dame University

PENNSYLVANIA

Newark

Jersey City

New York City

Pro Football Hall of Fame

Princeton University

TIMES SQUARE

Boone

Clinton

De Kalb

Aurora

Joliet

Merriam

Churubusco

STURGIS HOUSE

Trenton

Denison

DIXON

South Bend

Van Wert

Canton

East Liverpool

Pittsburgh

Bedford

Amish Country

York

The Blob

MAKES MAKES

Omaha

TAYLOR'S

Smith Brothers General Store

RIP

Uncle Sam's Grave

Fort Wayne

BALYEAT'S chicken

Chester

Newell

Gettysburg Battlefield

Downington

Philadelphia

LINCOLN

Made-Rite

Lothson's Karry-out Chicken

Cindy's Diner

Mansfield

Homer Laughlin China Company

Westinghouse Bridge

Elaine's Shoe House

IOWA

ILLINOIS

INDIANA

OHIO

WEST VIRGINIA

VIRGINIA

MISSOURI RIVER

MISSOURI

KENTUCKY

NORTH CAROLINA

MISSISSIPPI RIVER

TENNESSEE

ARKANSAS

SOUTH CAROLINA

GEORGIA

ALABAMA

Map by David Cain

The

LINCOLN HIGHWAY

Coast to Coast from Times Square to the Golden Gate

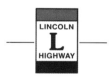

MICHAEL WALLIS

and

MICHAEL S. WILLIAMSON

W. W. NORTON & COMPANY

NEW YORK · LONDON

For information about permission to reproduce selections from
this book, write to Permissions, W. W. Norton & Company, Inc.,
500 Fifth Avenue, New York, NY 10010

For information about special discounts on bulk purchases, please contact
W. W. Norton Special Sales at specialsales@wwnorton.com or 800-233-4830

Excerpt from "Joliet" in *Cornhuskers* by Carl Sandburg,
copyright © 1918 by Holt, Rinehart and Winston and renewed 1946
by Carl Sandburg, reprinted by permission of Harcourt, Inc.

MANUFACTURING BY R. R. DONNELLEY
BOOK DESIGN BY JUDITH STAGNITTO ABBATE / ABBATE DESIGN
PRODUCTION MANAGER: ANNA OLER

Library of Congress Cataloging-in-Publication Data
    Wallis, Michael.
The Lincoln Highway: coast to coast from Times Square to the
Golden Gate / Michael Wallis and Michael S. Williamson.
        p. cm.
    Includes bibliographical references.
    ISBN 978-0-393-05938-0 (hardcover)
    1. Lincoln Highway—History. 2. Automobile travel—United States.
3. United States—Description and travel. 4. Lincoln Highway—
Pictorial works. I. Williamson, Michael, 1957– II. Title.
    HE356.L7W26 2007
    388.1'2209373—dc22
                                                        2007006025

W. W. Norton & Company. Inc.
500 Fifth Avenue, New York, N.Y. 10110
www.wwnorton.com

W. W. Norton & Company Ltd.
Castle House, 75/76 Wells Street,
London W1T 3QT

1 2 3 4 5 6 7 8 9 0

BT 6/22/07

TO ANNE GARRETT,

A DAUGHTER OF THE ROAD

CONTENTS

The Palisades, just west of Green River, WY.

INTRODUCTION

Mister Lincoln's Highway

Nothing is predictable about a trip down the Lincoln Highway. This is true whether travelers drive the 3,000-plus miles from Times Square to the Golden Gate Bridge or whether they make the journey eastbound. It is also true even if

a traveler only goes halfway or just cruises through part of one of the thirteen states the historic highway touches. The venerable Lincoln promises the quintessential road trip for all those willing to steer clear of the banal and the humdrum.

The Lincoln is a route for travelers, not for tourists. Tourists flock to the franchise eateries and the chain motels because they know what to expect. They won't take a chance, even if it might lead them to a memorable place or a person they will never find again. Tourists

THE LINCOLN HIGHWAY IS A TEXACO TRAIL

have a tendency to gawk at history and culture from afar. They do not wish to get too close or take risks. Interstate highways and turnpikes are their made-to-fit courses of choice.

Travelers, on the other hand, are more apt to enjoy a cruise on the Lincoln Highway. People who hanker for the hidden places off the well-beaten tourist path will invariably find this remarkable highway much to their liking.

These travelers have come to learn that the interstates, the turnpikes, the superslabs are straight roads. Long

RIGHT *Cover of* Motoring with a Kodak, *1910.*

BELOW *The front page of the automobile section of the* San Francisco Examiner *on June 20, 1915, declared, "Lincoln Highway of Vast Importance to Entire United States."*

San Francisco Examiner

Automobile Section

LINCOLN HIGHWAY OF VAST IMPORTANCE TO ENTIRE UNIT

Man Who Developed Idea Is Enthusiastic After Having Traversed Road Across Continent From

Henry B. Joy, at Ferry Building, finishing last lap of trip from New York over the Lincoln Highway.

HENRY B. JOY

before the Lincoln Highway came into being, the renowned English artist and poet William Blake best summed up these kinds of roads when he wrote: "Improvement makes straight roads; but the crooked roads without improvement are roads of genius."

The Lincoln Highway is such a road. It is a crooked path—curving and bent, even sometimes warped—but it is also a road that reflects the glorious diversity, the multifaceted heritage, indeed the exceptional genius of what America was and what it promises to be.

It is so fitting that this historic road was named in honor of Abraham Lincoln, the sixteenth president of the United States. Lincoln, who during the course of his life resided in Indiana and Illinois—two future Lincoln Highway states—is obviously best remembered as a masterful political figure who guided the nation through the ravages of the Civil War. Yet in his earlier life, before he took up the practice of law, Lincoln also was a self-taught surveyor for three years in Sangamon County, Illinois.

Young Mister Lincoln performed many surveys of private properties and municipal developments, but some of his most interesting efforts involved the new roads on which he worked. One of the projects was a twenty-seven-mile road north of Springfield, which earned the gangly surveyor $28.75 for his services. It was not a straight road because Lincoln skirted farm fields and other landmarks and cleverly made sure that the road went right through the heart of his adopted hometown of New Salem.

A few years later, as a lawyer in Springfield, Lincoln rode far and wide on the crude roads and trails of mid-nineteenth-century America. He represented several landowners fighting the creation of straight-line roads that threatened the valuation and integrity of their acreage. With Lincoln's legal aid, the plaintiffs were able to save their lands by having the county road relocated along the outskirts of their properties.

Not that the future president was against the coming of the roads, especially improved ones. He knew the problems that farmers, settlers, and travelers faced while moving through the hardscrabble countryside. While still a political novice in the early 1830s, Lincoln spelled out his thoughts in an early platform speech when he announced: "The poorest and most thinly populated countries would be greatly benefited by the opening of good roads, and in the clearing of navigable streams."

More than eighty years later, just such a highway would be born. On September 12, 1912, Carl G. Fisher, a prominent Indiana business leader and the founder of the Indianapolis Motor Speedway, conceived the idea of connecting a "hard-surfaced, improved highway" from the Atlantic to the Pacific. Calling his brainchild "The Coast-to-Coast Rock Highway," Fisher hoped that he would find financial support from leaders of the automotive industry to build the first transcontinental automobile route.

Later that same year, Henry B. Joy, president of Packard Motor Car Company, proposed to Fisher

that the coast-to-coast highway serve as a memorial to the nation's beloved Abraham Lincoln. On July 1, 1913, the Lincoln Highway Association was officially organized. The route was made public on September 14, 1913, and was dedicated on October 31, 1913, when bonfires, speeches, fireworks, parades, and street dances were held in hundreds of cities and towns in all thirteen states along the route.

As grand as these celebrations were, they would not last long. Although numerous guidebooks and tourist publications would continue to proclaim the virtues of this once-newfangled highway well into the 1920s, the handwriting was already on the wall and the nation's named roadways would be converted to numbered highways by the end of the decade. On September 1, 1928, the last major promotional activity on the Lincoln Highway occurred. On that date, thousands of Boy Scouts placed approximately 3,000 concrete markers at sites along the route.

Although the Lincoln Highway Association eventually disbanded and

BELOW

Ad from the 1916 Lincoln Highway Guide boasting that Bowser "will supply the life blood of your automobile at every stopping point on the Lincoln Highway."

Tips for travelers on "The Main Street of the Nation," 1941.

new highway signs with numbers were posted in all the states between the terminal cities, the Lincoln Highway faded from national consciousness but did not die. People who lived along this corridor of concrete, asphalt, and dirt recognized that their very existence depended on the road's perpetuation. And by the 1980s, a new generation of travelers was born. They learned—often with great delight and wonder—that this so-called relic of America's past was worth rediscovery.

Thus the Lincoln Highway Association was reborn, grassroots preservation efforts were launched, and important surviving stretches of the original Lincoln Highway and many sites on the path were saved for future generations. The various incarnations of the old road are just as crooked as ever. And as this revival continues to take hold, the Lincoln Highway is becoming as much a state of mind as it remains a road of genius.

—MICHAEL WALLIS
Tulsa, Oklahoma
September 2006

THE COSTLIEST MEMORIAL EVER PLANNED---
The Great Lincoln Highway

The Total Length of This Road Is 3,384 Miles---Only 200 Longer Than the Shortest Coast-to-Coast Railroad and 14 Miles Longer Than the Telephone Line

LINCOLN HIGHWAY TO NEW YORK 3,384 MILES

Chapter One

NEW YORK

High noon in Times Square, "New York, New York," as the song proclaims, and every sense is on alert. The aromas of fancy cologne, cut flowers, and grilled shish kabob merge with car exhaust and reeking garbage to create a scent distinctive to

Gotham. Automobile engines rev, tires squeal, trucks grumble, and taxi horns jolt the pedestrians—a few even in "vagabond shoes." In this city that actually boasts of its insomnia, Times Square is the essence of New York. It is a city perpetually in a hurry—hungover, brash, sweating like a stevedore, and constantly in motion.

Enormous lighted signs and bands of candy-colored neon, as if blinking to a disco beat, cling to soaring glass towers, not even waiting for nightfall to flash their messages. Out-of-towners,

Times Building, New York City.

instantly recognizable, are the ones with their mouths slightly ajar, actually *waiting* for traffic lights to change at a crosswalk. Sidewalks are clogged with gawking tourists armed with cameras and maps, and sailors prowling midtown in their whites. Barking vendors, theatergoers hunting bargain tickets, street portrait artists, and leggy, wannabe models join the fray, as do hapless souls with wan stares who effortlessly fade into the city's mayhem.

LEFT

Vintage postcard of the Times Building, New York City.

About some places it is said that time stands still. Times Square is not one of those places. It is New York's rumpus room. It is, as it has often been described, the crossroads of the world. Time does indeed start here. So does the beginning of a road trip. Ahead are more than 3,300 miles of macadam, pavement, and even a few dirt roads constituting the Lincoln Highway, which cuts through four time zones and thirteen states.

The Lincoln Highway runs east and west. It begins or ends in New York City, depending on the direction of travel. The same can be said for San Francisco, the highway's anchor city in the west. Open-road travelers with pioneer ties to the age of Manifest Destiny tend to look westward and often begin their cross-country trek in the east. It really doesn't matter. The journey itself—the experiences and discoveries along the way—is what's really important, not the destination. The act of "getting there" is what any road trip is all about. Otherwise there's no sense leaving.

Today's travelers soon discover that of the thirteen states the highway touches, New York has the smallest segment. There is not quite one mile of the Lincoln Highway in all of New York, but it is more than enough to jump-start a journey on America's first transcontinental artery. Starting at Times Square, the original route of the Lincoln extended west along 42nd Street until travelers reached the Hudson River, where the Weehawken Ferry carried them to the New Jersey shore.

If anything, the Times Square terminus always was and still is completely ceremonial. Yet the forward-thinkers who formed the Lincoln Highway Association in 1913 already knew, even before the exact routing across the nation was finalized, that the highway's eastern end would have to be in New York. They figured that to provide cachet for a project as ambitious as America's first cross-country highway, the starting point had to be particularly significant. Times Square, already beginning to be regarded as a confluence of world culture, became that perfect symbol.

The area that ultimately became Times Square was well-trod ground long before Peter Minuit and his Dutch colonists made their celebrated deal with the Lenape Indians in 1626 and purchased the island of Manhattan for the equivalent of $24. Tribal people had already developed fields and campsites all along an extensive network of trails, including one that ran the length of the island.

Many years later, the British—who made Manhattan their headquarters during the Revolutionary War—dubbed a deserted Indian site near the well-worn trail Long Acre, the name of London's carriage district. In 1776, when American forces marched up the old Indian trail, they made a brief stand against the British troops at Long Acre before hastily retreating to the high ground that is today's Central Park.

As New York pushed northward from lower Manhattan and evolved into a nineteenth-century metropolis, Long Acre eventually became Long Acre Square, a name that stuck throughout the 1800s and into the early twentieth century. Then *New York Times* publisher Adolph S. Ochs moved his newspaper headquarters into a new twenty-five-story tower in the middle of Long Acre Square, at the convergence of 42nd Street, Broadway, and Seventh Avenue. Once a center for livery stables and harnessmakers, the area was in rapid decline until Ochs persuaded the powers that be to build a station there for the first underground line of the subway system. This move was destined to make the district a major commercial and cultural center.

To mark the official opening of the Times Building on New Year's Eve, 1904, Ochs hosted a daylong street party that culminated with a lavish fireworks display. The event proved so successful that New Yorkers no longer rang in the New Year at City Hall but gathered instead at Times Square. Within a few years, the increasing throngs and the danger of fireworks prompted Ochs to change the event. Instead of pyrotechnics, an illuminated glass ball weighing more than four hundred pounds was lowered from the flagpole on top of the tower at the stroke of midnight to signal the birth of the new year.

On April 8, 1904, Mayor George B. McClellan, Jr.—the namesake son of Abraham Lincoln's favorite Civil War general—officiated at the renaming ceremony, and Times Square entered the national consciousness.

From the start, Times Square had its detractors. An obvious critic was the *New York Herald*, a rival newspaper headquartered just to the south on 34th Street in Herald Square, at the intersection of Broadway

LEFT

A ceremonial dip in the Atlantic Ocean at Brighton Beach before a 1914 cross-country promotional trip for the Saxon Motor Car Company. Note the Lincoln Highway emblem on the car door.

THE HOUSE OF HOSPITALITY

Hotel LINCOLN ~ NEW YORK CITY

RIGHT *The Hotel Lincoln on 45th Street in New York City was built in 1928 during Times Square's hotel boom. The building now houses the Milford Plaza Hotel.*

and Sixth Avenue. "The old name is a good one," objected a 1904 *Herald* editorial. "The new name is awkward because of the letter 's' doubled in the middle of it, it cannot be properly pronounced without an effort, and even then it is not pleasing to the ear."

Apparently no one agreed. Folks could pronounce the name just fine, and it stuck even after the *Times* outgrew its lofty tower and moved slightly north in 1913, the same year the Lincoln Highway was made official. Within a decade, Times Square became the busiest subway-station complex in the city and endured several incarnations— much like the venerable highway it anchors in the east.

Along with its new name, Times Square earned a reputation that was both dazzling and notorious. Before World War I and through the Roaring Twenties and beyond, it was the nation's entertainment hub, hosting the finest theaters in the city. Even during the years of Prohibition, great crowds flocked to the area to take in the shows and music halls, dine at popular restaurants, stay in fancy hotels, and bask in the glow of lights so bright that the stretch of Broadway through Times Square was nicknamed "The Great White Way." In 1930, the Times Square area housed twenty high-rise hotels.

Yet even during those glory days, Times Square also was known as a destination for carnal pleasures. Sex and vice were big draws as far back as the late 1800s, when many brothels began to move uptown and soon lined the streets. One block came to be called "Soubrette Row," after the coquettish French prostitutes operating there who were said to be willing to do things the American ladies were not willing to do—if the price was right. Harlots from a range of backgrounds, including some off-duty showgirls (or "chorines," as they were then called), worked the square, parading up and down 42nd Street and Broadway in broad daylight. Clergy from nearby churches complained that the painted ladies brazenly solicited favors from male churchgoers following Sunday services. Beat cops sometimes harassed, if not busted, the prostitutes but rarely bothered the "sporting men."

In 1909, there was a short-lived campaign to instill civic pride and "confound mudslingers," as the *New York Times* put it. The newspaper went on to explain that toward that end, a fifty-foot-tall plaster statue of a woman—who became known as "Purity"—was to be erected in Times Square as a symbol of the city. The snow-white figure "of majestic size and mien, somewhat angry and even disgusted at the slander and unjust fault-finding she has been objected to," stood for just two months in the triangular traffic island at Times Square before workmen pulverized the heroic figure into a pile of dust. It seems that Miss Purity was a daughter of Tammany Hall, and when the political machine did not fare well in the 1909 elections, she quickly outlived any usefulness as a vote-getting prop.

Before Miss Purity enjoyed her fifteen minutes of fame, Times Square had already become a lure for more than pleasure seekers. That became evident when several automobile dealerships sprouted along Broadway just north of the square. They catered to an exclusive clientele, since autos had not been

Treat yourself to the ASTOR

It's the only great hotel entering right on Times Square.

Save time
Save money
Save taxis

ABOVE *Astor Hotel ad from the 1933* A.L.A. Automobile Green Book, Road Reference and Tourists' Guide. *The Astor was the control station in New York for Lincoln Highway travelers.*

commercially available very long and were thought of as playthings of the affluent. Nonetheless, all eyes were on New York on February 12, 1908—Abraham Lincoln's birthday—when "the race of the century" was staged, with Times Square as the starting point.

On that morning, a total of six audacious contestants representing four countries—France, Italy, Germany, and the United States—entered the 22,000-mile-long race from New York to Paris. They roared off in swirling snow, bolstered by a cheering crowd of 250,000 well-wishers. Their race route westward across the continent followed

Times Square, New York City, N. Y

NEW YORK

Adirondack
Mts.

ALBANY

Niagara
Falls

Finger Lakes

Catskill
Mts.

New
York
City

The EMPIRE State

BIRD in HAND-HANGOVER BREAKFAST...
For the Morning After the Night Before

TOMATO JUICE
TWO RAW EGGS
DRY TOAST
BLACK COFFEE
ASPIRIN
and
OUR SYMPATHY

50¢

much of what would become the Lincoln Highway through Pennsylvania, Ohio, Indiana, Illinois, Iowa, Nebraska, Wyoming, Utah, Nevada, and California.

From San Francisco, the autos were shipped by steamer to Seattle and then driven to Alaska, followed by a Bering Strait crossing to Siberia and then the long ride to Paris. Some entrants ran into serious problems and had to change plans. Given the condition of the roads at that time, the going was very tough. Even in the continental United States, there were likely to have been almost no gas stations, garages, or paved roads. Only three contestants managed to finish, including the winner—the lone American racer, who arrived in Paris 170 days after leaving Times Square. Not only did the race spark the public's imagination and desire to take to the open road, but the resulting notoriety helped build the case for Times Square to serve as the launching pad for the Lincoln Highway just five years later.

By September 14, 1913, when the official Lincoln Highway route from Times Square to San Francisco's Lincoln Park was announced, the bumpy journey in this era before routine automobile travel had improved little. Although few Lincoln Highway travelers actually started their cross-country trek in Times Square, the tremendous symbolism it evoked was critical to the entire road. Some have said that New York meant more to the Lincoln than the highway ever meant to New York, and perhaps that's true. Nevertheless, West 42nd Street, from Times Square to the banks of the Hudson, remained marked as the Lincoln Highway well into the 1920s, even though the last concrete post markers erected in 1928 completely detoured New York.

By the end of that decade, significant change had occurred in the exit route from Manhattan and into New Jersey. For fourteen years after the Lincoln Highway became operational in 1913, travelers departing Times Square had only one option for reaching New Jersey—to proceed westward on 42nd Street to a ferryboat that crossed the Hudson diagonally to a slip at Weehawken. But as early as 1906, a coalition from New York and New Jersey had sought to create an alternative method of getting people across the river. The rapid increase in vehicular traffic spurred on this joint commission, a precursor of today's Port Authority. In 1913, they decided to build a tunnel from downtown Manhattan beneath the Hudson to New Jersey.

In 1920, construction began on the tunnel that eventually would be named for Clifford Holland, chief engineer of the project. The work was both laborious and treacherous. Tunnel construction workers, called "sandhogs," worked for seven years to get the job done. They hauled out mud, blasted through rock, and lined the tunnel with cast-iron steel and concrete. Many succumbed to the bends, and at least thirteen workers perished during construction.

Finally the two "sandhog" teams "holed through," and when they met in early 1927, the two brothers leading the men shook hands to a chorus of cheers. President Calvin Coolidge, using the same key that had opened the Panama Canal, formally opened the Holland Tunnel, a

few miles south of 42nd Street, at midnight on November 13, 1927. The final project cost was $54 million.

In 1927, ferry traffic between New York and New Jersey peaked at a staggering twenty-seven million passengers. That number steadily declined with the opening of the Holland Tunnel that year, followed by the opening of the George Washington Bridge in 1931 and the Lincoln Tunnel, a few blocks from Times Square, in 1937. In 1959, the New York Central Railroad, the last owner of the ferries operating between Weehawken and Manhattan, discontinued service, ending 259 years of constant operation.

The Holland Tunnel had no positive impact as far as the Lincoln Highway boosters were concerned. They anticipated the highway's demise as early as 1925, when plans were unveiled for the new federal system that called for doing away with all highway names and replacing them with numbers. At the close of 1927, the Lincoln Highway Association ceased to exist, and by the onset of the Great Depression, the highway was referred to in the past tense in New York.

Ironically, about the same time, Times Square was beginning a long decline of its own. The Depression and then World War II had a tremendous impact on the "crossroads of the world." Theater owners, facing competition from cinemas sprouting all over Manhattan, were going broke and selling out. The age of "peep

LEFT *The New Amsterdam Theater, Times Square, New York City.*

shows," shops peddling cheap tourist trinkets, honky-tonks, and "dime museums" staging freak shows for the pleasure of society's bottom feeders became the rage. After the war, 42nd Street teemed with hookers, pimps, and hopheads, while travelers watched their back pockets as they hustled through the Port Authority terminal. The once-grand movie theaters became dilapidated, but just to the north, Broadway theaters continued to play to packed houses and Sardi's reigned as the celebrity restaurant. Damon Runyon, Toots Shor, and Eddie Cantor were no longer relevant.

Occasionally an image surfaced to make Times Square still look worthy of its self-appointed position as the center of American culture and celebration. There was *Life* magazine photographer Alfred Eisenstaedt's euphoric snap of a nurse being kissed by a sailor in Times Square on V-J Day in 1945, or the hip 1955 Dennis Stock photo of James Dean hunched over in his black trench coat, hands shoved deep in his pockets, cigarette dangling from his lips, walking in a rainy Times Square that beckons with a misty come-hither air.

The famous "Zipper"—the outdoor message board emblazoned above Times Square that became a twentieth-century icon—constantly spelled out breaking news of the world almost as it happened. Even during its most decrepit years, Times Square remained a comforting beacon to New York's masses and was the place to go whenever something good or bad took place. Throughout the century, people still went there to celebrate the endings of wars and

World Series victories, and faithfully to watch the Waterford crystal ball drop every New Year's Eve.

In the 1950s and 1960s, the character of the area soured even more. As suburban flight and television took a toll on the already rowdy social and cultural scene, Times Square spawned dirty bookstores, porn shops, grindhouse cinema, perverts, rough trade, and teenage runaways. The Beats chronicled Times Square, as did John Rechy, an El Paso–born author, in his novel *City of Night*, a story of loneliness and the search for love in the underbelly of New York. And after the Age of Aquarius dawned, the world saw the Times Square of Joe Buck (*Midnight Cowboy*) and of Travis Bickle (*Taxi Driver*).

BELOW
The original Lincoln Highway route crossed the Hudson River from New York City to Weehawken, NJ, via the Weehawken Ferry. Service ceased in the 1950s and was resumed in 1986.

The world also saw the Times Square of sordidness and sleaze that intensified in the 1970s and 1980s into a haven for crack whores, drug dealers, runaways, chicken hawks and their boys, and society's most marginalized souls.

But then, in the 1990s, Times Square evolved, miraculously to many, yet again. It became legit. Corporate America heard the city's call for a cleanup, and the big companies came running, along with all the out-of-towners. The Camel Man, blowing smoke rings around the clock for decades, was no longer acceptable. Walt Disney and Toys "R" Us came to play big

time, and they stayed. Ronald McDonald set up shop. So did network television and megahotels with sushi bars, spas, multiplex cinemas, and fitness centers. Generic America is alive and well in Times Square.

Meanwhile, the Lincoln Highway—the road New York once dismissed—also is alive and well. There has been no attempt to memorialize the historic path in the Big Apple, and no signs or markers indicate its existence, but the Lincoln is there. It starts and stops in Times Square and then goes to New Jersey. It moves under aliases, but it is the Lincoln, after all.

Travelers may take the Holland Tunnel if they wish, but in 1986 the Weehawken Ferry was reincarnated and makes its determined runs back and forth across the majestic Hudson. Hard-core Lincoln Highway travelers who start in New York know that the ferry only carries pedestrians and not vehicles, but they don't seem to care. They park their cars on the New Jersey side of the river, take the ferry to Manhattan, and then they return. They sit on a metal bench or stand at the rail as the ferry churns through the coffee-colored water and they bid New York farewell. Behind is the serrated skyline of Manhattan; ahead, an old highway that has paid its dues waits patiently atop the steep Palisades at Weehawken, guarding the Jersey shore.

LEFT *Big, bright, colorful signs are actually required of advertisers in Times Square.*

BELOW *Times Square has several headline news crawls known as "Zippers." The Zippers can be a magnet for crowds in good and bad times, as they were in the days following the 9/11 terrorist attacks.*

WELCOME TO NEW JERSEY

Chapter Two

NEW JERSEY

New Jersey's rocky Palisades rise like primeval sentinels on the western margin of the Hudson, the first of the great rivers Lincoln Highway travelers encounter on their westward journey to the Pacific shore.

Molded by the ancient river and seasoned over the eons by wind and rain, the Palisades were formed millions of years ago by a great sheet of ice bulldozing molten rock that emerged cool and solid from deep within the convulsing earth. In the wake of that distant time, when ice covered much of the land, the retreating glaciers overran the landscape, carved out lakes, rerouted streams, deepened the Hudson, and created the bedrock of New Jersey and Staten Island.

New Jersey gave Manhattan its backbone and in the fullness of time allowed monstrous skyscrapers to shoot into the firmament over midtown. That, at least, is what some geologists maintain, as did author John McPhee in his 1983 book *In Suspect Terrain*:

The Wisconsinan ice sheet, arriving from the north, had come over the city not from New England, as one might guess, but primarily from New Jersey, whose Hudson River counties lie due north of Manhattan.

LEFT *Jackie Robinson statue, Journal Square, Jersey City, NJ.*

Big boulders from the New Jersey Palisades are strewn about in Central Park, and more of the same diabase is scattered through Brooklyn. The ice wholly covered the Bronx and Manhattan, and its broad snout moved across Astoria, Maspeth, Williamsburg, and Bedford-Stuyvesant before sliding to a stop in Flatbush.

A New Jersey native, McPhee was born and educated in the Lincoln Highway town of Princeton in 1931. For most of his life, he made his home less than ten minutes away from where he grew up. In reflecting on his home state, McPhee likened the vehicles speeding back and forth on the New Jersey superslab connecting New York and Philadelphia to "peas in a pea shooter." He clearly understands that there are slower roads to take, such as the routings of the Lincoln. He knows that New Jersey offers ocean beaches, such as in exclusive Deal or funkier Asbury Park; the Pine Barrens; small towns locked in time; and people, in touch with the quaintness of New England, who practice the hardworking values of the Midwest, which lies ahead.

McPhee knows furthermore that New Jersey often falls victim to misleading stereotypes and well-hammered clichés. A few of them have been earned but many have not. Mention New Jersey to some people and images of toxic-waste dumps, obnoxious accents, and *Sopranos*-like hit men come to mind. New Jersey may not be Dorothy's Kansas, but it's definitely not "the armpit of America," as it was once called. New Jersey is the fourth smallest state in size but the most densely populated state in the country, which means that all those who choose to live there must know something the Jersey critics don't know.

How could a state that gave the world Sinatra and Springsteen be all bad? Besides those two warblers, New Jersey has provided sanctuary for a wide range of notables. The list of some of the famous who have called New Jersey home is as diverse as the state: Bud Abbott and Lou Costello, Count Basie, Stephen Crane, Vince Lombardi, Merle Streep, Joyce Carol Oates, Bon Jovi, Thomas Edison, Woodrow Wilson, Albert Einstein, Jack Nicholson, and Dorothea Lange.

New Jersey produces arguably the tastiest beefsteak tomato anywhere—and was referred to as the Garden State long before it became associated with industrial smoke and interstate fumes. It is home to some of the nation's finest institutions of higher learning and is rich with history dating from long before the American Revolution. But experiencing all that New Jersey offers requires getting off the superhighways and sticking to old roads, such as the time-tested Lincoln Highway. For that reason, when cruising central New Jersey, travelers who aren't out just to "make time" will avoid the tedious New Jersey Turnpike as much as possible. All along the Lincoln in Jersey lie gritty cities, quaint towns and villages, centuries of rich history, and, yes, ghosts.

According to state lore, some ghosts may appear even before the ferryboat docks at Weehawken, or the perpetual stream of traffic clears the Jersey end of the Lincoln Tunnel. Before dealing with ghosts,

however, there are options to consider—travelers may either take the modern version of the Lincoln or retrace the historic route by scaling the Palisades on Pershing Road. Most purists opt for the old way.

The Palisades hoard secrets and conceal phantoms of times gone by. Those rocky cliffs and jagged slopes splashed with vegetation have long attracted both the living and the dead. On bright mornings, even the legendary Jersey Devil—a hideous flying creature with hooves, said to dwell in the Pine Barrens to the south—might be tempted to make an appearance at the Palisades for a peek at the Manhattan skyline glinting in the sun.

Plenty of characters and creatures have left their prints on the Palisades, including the earliest human dwellers who fished the river and hunted the forests and thickets. They fashioned tools and weapons from the Palisades rock, as did the tribal people who followed them. In 1609, Henry Hudson marveled at the towering stone cliffs when he explored the river (later named for him) with his Dutch and English sailors on the eighty-ton ship the *Half Moon*.

Ever since New York City sprang up between two rivers, its citizens have been drawn to the high ground of the Palisades, where comfortable homes were built by the wealthy for weekend escapes from the sweltering city. For years, a river walk on the Jersey bank was a popular respite from crowded Manhattan. Many of those who crossed the Hudson stopped at Sybil's Cave, just north of modern-day Hoboken. When the cave was dug out of the cliff in 1832, a natural spring was found. Parched hikers went to the cavern and paid a penny a glass to quench their thirst with water so cold it hurt their teeth.

RIGHT *Loew's Jersey Theatre, Journal Square, Jersey City, NJ, circa 1932.*

Sybil's Cave made headlines in 1841, when the brutalized body of a young woman—of course described as "beautiful" in the nineteenth-century tabloids— was found floating near the entrance. The crime and resulting publicity boosted business for Weehawken and Hoboken as sightseers came in large numbers to view the scene. Edgar Allan Poe immortalized the crime in one of his stories, although he changed the location to Paris.

The cave closed in the 1880s, when the supposedly medicinal water was found to contain traces of sewage and was declared unfit for human consumption. The entrance to the cave was sealed, and for a while a tavern operated just outside. Ultimately, Sybil's Cave became part of local lore and legend. Then, around 2004, the cave was rediscovered just off Sinatra Drive, not far from a popular fishing pier. Excavation work began and plans were formed to bring the once-infamous attraction back to life.

Like the Weehawken Ferry, the cave has come full circle and is further proof that history, especially if it is sensational, can always entice the curious. All along the Lincoln Highway, as with so many spots in America, are death sites, crime scenes, battlegrounds, and the settings of natural and manmade disasters that have become popular tourist attractions.

One death site has always lured travelers to the Palisades just below the township of Weehawken. At the southern end of a narrow promenade on John F. Kennedy Boulevard East—or simply Boulevard East, as the locals prefer—is a bronze bust of Alexander Hamilton. It commemorates the most famous duel in American history, which took place just after dawn on July 11, 1804, when Aaron Burr, the sitting vice president of the United States, mortally wounded Hamilton, the nation's first secretary of the treasury and Burr's most ardent political antagonist.

LEFT *Loew's Jersey Theatre, Jersey City, NJ.*

Shot through the hip with the bullet lodged in his spine, Hamilton was taken back to New York, where he died in agony the next day in a friend's Greenwich Village home. A funeral procession wound through Wall Street to the yard of Trinity Church, where Hamilton was laid to rest. Although Burr eventually was indicted for murder, he was never prosecuted. He completed his term of office and later was implicated in further political intrigue that led to his being tried and acquitted of treason. He spent his final years in a Staten Island hotel, where he died at the age of eighty in 1836. Burr was buried in Princeton, not far from the highway named for Lincoln, another American politician whose life was ended by a gunshot wound.

Debate has long raged about the precise location of the Weehawken dueling grounds where Burr and Hamilton squared off but also where many other celebrity duelers defended their honor, including DeWitt Clinton, governor of New York and "Father of the Erie Canal," as well as naval hero Commodore Oliver Hazard Perry. Clinton and Perry survived their contests, as did eleven participants of the eighteen known duels fought there before dueling was banned in 1845. One of the casualties was Hamilton's nineteen-year-old son, Philip, who was shot and killed in 1801 on the same ground and with the same pistols that were used three years later in his father's duel with Burr.

In 2004, to mark the 200th anniversary of the duel, descendants of Hamilton and Burr performed a reenactment. Douglas Hamilton, an IBM salesman from Ohio, and Antonio Burr, a New York psychologist, represented their famous ancestors. Precautions were taken to ensure that no live ammunition was present, and the proceedings were described as cordial. Historical plaques were erected at the Hamilton monument and the big rock where, according to Weehawken legend, the wounded Hamilton rested his head after being shot. The boulder was moved to the site long ago, well before shoreline reclamation and railroad construction destroyed the actual dueling grounds—described as a grassy shelf located near the base of the Palisades and accessible by a path leading from the Hudson River.

It is well known that this lofty spot offers one of the best views of midtown Manhattan. Wedding parties show up for portrait sessions, taking full advantage of the magnificent setting and backdrop. No wonder Washington Irving was known to take refreshing catnaps at this very spot when visiting friends who lived close by. Joggers, dog walkers, and locals from this gentrified neighborhood of Victorian homes often outnumber Lincoln Highway travelers who stop at the monument.

On summer evenings—above the marinas, condos, restaurants, and hotels that have sprouted below the cliffs in the old railroad yards along the river—couples snuggle in parked cars and on the benches. Across the Hudson, the twinkling necklace of millions of office-building lights joins the radiant peaks of the Empire State and Chrysler Buildings and creates a glow that hangs over the city and the river. For some, it is a night light showing the way home; for others—those with the urge to see more—it is a beacon that reveals the best path to follow.

A jaunt across central New Jersey can take forever, depending on which roads motorists choose. Turnpike commuters facing peak traffic may turn either suicidal or homicidal. There also are people who just want (or need) to get through Jersey. They pause only for gas, pit stops, or a swing through an all-you-can-eat buffet. It's an altogether different story if a veteran traveler is behind the wheel. Although New Jersey may contain just sixty-four miles of the Lincoln Highway between Weehawken and Trenton, every one of those miles can count. Those who have time on their side, a sense of history, and a modicum of curiosity stick to the Lincoln.

Sometimes, however, this is not an easy task. The original routings of the Lincoln, like the alignments of other older American highways, can be difficult to find or follow in such urbanized areas as the string of densely settled New Jersey cities just beyond New York. Yet fear of getting lost on a road is much like fear of getting lost in a book or a movie. As funny as it sounds, sometimes getting lost can be good. There are travelers who consider getting lost an art. It can be a balm for the soul, allowing those who are lost to learn more about themselves by altering the predictable course of life. Those who follow the circuitous route of the Lincoln through Jersey City, Newark, Elizabeth, or anywhere else along the old road, must keep in mind that the only people who never get lost are those who never leave home.

While not concerned about going astray, travelers still scrutinize vintage Lincoln Highway maps and newer guidebooks as they leave Weehawken and make their way toward Jersey City, the state's second largest city. Now the scavenger hunt really starts. All eyes scan the streets and neighborhoods for landmarks, bizarre signs, historic sites, and examples of commercial archaeology scattered among the ever-changing cityscape. Some of the old familiar places, such as Roosevelt Stadium, exist only in memory.

Located on the east shore of Newark Bay in Jersey City, the art deco stadium was built in 1936 as a Works Progress Administration (WPA) project and named for President Franklin Roosevelt. It officially opened April 23, 1937, as the home of the Jersey City Giants, a farm club for the New York Giants.

Over the years, the stadium also welcomed some of the boxing world's greatest fighters, including Max Baer, Sugar Ray Robinson, Jersey Joe Walcott, and Ezzard Charles. Still, the most historic event ever to take place at Roosevelt Stadium came on April 18, 1946. That afternoon—just shy of the stadium's tenth anniversary—a determined twenty-seven-year-old Californian named Jackie Robinson took the field for the visiting Montreal Royals and became the first black player in the modern era of organized professional baseball.

Some of the sellout crowd on hand greeted the young man's debut with boos the first time he stepped to the plate. Robinson responded by putting on a hitting, baserunning, and fielding clinic. He hustled out two bunt hits, smacked another single and a homer, scored four runs, and stole a pair of bases in Montreal's 14–1 rout of the home-team Giants. By game's end, the heckling had turned to a chorus of cheers, and within a year Jackie Robinson was on his way to a Hall of Fame career with the Brooklyn Dodgers.

Roosevelt Stadium hosted hundreds of minor-league ball games for other major-league teams after the New York Giants moved the franchise in 1950. For a short stint, the Brooklyn Dodgers used the stadium as their home field before moving to Los Angeles. By the early 1970s, the biggest crowds at Roosevelt Stadium came not for hardball but for music concerts. Among the more memorable performers were the Grateful Dead, Pink Floyd, Eric Clapton, Tony Bennett, and the Beach Boys and their then-unknown opening act, the Eagles.

In 1985, with baseball long gone, event attendance dwindling, and the facilities in disrepair, Roosevelt Stadium was demolished. One seat was sent to the Baseball Hall of Fame and another went to the

Smithsonian Institution. A housing development named Society Hill opened on the site in 1987. In 2004, another Roosevelt Stadium—this one in neighboring Union City—met a similar fate and was torn down to make room for a new high school and athletic complex.

The past, however, has not been forgotten in Jersey City. A bigger-than-life statue of Jackie Robinson has a place of honor in Journal Square, once the commercial heart of a downtown that turned derelict. That changed in the late 1990s and early 2000s, when an outbreak of

RIGHT *The chandelier in the lobby of the Stanley Theater in Jersey City, NJ, used to hang from the ceiling of Manhattan's original Waldorf-Astoria Hotel, which was torn down in 1930 to make way for the Empire State Building.*

civic pride sparked a widespread building boom and overhaul of historic properties. Classic office towers were renovated and downtown neighborhoods began experiencing rapid gentrification as professionals weary of high prices in Manhattan moved into apartments and Victorian brownstones. In the wake of the September 11, 2001, terrorist attacks in New York, several financial institutions and investment firms expanded operations or relocated to Jersey City.

The Stanley Theater opened on Journal Square in 1928 with 4,300 seats, making it the second largest theater on the East Coast, just behind New York's Radio City Music Hall. In 1978, the big Wurlitzer organ fell silent when suburban flight so decreased ticket sales that the Stanley closed its doors. The grand old building still stands, however; since 1983, it has been used as a meeting hall for Jehovah's Witnesses. Another grand movie palace—Loew's Jersey Theatre—opened in 1929 and presented thousands of movies and live stage shows. Jack Benny, Bob Hope, Cab Calloway, Jean Harlow, and Burns and Allen were just a few of the big stars who took the stage at Loew's before it closed in 1986. As the majestic building awaited the wrecking ball, local citizens put their collective foot down and stopped the demolition. In 1993, the city purchased the building, and extensive renovations have brought Loew's back to life, hosting a variety of films, musicals, plays, children's programs, and concerts.

Besides the cultural landmarks, other famous Jersey City sites beckon. The Colgate Clock—touted as the largest in the world at fifty feet in diameter, with a minute hand weighing 2,200 pounds—still faces Lower Manhattan, as it has since 1924. And "The World's Largest Cat" grins from its rooftop perch beneath the Holland Tunnel viaduct. Nineteen feet long, the 500-pound bundle of fiberglass supposedly was created in the 1950s for a Macy's Thanksgiving Day parade. Although out of the reach of vandals, the cat grows more decrepit with each passing day, and its many fans pray that not all of its nine lives have expired.

Besides the enormous clock and cat, Jersey City is where the first of the Abraham Lincoln statues greets motorists. South of Journal Square, at the intersection of JFK Boulevard and Belmont Avenue, this bronze statue of Lincoln—clad in a fashionable light-green patina suit—sits in a state of perpetual contemplation of the entrance to Lincoln Park, just as he has since 1930. Created by sculptor James Earle Fraser—the artist who designed the nickel with a buffalo head on one side and an Indian head on the other—the Lincoln statue was placed at this specific location because it was on the original Lincoln Highway.

The Lincoln Association of Jersey City commissioned Fraser to do the statue, given his Lincoln Highway connection dating back to the early years of the road. Fraser's famous *End of the Trail* sculpture was considered the most popular work of art at the 1915 Panama-Pacific International Exposition in San Francisco—the impetus for early travelers to use the newly christened road. After winning the exposition's Gold Medal, Fraser hoped to cast the statue in bronze and place it near the new highway's terminus overlooking San Francisco Bay. Alas, World War I intervened, wartime materiel demands ended that plan, and soon the statue of the forlorn Indian drooping on his horse was discarded. For years, it slowly deteriorated in a California park until 1968, when the National Cowboy & Western Heritage Museum in Oklahoma City acquired it and restored the original plaster statue. Today Fraser's work is the focal point of the museum, located near another famous highway—U.S. Route 66. "The Mother Road," as John Steinbeck dubbed Route 66, intersects with the Lincoln Highway in Illinois, many miles to the west of New Jersey.

Following a stop at Fraser's statue in Lincoln Park, the open road beckons, as does yet another statue of President Lincoln just down the old highway in New Jersey's largest city, Newark, now experiencing a major revival of its own. But to reach the next Mister Lincoln, travelers first must cross a pair of drawbridges over the Passaic and Hackensack Rivers and the vast Jersey Meadows (or Meadowlands). Much of the scenery here has changed since Arbor Day 1914, when Newark Motor Club officials planted trees and shrubs along the old Plank Road, soon renamed the Lincoln Highway, between Jersey City and Newark.

To the north, travelers cannot miss seeing the almost sculptural black steel of the Pulaski Skyway—named for General Casimir Pulaski, the Polish-born hero of the American Revolution—the most expensive bridge of its day when completed in 1932 at a cost of $20 million and the lives of fifteen construction workers. The 3.5-mile-long elevated span crosses the two rivers and marshlands and acts as the major commuter route between the state's two biggest cities. It was not part of the Lincoln but was intended as a bypass. Nonetheless, some Lincoln wayfarers include a short but architecturally rewarding side trip on the Jersey City side beneath the Pulaski Skyway.

Below the steel girders on U.S. 1, just south of its intersection with Newark Avenue, stands the giant Muffler Man, dressed like a lumberjack and clutching a roll of green industrial carpet in an attempt to draw customers into the carpet store behind him. Thousands of commuters crawling along the highway and standing or sitting on the elevated trains pass him every day. In the late 1990s, he gained fame as a pop-culture icon when the producers of *The Sopranos*, the hugely popular HBO television series, included a shot of him, as well as the Pulaski Skyway, in the opening credits. The Jersey giant—who might be more at home on a Texas highway—was one of many such figures created in the 1960s by a fiberglass firm in California to help sell mufflers for a chain of gas stations. Like some of his surviving brothers, the big guy changed careers after his muffler-selling days ended. Throughout the country, mostly on the older roads and vintage highways, other Muffler Men still stand tall, dressed in vintage garb as Indians, cowboys, soldiers, pirates, or even space men.

Savvy travelers realize the value of probing all layers of history and culture along the shoulder of a highway, but that means in New Jersey as well as farther west, jumping back and forth in time between, say, the American Revolution and the Industrial Revolution; between the family farms still struggling to hold on and the high-tech centers emblazoning the future. Oddly enough, a little stop at the Muffler Man acts as a transition—a palate cleanser between the two sitting Lincoln statues as travelers enter Newark.

Like so many other cities, much of Newark is not what it used to be. Some of the city's most revered architectural jewels are long gone. The Paramount, last of the city's theater palaces, still stands, but in name only. Small retailers operating out of the lobby come and go, and only the once-brilliant marquee is left as a reminder of a theater that seated more than 2,000 people.

Newark Penn Station, however, remains a major transit hub, as it has since 1935, and the dapper Robert Treat Hotel, opened in 1916 just in time to host President and Mrs. Woodrow Wilson, is a refurbished city landmark. Named after the founder of Newark, the hotel is one of scores of Lincoln Highway properties in New Jersey listed on the National Register of Historic Places. The most impressive part of the original hotel was the lobby, where huge columns combined with intricate lighting features over white marble steps, tile floors, and lavish rugs. The lobby also had plentiful lounge space, large palms and potted plants, and writing desks and tables on a balcony for afternoon tea.

Another property on the prestigious heritage list is the Lincoln statue on West Market Street, in front of the old Essex County Courthouse. The large bronze likeness

of Lincoln can be seen some way off by travelers making their way to the "Four Corners" at Broad and Market. This is the heart of the city, as it always has been. For many years, including during the heyday of the Lincoln Highway, the Four Corners was widely considered one of the busiest if not *the* busiest intersection in the nation.

The original routing of the Lincoln turned left at Broad Street, close to the statue that remains a favorite of Lincoln Highway enthusiasts. Unlike the so-called Mystic Lincoln in Jersey City, the statue in Newark is more inviting. It depicts Lincoln at ease, with his trademark stovepipe hat next to him

ABOVE

The Wilson's Carpet Muffler Man under the Pulaski Skyway in Jersey City, NJ, was featured in the opening credits of the HBO series The Sopranos.

RIGHT *Gutzon Borglum's seated Lincoln statue overlooking the "Four Corners" of Market and Broad Streets, downtown Newark, NJ.*

on the bench. Dubbed the "Children's Lincoln," the statue has an ample lap that has held countless children and perhaps some adults since 1911, when the remarkable artist Gutzon Borglum seated him there.

Best remembered for his monumental granite carvings of four U.S. presidents on Mount Rushmore in South Dakota, Borglum greatly admired Lincoln and named his own son after him. The sculptor carved a striking marble bust of Lincoln for the rotunda in the nation's Capitol, but it was the seated Lincoln at the Four Corners that remained his favorite.

It seems the perfect place for the sixteenth president. His sad bronze eyes behold a city much changed since the time when Market Street was a Hackensack

Indian trail and long before Broad Street appeared on a city map in 1667. Puritan settlers and German brewers walked those avenues, and General George Washington marched his troops down Broad Street in retreat from New Jersey. Years later, more soldiers marched the same route when the bloody Civil War erupted. Horse-drawn trolleys rumbled right down the center of Broad Street, and elm trees grew so large that their canopies formed a green corridor.

Newark boomed and the population kept growing through the first half of the twentieth century. By the early 1920s, the city had more than sixty live theaters and almost fifty movie houses. In 1927, it was said that Newark was destined to become the greatest industrial center in the world, and it simultaneously beckoned thousands of immigrant and newly settled Jewish families. Newark native Philip Roth, its greatest twentieth-century writer, brilliantly depicted this in his 2004 evocation of 1930s Newark, *The Plot Against America.* Just after World War II, Newark hit its peak. Local legend boasts that when the pop artist Robert Rauschenberg left Texas to seek fame and fortune, he mistakenly got off the bus in Newark and stayed a week before he realized he wasn't in New York City.

Starting in the 1950s, all of that changed with the opening of the New Jersey Turnpike. This 118-mile toll road, completed in 1951, connected New York City to Philadelphia and Delaware, slashing through traffic-choked New Jersey with little regard for the land or the people. The four-lane superhighway (and its subsequent growth to a dozen lanes) may have saved commuters time, but there was an exorbitant price to pay over and above the original $255 million shelled out for construction. The New Jersey Turnpike bullied its way through farms, tidal flats, marshes, little towns, and established city neighborhoods without the slightest regard for the environment, the fragile fabric of urban neighborhoods, or the state's rich heritage. Newark was impacted and so was the neighboring city of Elizabeth, where the turnpike brazenly sliced the city in two.

A horrific 1967 riot, caused by a racial incident and fueled by rampant poverty and overcrowding, further tarnished Newark's reputation and led to wholesale white flight to the suburbs. The decline of Newark continued in the 1970s and 1980s. In his earlier novel *American Pastoral*, which won the Pulitzer Prize in 1998, Roth takes his hometown to task. In describing the city's despair, the book's protagonist explains that Newark "used to be the city where they manufactured everything, now it's the car theft capital of the world. . . . there was a factory where somebody was making something on every side street. Now there's a liquor store on every street—liquor store, a pizza stand, and a seedy storefront church. Everything else is in ruins or boarded up."

The Four Corners intersection is not the same as it was when Lincoln took his seat on the bench so long ago. Along the wide avenues, small retail shops peddle cheap wigs, shoes, furniture, and beauty products. During the day, vendors and shoppers fill the sidewalks, but by nightfall things grow still, and most shops close for the evening. Yet there remains a hope that is both powerful and growing. The same year that *American Pastoral* was published, a stunning performing-arts center was built as the first step on the city's road to revival. More revitalization work followed in downtown and the adjoining neighborhoods. By the first decade of this century, the city's population increased for the first time since the late 1940s, and the crime rate, while not enviable, had dropped slightly.

Indeed, for people cruising the old road there is always the chance that the next time they pass this way, Newark will have evolved even more. But there is an even better chance that the statue of Abraham Lincoln will still be at the Four Corners with kids eagerly climbing his shoulders.

From Newark, the route quickly reaches Elizabeth, the first state capital and the hometown of crime novelist

Mickey Spillane and Admiral William "Bull" Halsey, Jr., to name but two former citizens. An industrious populace helped put Elizabeth on the map, and for a long time Singer Sewing Machine kept it vibrant.

Heading southwest, the Lincoln connects with current New Jersey State Route 27, which meanders down to the historically fascinating city of Trenton, the state capital and the last Lincoln Highway city in Jersey before crossing the Delaware River into Pennsylvania. The original Lincoln route between Elizabeth and Trenton included stretches of road used as Indian footpaths and highways since the seventeenth century. The old road goes by various aliases but is often still called the Lincoln in several places.

It is obvious when one takes this long stretch that New Jersey's boast about having more diners than any other state is true. At one time the state was home to more than a dozen diner manufacturers. Roadside diners dot the shoulders of the road through Rahway, Iselin, Menlo Park, Metuchen, New Brunswick, Highland Park, Franklin Park, Kingston, Princeton, Lawrenceville, and Trenton. While diners are appealing for those who love nostalgia, the history of the region conveys a sense that New Jersey is anything but ephemeral or superficial. Almost every township, in fact, retains historic homes and sites that date back to the American Revolution—when a coach ride on the King's Highway from Newark to Philadelphia took at least a week.

In 1954, Raritan Township changed its name to Edison to honor Thomas A. Edison, the famed inventor who in 1876 set up his home and research lab in a defunct real estate development called Menlo Park. During eight years in his lab on Christie Avenue, Edison and his staff dreamed up the phonograph and the electric light and received more than four hundred patents. After his wife died, Edison—appropriately called "The Wizard of Menlo Park"—packed up and moved to more spacious research facilities in West Orange, New Jersey. Today visitors can duck into a small museum displaying some Edison memorabilia and stroll

on a woodland path where it was said Edison did some of his best thinking. There is also the 129-foot Thomas Alva Edison Memorial Tower, topped by a great lightbulb that sometimes is illuminated.

Several miles to the southwest, the lights burn brightly in New Brunswick, where actor Michael Douglas was born, as was World War I poet Joyce Kilmer, who never saw anything lovelier than a tree. The main campus of Rutgers University is in New Brunswick, and it was there in 1869 that Rutgers took on its neighbor, Princeton University, in what is billed as the first intercollegiate football game. The home team won, 6–4, in what one Rutgers player described as a contest "replete with surprise, strategy, prodigies of determination, and physical prowess."

By the mid-1920s, college football had become a national game; at the same time, the entire route of the Lincoln Highway through New Jersey was paved with concrete—including a section

LEFT *The White Diamond Diner, Linden, NJ.*

LOWER LEFT

The Edison Memorial Tower at the site where Thomas Edison perfected the electric lightbulb, Menlo Park, NJ.

T-17—Night View of State Street West from Broad Street, Trenton, N. J.

3B-H327

NEW JERSEY
the GARDEN State

120 MILES OF SEASHORE

linking Franklin Park and Kingston that was built by convict labor from the state penitentiary. Between Kingston and Princeton lies Carnegie Lake, a gift of Andrew Carnegie that was formed in 1906 by a dam on the Millstone River. The artificial lake attracts passersby as well as Princeton students. The prestigious Ivy League school, founded in 1746 and known these days as the highest-ranked university in the country, is rich in historical lore. In the middle of the campus stands a fifty-foot-tall limestone Battle Monument, commissioned in 1908 but not completed until 1922. Commemorating the 1777 Battle of Princeton, it depicts not only Washington leading his troops into battle and victory but also the death of General Hugh Mercer. On the sides of the monument are the seals of the United States and the original thirteen states.

Campus visitors can also check out the many gargoyles perched on the university library, dormitories, and academic halls. The decorative carvings have such whimsical names as *Flute Player*, *Chained Dragon*, *Football Runner*, *Benjamin Franklin*, *Dinosaur Head*, *Goblin with a Shell*, and *Man with an Open Mouth*. In a direct link to the Lincoln Highway, a gargoyle called *Monkey with a Camera*, looking down from a prominent arch, was carved by Gutzon Borglum, the sculptor who created the sitting Lincoln statue in Newark.

The most famous of the Princeton gargoyles is *The Joy Ride*, on the east wall of the Graduate College. When it was installed in the 1920s, it reflected the fashions of the time. The *New York Sun* described the female frieze as "a student abandoning care in favor of an automobile and a gay companion. She's quite modern, this young lady. Note the cigarette, the bobbed hair, and the expression of unconcern as her 'boy friend' manipulates the steering wheel with a single dexterous hand." F. Scott Fitzgerald, a former Princeton student, would be proud.

The Jersey joyride ends soon enough beyond leafy Princeton and Lawrenceville at Trenton. Established by Quakers in 1679, Trenton was the site of Washington's first victory during the American Revolution. On December 25, 1776, he and his army crossed the ice-clogged Delaware River from Pennsylvania to Trenton and defeated the Hessian troops garrisoned there as they slept off their holiday drink. In 1784, Trenton briefly served as the national capital of the fledgling United States, but Southerners preferred a location nearer to the Mason-Dixon Line, so the permanent capital was created in Washington. In 1790, Trenton settled for being New Jersey's capital.

Lincoln Highway travelers face a river crossing of their own at Trenton. Over the years, different bridges were used because of various re-routings, but the current span displays the famous "Trenton Makes—The World Takes" sign. The huge lighted sign calls attention to a city that was a major manufacturing center and supplied both national and international markets with tools, rubber, linoleum, watches, wire rope, steel, glass, clothing, and many other products. That was an era when travelers accustomed to slower travel knew at Trenton that they had hit the halfway point between "The City that Never Sleeps" and "The City of Brotherly Love."

The Delaware River, forming the boundary between New Jersey and Pennsylvania, rises on the western slopes of the Catskills in eastern New York and flows down from broad Appalachian valleys. The river meets the tidewater at Trenton and continues beneath the "Trenton Makes" bridge on its journey to Delaware Bay and the open sea. Crossing the river in evening shadows, travelers peer at the water reflecting the lights in hopes of seeing something special.

In 2005, they did. When a solitary beluga whale was spied swimming in the Delaware at Trenton, sightseers came from as far as Canada. A local barber put a sign in his window reading, "We Do a Whale of a Job!" Bakeries made batches of whale-shaped cookies. For several days, the whale watch continued. The gawkers also listened for the beluga's high-pitched whistles and birdlike calls that account for its "sea canary" nickname. The whale stayed a while and then left, with everyone hoping that it swam downstream past Philadelphia and back to the sea.

Just across the Delaware is Pennsylvania, the third Lincoln Highway state, and a waiting motel bed. Sleep brings dreams of rocky cliffs, dueling pistols, fiberglass giants, gargoyles, two Lincolns keeping watch, and the song of a "sea canary" going home. What New Jersey makes, the traveler takes.

BELOW *Sign at the base of the Calhoun Street Bridge over the Delaware River in Trenton, NJ.*

Calhoun Street Bridge, Lincoln Highway, Trenton, N. J.

LEFT *The Calhoun Street Bridge, built in 1884, connects Trenton, NJ, with Morrisville, PA. The bridge was officially part of the Lincoln Highway until 1920, when the highway routing was moved to the free Lower Trenton Bridge.*

LOWER LEFT

A 1920s vintage view of the Calhoun Street Bridge, Trenton, NJ.

Welcome to PENNSYLVANIA

State Capital in Harrisburg

State Flower
the Mountain Laurel

Chapter Three

PENNSYLVANIA

Barely into Pennsylvania, travelers are headed westbound on U.S. 1—the assumed name for the Lincoln Highway in these parts since 1925. If they crave real coffee, it's worth waiting for freshly brewed java stronger than coffin varnish,

available at the many diners that lie ahead.

Then, just beyond Morrisville—the first Lincoln Highway town in Pennsylvania— appears a vintage building with a profile of Abraham Lincoln painted over the entrance and, in large black letters, the words:

**LINCOLN GARAGE
DON'T CUSS, CALL US**

No need for any discussion. Coffee can wait. There are stories worth hearing just inside a garage that has more

grease than grace. Stacks of tires, drums of lubricant, and all sorts of automotive paraphernalia surround the work area. There also are plenty of tools and a sign requesting that no one ask about borrowing them. A mechanic in oily coveralls labors over an ailing Chevy. Doris Day croons from a radio in an office where garage owner Gene Bellardo sits at his desk pawing through piles of papers. Without rising, Bellardo looks over his eyeglasses at curious strangers interested in a garage named for the man who gave the road outside its

LEFT

Lincoln Garage, Langhorne, PA.

name. Following introductions and some ritual small talk, questioning starts and Bellardo is happy to oblige.

"I like Lincoln," he says when asked about the name of his place. "I've always liked Lincoln. He was the best president we ever had—maybe the best one that we'll ever have." No one disagrees. "Both my grandfather and my father adored Abraham Lincoln. That's why we named this business after him, and then on top of that we're located right here on the Lincoln Highway—the main artery in the U.S.A." Bellardo turns down Miss Day just a little and wipes his glasses with a fairly clean shop

towel. "You know, it's kinda funny. I've heard that name Lincoln every single day of my life and I still like it."

He explains that his grandfather, Joseph Bellardo, came to America from Italy and started a home-building business with his brother. Then, around 1925, Joseph helped his son Henry—Gene's dad—establish the garage, which has been in the family ever since. "Our family is big and it seems everyone works in garages," says Bellardo. "It's gotta be in your blood." Other than when he served a hitch as a military policeman patrolling tough army towns in Georgia in the early 1950s, Bellardo has been at the garage.

Besides servicing stricken vehicles, the Lincoln Garage is known as one of the oldest and most reliable wrecker services on that stretch of highway. Big tow trucks parked out front are gassed up and available twenty-four hours a day, every day of the week, in case a stranded motorist needs help or a bloody wreck has to be removed. "You know that slogan of ours has been around a long time, and it really caught on," laughs Bellardo. "Even now, when we pull up to an accident scene, the first thing the people we're there to help say is, 'Don't cuss, call us.'"

Patriotic signs and pictures of Lincoln adorn the office walls. There also are lots of pictures of horses. Bellardo admits that horses are one of his three passions—along with cars and Abe Lincoln. After a quick tour, he retreats to his desk and turns up the radio. The medley of Doris Day tunes is still playing.

Driving the Lincoln across Pennsylvania, like listening to Doris Day, can be a fine sentimental journey for a lot of travelers. Along the 350 miles of the Lincoln traversing the state—through Philadelphia, Amish country, Gettysburg, the Alleghenies, and Pittsburgh—old memories are revived and new ones are made. Pennsylvania represents a critical part of the nation's highway history, and much of it was created in Bucks County—the first county travelers come to after crossing the Delaware. Like elsewhere in Pennsylvania, the relationship of Bucks County to roads goes back long before the county was established and the United States of America was even a dream. Some of that road history, however, was made in the mid-twentieth century, when automobiles became more widespread. Bucks County, like the entire state, was impacted by the creation of the Pennsylvania Turnpike. Conceived and constructed during the Depression and opened in 1940, the turnpike was the first long-distance rural freeway in the nation and is considered the "Grandfather of the Interstate Highway System." It was the first roadway in the country with no cross streets, railroad crossings, or traffic lights. The original turnpike featured seven tunnels that bored through the steep Pennsylvania mountains. The Pennsylvania Turnpike became the ideal escape route from the cities, but at the expense of the scores of small towns and hamlets that were bypassed along the way.

By the early 1950s, Levittown—one of William Levitt's sprawling, mass-produced suburbs—was well underway in Lower Bucks County, where blue-collar steelworkers needed affordable housing. Thankfully, the cookie-cutter culture spawned in the 1950s and perfected over the next few decades did not fully engulf the shoulders of the Lincoln in Pennsylvania. While there are plenty of franchise eateries and chain stores, just as in the cities and suburbs, there remain many honest-to-goodness independent businesses such as the Lincoln Garage. Gene Bellardo is just one example of the kind of individual Franklin D. Roosevelt must have had in mind when he advised, "Don't speak with your banking friends or your chamber of commerce friends, but specialize in the gasoline station men, the small restaurant keeper, and farmers you meet by the wayside."

Plenty of these wisdom keepers—some of whom have never left their town except to go to war or on a honeymoon—thrive on the Lincoln Highway in

ABOVE *The Airplane Diner, Penndel, PA, was demolished in 1995 and the airplane removed.*

Pennsylvania and in the other dozen states through which it passes. Lincoln Highway travelers meet these wayside folks in hundreds of locales, including the borough of Langhorne, west of the Lincoln Garage and beyond historic Fallsington. In colonial times, Langhorne was a major hub of Bucks County for stagecoaches transporting passengers between Trenton and Philadelphia. The town experienced spurts of growth well into the twentieth century, when wealthy Philadelphians built large homes in the area despite the bothersome four mph posted speed limit that was duly noted in the Lincoln Highway Association's 1915 road guide. A lot has changed besides the speed limit in Langhorne, but not the good service at the Blue Fountain Diner, on a stretch of Business U.S. 1 that still is called the Lincoln Highway. Since 1966, untold numbers of travelers, truckers, and locals have been nourished in this diner built by the Fodero Dining Car Company, a New Jersey manufacturer that went out of business in 1981.

The Kokkinos family, owners of the Blue Fountain, turn out meals that have to compete with fast-food fare served in Styrofoam boxes at the franchise joints servicing the Pennsylvania Turnpike and superhighways that bypass life in the slower lanes. The notion of real food—a veal cutlet, a bowl brimming with split pea soup, some rice pudding, and baked macaroni—is compelling. The diner lures in its share of hungry families, the after-church crowd, teenagers celebrating a football game, and shift workers.

Most dependable diners feature twenty-four-hour service, seven days a week, and the Blue Fountain is no exception. All baking is done on premises, prices are reasonable, and if people leave the place hungry, they have only themselves to blame. Travelers getting their morning coffee fix have plenty of breakfast choices— creamed chipped beef, cheese blintzes, steak and eggs, Belgian waffles, corned beef hash, short stacks, and bagels. Sometimes a bowl of steamy oatmeal makes the cut. Muureen Murks, a waitress for thirty years, delivers the freshly cooked oatmeal accompanied by a small pitcher of warmed milk. That simple touch—warmed milk—results in well-deserved tips and satisfied customers ready to take to the road once more.

Older customers come, too—some who have spent their lives in the community and remember when the big show in town was the Langhorne Speedway. Opened just off the Lincoln Highway in the mid-1920s to celebrate the Philadelphia Sesquicentennial, the one-mile dirt track was built on top of marshland and underground springs. That meant the surface was always wet and soft except in the dead of summer, when the mud baked and the ground cracked. A perfectly round circle with no straightaways, the speedway earned two nicknames: "The Big Left Turn" and "The Track That Ate the Heroes." A downhill section just beyond the starting line was so steep and rutted that drivers called it "Puke Hollow." Langhorne was a tough track, yet some of the best racers showed up to give it a whirl, including Mario Andretti, Eddie

Sachs, and Bobby Unser. Racing legend A. J. Foyt won the last race on dirt at the speedway before it was paved in 1965, the year before the Blue Fountain opened. From then on, many of the spectators as well as the daring drivers showed up at the diner for post-race suppers. That ended when Langhorne's reputation as one of the most dangerous tracks in motorsports started keeping away even the boldest daredevils. When the speedway was razed in 1971, a shopping mall took its place.

Philadelphia is ahead, but first come Neshaminy, Penndel, and Bensalem, the southernmost township in Bucks County. This area is the home of the Neshaminy Mall, one of the first malls built in the United States, as well as the Growden Mansion, where the ingenious Ben Franklin supposedly flew his famous kite. There are various generations of old-road and optional routes to consider taking, but the U.S. 1/ Roosevelt Boulevard path is the best one for old-road travelers to follow into Philly. It is one of the largest Lincoln Highway cities, and its residents don't mind using the nickname "Philly"—unlike their counterparts at the other end of the highway in San Francisco, where anyone using "Frisco" is fingered for a newcomer.

From the Lincoln Highway's inception, cross-country travelers often took the time to visit such Philadelphia landmarks as the Liberty Bell, Independence Hall, and the U.S. Mint. Hardly any visitors, however, stopped at an ominous site just off Roosevelt Boulevard in northeast Philadelphia. Established in 1907 as the Philadelphia State Hospital at Byberry, this infamous asylum housed patients ranging from the mentally challenged to the criminally insane until it was finally shut down in 1990. Better known as the Byberry Mental Hospital, after the township where it was located, the institution was built on acreage once owned by Benjamin Rush, a signer of the Declaration of Independence and member of the Continental Congress. Rush also was a physician known as "The Father of American Psychiatry," for his innovative treatment of mental illness, which Rush considered a disease that could be cured with proper treatment.

Despite the early advances made by Dr. Rush, for many years the mentally ill were poorly treated and often shackled like criminals. By the early 1900s, conditions had not improved much. The patient population grew so rapidly that Byberry steadily deteriorated, despite construction of new facilities, including a morgue. The hospital remained overcrowded and understaffed. Reports of rampant abuse, killings and suicides, and straitjacketed patients housed in dark cells for long periods of time led to periodic cries for help, but little action resulted.

In both an exposé published in *Life* magazine and his 1948 book *The Shame of the States*, social reformer and journalist Albert Deutsch described the horrible conditions he witnessed at Byberry. "As I passed through some of Byberry's wards," wrote Deutsch, "I was reminded of the pictures of the Nazi

concentration camps. I entered a building swarming with naked humans herded like cattle and treated with less concern, pervaded by a fetid odor so heavy, so nauseating, that the stench seemed to have almost a physical existence of is own." The historic hospital was finally closed in 1990, and the remaining patients were transferred to improved treatment facilities.

Almost immediately, looters ripped out the copper pipes and stole anything of value from the abandoned buildings. Vandals smashed windows and covered the walls with graffiti and obscenities. Others came, including homeless people looking for shelter, thrill-seeking teenagers, and urban explorers eager to probe the tunnel system beneath the complex. Rumors of satanic cults performing animal sacrifices and bizarre tales of supernatural occurrences circulated, and soon Byberry was the subject of urban legend. Lincoln Highway travelers even stopped to get quick snapshots of the place. More recently, plans were unveiled to transform the Byberry site into a residential and commercial complex; in June 2006, the development was underway.

At last the ghosts were stilled, and Dr. Benjamin Rush—who showed that mental illness can be treated with kindness—could sleep in peace at the Old Christ Church Burial Ground, joining four other signers of the Declaration of Independence, including Ben Franklin. Die-hard Lincoln Highway fans may wish to pay their respects at the old graveyard and then perhaps genuflect at other prominent points of interest by taking the original alignment of the route to downtown Philly. That means turning south off Roosevelt Boulevard onto Broad Street, which runs to Penn Square and puts visitors within easy reach of many historical sites.

Travelers continuing their trek out of the city follow Lancaster Avenue through neighborhoods of row houses, corner bars, paved schoolyards filled with children, and small grocery stores. Gradually the cut-rate liquor stores, movie theaters converted to churches, and unpretentious diners serving barbecue and homemade bread give way to expensive auto dealerships, smart cafes and coffeehouses, and jewelry shops selling Rolex watches. These well-established western suburbs make up a succession of affluent communities known as the Main Line—after the main line of the Pennsylvania Railroad.

First comes Wynnewood, a community named in 1691 for Dr. William Wynne, the personal physician of William Penn, the Quaker visionary who founded Pennsylvania. The adjacent community of Ardmore was the home of the Autocar Company, an early motor-vehicle manufacturer and supporter of the Lincoln Highway. Ardmore's Suburban Square, one of the nation's first shopping centers anchored by a branch of a major department store, attracts old-money shoppers just as it has since 1928.

About ten miles northwest of Philadelphia lies Haverford, site of Haverford College, founded by Quakers in 1833 and consistently rated as one of the top liberal arts colleges in the nation. Haverford maintains a strong relationship with Bryn Mawr College in the nearby town of Bryn Mawr, which gave the school its name, meaning "big hill" in Welsh. Founded in 1885, Bryn Mawr was the first women's school of higher learning to offer graduate degrees, including doctorates. It also is one of the four remaining of the seven prestigious women's liberal arts colleges, dubbed the "Seven Sisters," that has not become coeducational. There is no shortage of scholars or athletes on this portion of the road, as it continues to the community of Rosemont, home of Rosemont College, and then to Villanova and the campus of Villanova

University, with its excellent academic reputation and strong tradition of turning out basketball champions.

Hungry university students and athletes—and some professional sports stars, mostly basketballers, who reside in Villanova—make frequent fuel stops at Minella's Diner, a short drive down Lancaster Avenue in Wayne. Named for former owner Minella Zoto, the diner, like the old road, survived its share of transformations. Originally Minella's was housed in a 1964 Fodero diner, but a diner built by DeRaffele Manufacturing replaced it in 2003. The switch had no impact on the food. Still family owned and operated, the diner's booths stay filled with loyal customers, moviegoers en route to the Anthony Wayne Theater, and road-weary travelers. They come to share a meal with friends or to celebrate a victory, but most of all they come to wolf down fried-egg sandwiches, beef stew, stuffed cabbage, short ribs, or one of the other offerings on the lengthy menu. Those who just can't decide can always opt for the Main Line Special—two pancakes, two eggs, link sausage, and bacon. Some even save room for banana cream pie. Undoubtedly, some sliced London broil and a spot of freshly brewed tea would have calmed the town's namesake, General Anthony Wayne—the American Revolutionary War commander nicknamed "Mad Anthony" for his frequent temper tantrums.

West of Wayne, the road soon reaches the communities of Strafford, Devon, and Berwyn. The end of the Main Line is near, but first there is

LEFT

*Chef McJon
prepares a
Blobwich,
Downingtown, PA.*

BELOW

*The Blobwich,
Downingtown, PA.*

Paoli, named after a popular local tavern honoring General Pasquale Paoli, a Corsican patriot who made a lasting impression during a St. Patrick's Day celebration. Finally there is Malvern, the site of the Paoli Massacre during the Revolution; it is always considered the last stop on the Main Line.

Travelers moving westward from Malvern ride on layers of road history. From Philadelphia to Lancaster—stretching for more than sixty miles through densely settled suburbs, country hamlets, and growing fields—the Lincoln Highway follows the old Philadelphia and Lancaster Turnpike, now called U.S. 30. Like all highways, the Lancaster Pike was the result of public demand for a new and improved roadway.

When completed in 1795, this first real American highway linked New York, the largest city on the continent, with Philadelphia, the largest inland city in the new nation. The Commonwealth of Pennsylvania lacked the resources to build such a road, so it was constructed with private funds, and thirteen tollgates were established along the highway. Travelers and stockmen paid a fee before a long pole (or "pike") blocking the entrance was raised, allowing them to pass. The crushed-stone roadbed was so solid that it was used into the twentieth century, and fees were charged until 1919, six years after it became part of the Lincoln Highway.

Perhaps with images of Conestoga wagons lumbering down this same route so long ago, travelers going farther into Chester County arrive at Frazer, ten miles southwest of historic Valley Forge, followed by Glenloch and Exton, at the intersection of U.S. 30 and Pennsylvania Route 100. At Downingtown, the east branch of Brandywine Creek slices through the town from east to west, and Business Route 30—the Lincoln—divides the town north and south. Originally called Milltown, after the War of 1812 it was renamed Downingtown for local industrialist Thomas Downing. The locals like to remind visitors that Downingtown was a waypoint for escaped slaves fleeing to Canada on the Underground Railway, and that President Lincoln's funeral train passed through in 1865. It should be noted that the 1958 sci-fi cult classic *The Blob* was filmed in and around Downingtown.

Although Philadelphia is still within easy commuting distance, the landscape is changing and the countryside opens up. Stone houses that sheltered generations of families stand as sturdy as ever in the village of Thorndale and the once-booming steel-mill town of Coatsville, where during the Civil War steel plates were hastily fabricated for the ironclad *Monitor*. At Sadsburyville, lucky travelers may spy a carved milestone marker left over from the era when this was the Lancaster Pike. While the sixty-two-mile-long turnpike was being built in the late 1700s, stones were set in the ground every mile, usually on the north side of the road. Through the years, the stones have been removed by road crews, farmers, or souvenir hunters, but some remain along the way. They have been found in front of a suburban home, near Villanova University, behind a guardrail, by a gas station, and in a parking lot. The milestone at Sadsburyville is beneath a line of cedar trees across the road from the remnants of Drake's Spanish Court, built in 1940 as a motorists' lodge.

The road leaves Chester County and enters Lancaster County, carrying travelers through the heart of the scenic Pennsylvania Dutch Country, a region known for communities of people who remain devoted members of the Amish, Mennonite, and Brethren faiths. Often referred to as "The Plain People," because of their unadorned lifestyle and ascetic religious customs, they work their fertile fields just as their German and Swiss ancestors did when they established their farms in the early 1700s.

The Pennsylvania Turnpike slashes across the northern part of the territory, but because of the picturesque countryside and abundance of attractions along the Lincoln Highway route, many travelers steer clear of the turnpike. This practice—known as *shunpiking*—has been routinely followed in various parts of the country ever since people had the choice between taking a free road or paying to take a more direct route. Many travelers no longer boycott turnpikes simply to evade forking over money. Shunpikers avoid the turnpike in order to drive roads offering a slower pace through scenic landscapes with glimpses of old stone taverns, covered bridges, and farms and orchards framed by mountains. The Lincoln Highway is such a road. And with the growing interest in heritage and cultural tourism, guided shunpiking tours attract more people ready to travel two-lane roads that weave through living history. In some instances, tour guides even provide a picnic lunch in a hamper, just as in the early days of the Lincoln Highway.

Lining both sides of the road through the towns of Gap, Kinzer, Vintage, Leaman Place, Paradise, Soudersburg, and Ronks are antiques and quilt shops, tidy farms, historic sites, and bed-and-breakfasts. There also are ample restaurants featuring dishes of the Pennsylvania Dutch (an Americanization of the word *Deutsch*, or German). On any given weekend—especially during summer and the glorious autumn season when leaves change color—traffic increases dramatically, with vacationers and big-city

LEFT *Amish buggy, Lancaster County, PA.*

RIGHT *Amish buggy, Strasburg, PA.*

antiques hunters looking for bargains. Visitors also come to see the Amish people on their home turf.

The Amish—easy to distinguish from outsiders—have been a big draw for a long time. The men are clad in dark suits and black or straw broad-brimmed hats; if they are married, they generally sport long beards. Amish women wear modest, solid-colored full-length dresses, a cape, and an apron. They do not own jewelry, and their uncut hair is worn in a bun concealed by a prayer cap or bonnet.

Lancaster County became a popular destination after the Civil War as authors and writers for *Atlantic Monthly* and other magazines began extolling the virtues of a trip to Pennsylvania Dutch Country. This trend continued into the twentieth century and only grew with the introduction of automobiles, allowing even more people to make the journey on the Lincoln Highway. In the late 1930s, *National Geographic* wrote up Pennsylvania Dutch Country as "the land of milk and honey" and "a garden spot of the world." Tourism officials reported that approximately 25,000 visitors came to Lancaster County in 1954, but that number skyrocketed over the next few decades.

In 1984, the release of the popular motion picture *Witness* put Lancaster County back on everyone's map. Yet the murder thriller—which made the Amish lifestyle an intricate part of the plot and was filmed in large part in Lancaster County—created mixed feelings among the Amish themselves. Some of them thought the film boosted the local economy, but others feared it was just another form of exploitation and misrepresented their way of life. Despite the criticism, however, travelers, sightseers, and just plain gawkers came in great numbers—and they kept coming. By the early twenty-first century, more than five million people were showing up each year to buy quilts, homemade jam, candles, baked goods, and fresh produce, and to sample all things Amish. Tourism remains a big business for Lancaster County and represents another cash crop for many local citizens. But, as some feared, it has come at a price, as cultures clash and the commercialization of the Amish threatens their austere way of life.

Traffic in itself poses a real danger to the Amish as they make their way from home to market in horse-drawn buggies. Although state law requires that they attach orange reflective triangles to their buggies as a safety precaution, some Amish find them offensive and have been fined for not complying. They prefer to follow the old custom of hanging lanterns on their buggies, and, perhaps out of deference to the law, using some gray reflective tape. Besides congested roads, the Amish must endure boorish sightseers, who treat them like theme-park characters and often trespass on their farms. Although the Amish uphold a strict prohibition against being photographed—particularly their faces—tourists think nothing of taking snapshots of families and individuals on foot or in passing buggies. "It kind of reminds me of being out west on Route 66 and seeing tourists take pictures of Indian people who obviously

BELOW

Amish dolls for sale at Dutch Haven, Soudersburg, PA.

don't want their picture taken," says one traveler during a roadside stop. He shakes his head in bewilderment as a tour bus disgorges camera-toting passengers eager to snap an Amish family scurrying away in their buggy.

Regardless of the cultural intrusions, the Amish still observe many time-honored religious traditions and customs, such as the rite of passage known as *Rumspringa*, which literally means "running around" in the Pennsylvania German dialect. The name is fitting. It describes a period of time (varying from a few months to years) when Amish boys and girls who have reached sixteen are allowed to explore the outside world and decide whether or not they want to be baptized into the Amish church. Some teens ultimately leave their community and never return, but a greater number make the commitment to stay and follow the strict guidelines of their faith. In the early twenty-first century, this trend—and the fact that most Amish families usually are quite large—resulted in the subdivision of some farms to accommodate members of the community. At the same time, the number of outsiders relocating to Lancaster County steadily increased, due to an influx of retirees from cities and young families who were interested in affordable housing and more than willing to commute.

With these changes came the problems plaguing much of rural America, but especially the Amish—shrinking farmland, rampant commercialization, rising land values, and declining farm income. Many Amish people stopped working their farms and set up retail shops and cottage industries turning out crafts, foodstuffs, and other products for the tourist trade. Some farmers even stopped raising and curing tobacco, a popular but labor-intensive crop in Lancaster County since the American Revolution, used in cigars known as Amish Palmas. Others made money by giving buggy rides or opening their homes to feed ravenous sightseers sauerkraut, ham loaf, apple dumplings, and chicken pot pies. Regrettably, others have chosen to produce puppies en masse, although recent crackdowns have curbed the situation. These so-called puppy mills even spurred animal activists to erect a giant billboard along the highway that reads, "Welcome to Lancaster, Home to Hundreds of Puppy Mills."

A significant segment of the Lancaster County population continues to hold onto the reclusive way of life and at the same time deal with the mixed blessings of tourism. Travelers scooting down the highway are reminded of this when they see a bumper sticker that says, "What Happens in Rumspringa, Stays in Rumspringa." It is worth noting that the decal is on a car and not a buggy.

During a rest stop in Soudersburg, there is time to browse Dutch Haven, with a distinctive windmill on the roof. A popular road attraction since the 1940s, Dutch Haven brags that it has the largest Amish souvenir collection in Lancaster County. Inside is ample evidence that the boast can be backed up. Everything Amish—or at least what tourists perceive as Amish—is for sale.

Buyers may choose Amish hats and dolls, pine rocking chairs, birdhouses, T-shirts, postcards, hand-rolled soft pretzels, homemade root beer, and jars of jellies, jams, and chowchow relish. There are also books that explain Pennsylvania Dutch folklore. Included are home remedies and cures, superstitions and tall tales, weather lore, and such proverbs as, "Morning showers and old women's dancing do not last long,"

and "Whistling girls and crowing hens come to a bad end." There are no Palmas, pups, or whistling girls in sight at the Dutch Haven, but there is plenty of high-calorie shoo-fly pie. After downing a warm sample topped with a dollop of whipped cream, travelers may decide to ship one of the gooey Pennsylvania Dutch desserts to friends on the other side of the country.

Behind Dutch Haven stands the kind of zany roadside attraction that once could be found on most American roadways catering to tourists. Established in 1993, The Outhouse sells loads of gag gifts and features gimmicks such as a box with a sign telling visitors to peek in the hole to see the world's only two-headed pig. Of course, those curious enough to take a peek

find themselves staring into a mirror. The creamy fudge is a big seller; it is free to anyone over eighty—but only if accompanied by both parents. Just across the highway from Dutch Haven, the Soudersburg Motel looks as good as it did back in the 1950s; just a few miles to the south, at Strasburg, is another lodging option, the Red Caboose Motel. Surrounded by farmland, the Red Caboose attracts train buffs, who enjoy staying in one of the fully restored twenty-five-ton cabooses and waking up to the clippity-clop of a horse pulling an Amish buggy on a nearby country road.

But there is still plenty to see down the highway. Miller's Smorgasbord, a feeding stop since 1929;

BELOW AND OPPOSITE

Red Caboose Motel, Strasburg, PA.

Dienner's Country Restaurant; Jennie's Diner; and a slew of other eating places from Ronks through Lancaster tempt travelers hard put to avoid their temptations.

Lancaster (pronounced "*Lank*-a-stir" by the locals), the western terminus of the old Lancaster Pike, had the distinction of being the capital of the United States for one day—September 27, 1777, when the British captured Philadelphia, forcing the Continental Congress to flee. The following day, they moved farther west to York and set up a temporary capital there. Besides these two Pennsylvania cities having briefly served as the nation's capital, and both being on the Lincoln Highway, they have something else in common—a fondness for sweets. It was in Lancaster where the Rodda Candy Company invented Peeps, those sticky marshmallow chicks covered with yellow sugar that find their way into so many Easter baskets. York, of course, was where the York Peppermint Pattie ("Get the Sensation") was first created. Peeps are now hatched elsewhere, and Peppermint Patties have not been made in York for some time.

Following the Lincoln routing out of Lancaster, travelers breeze through Mountville to Columbia, where they cross the Susquehanna River to Wrightsville via the Veterans Bridge; a historical marker at its eastern end pays homage to the Lincoln Highway. The city of York is not far ahead, but first comes a stop in the borough of Hallam to visit one of the Lincoln Highway's iconic sites—the Haines Shoe House.

Located on Shoe House Road, just a short distance off Route 30, the Shoe House was built in 1948 by a flamboyant character named Mahlon Haines. A savvy promoter who knew the value of self-promotion, Haines presided over an empire of forty successful shoe stores when he commissioned the building of a house shaped like a huge workboot as an advertising gimmick and a lasting shrine to shoes. The wood-frame structure, covered with wire lath and coated in cement stucco, was built on five levels with three bedrooms, two baths, a kitchen, and a living room. Haines—the self-proclaimed "Shoe Wizard"—never lived there. Instead, he offered it to clients, honeymooners, and elderly couples free of charge. Haines even included a maid, a cook, and a chauffeur-driven auto for his guests during their stay

in his giant shoe. When Haines died in 1962, he left the Shoe House to his employees. After that, it changed owners several times and for a period fell into disrepair and ruin. In the early 2000s, a couple purchased the unusual structure and fully restored it. Now listed in the National Register of Historic Places, the Shoe House draws visitors from around the world. They pay a nominal fee to tour the building and grounds, which include a doghouse also shaped like a shoe; gobble ice cream made on the premises; and hear tales of the "Shoe Wizard." It is time well spent.

Just as in Lancaster and other larger cities on the route, the one-way streets in York pose obstacles. Travelers have to remember that it is not necessary to follow the exact path of the original Lincoln—and in many places that cannot be done. In York, for example, travelers in search of a good meal can stay on Market Street and scan the shoulders for the brightly shining lights of The Paddock. There are plenty of parked cars (but not too many), and a gut feeling—the best gauge on any road trip—says that this is the place to stop. A full-service bar up front, crowded with regulars, connects to the dining room. It's spacious, the chairs are comfortable, and in less than twenty seconds a waitress is standing tall, calling everybody "Sweetheart" and handing out free advice along with the ice water.

Helen Snyder is a waitress, but everyone who comes to The Paddock calls her "Sarge." She was born in Maryland six days before the bombing of Pearl Harbor in 1941. "I was born poor, but I've worked hard all my life," says

Sarge. "I've tended bar, cooked, and waitressed." Sarge explains that she once lived in Gettysburg, on the Lincoln Highway to the west. She worked at a nursing home and as a cook, and her husband managed a grocery store. Gettysburg was where their son was born. "I went to that battlefield every day for years," Sarge tells diners when she fetches their drinks. "It was like I had to go there." Orders are up. Dinner salads are green and crisp—no iceberg lettuce and no mealy tomatoes. Entrées follow—sizzling steaks that were never frozen and prime rib that's just right. The spectacular onion rings were made by the owner's wife. After dinner, empty dishes are cleared and there's still room for a big slice of apple pie à la mode.

Born in Greece in 1945, Jim Spanos, owner of The Paddock, came with his family to the United States in 1954. The family first lived in Brooklyn, and Spanos grew up in the restaurant business. In 1972, he and his wife moved to York to be near her parents. They raised three kids and bought The Paddock in 1983. They gutted the place, put it back together, and have been open ever since—serving regular customers, providing a place for ladies to play cards, and feeding hungry people just passing through.

"I am well aware of the importance of the Lincoln Highway," says Spanos. "And I'm proud that our restaurant is part of the road. Everyone is family on the road and also here in this place. We had a cook who died in the kitchen after working at that stove for forty-two years. Our employees are family. Maybe they're not blood, but believe me they are family."

After a restful night at the Modernaire Motel, with its big glass-block office window and curvy brick wall, a breakfast stop at one of the Maple Donuts shops in York is in order. Among the doughnut lovers who have frequented the bakery is "Zippy the Pinhead," the cult comic-strip character created by Bill Griffith in 1971. Zippy appears in hundreds of newspapers and has a devoted following eager to read his exploits as he visits roadside icons and other pop-culture sites, including the Modernaire and the Haines Shoe House. Some road warriors on the

Lincoln consider a Zippy recommendation as good as one from Duncan Hines, whose stamp of approval on a restaurant served as the national standard for dining excellence during the 1940s and 1950s.

Founded in York in 1946, Maple has fifty-eight varieties of doughnuts, ranging from glazed, jelly, and sugar to devil's food, peanut butter, and blueberry. Signs on the walls proclaim, "If you are drinking and eating doughnuts to forget, please pay in advance," and "As you travel through life, no matter what your goal, keep your

eye upon the doughnut, not upon the hole." Early morning regulars—mostly old men and women with lined faces and no place else to go—occupy every stool at the winding Formica counter. One of them is Mabel Rizzuto. Born in York in 1935 and a widow with five grown children, Mabel waitressed at Maple Donuts for years and still comes back. "Some people like me come here every day," she says. "Most come to sit and talk and some don't even talk but just sit. It's a real important place for people."

Travelers swoop down on an open table like ducks on a June bug. Soon they are washing down hot doughnuts with coffee and listening to snippets of the many conversations floating through the room. A talkative fellow on a sugar and caffeine high tells them of his iron-pumping session at a nearby gym. Between slurps of coffee, he explains that York became "Muscletown USA" in the late 1930s when York Barbell Company was founded, and he strongly suggests a visit to the company's Weightlifting Hall of Fame, a local attraction, along with all the downtown historical buildings and sites. Before he seeks another refill, the gym rat also puts in a plug for a tour of the Harley-Davidson assembly plant and museum, just off Route 30.

Beyond the city limits of York, the old Lincoln passes through the towns of Thomasville, Abbottstown, and New Oxford on its way to historic Gettysburg and the rest of Pennsylvania. This stretch of road is the Lincoln Highway Heritage Corridor (LHHC), established by the state to preserve, enhance, and promote the transportation heritage of the Lincoln Highway in a six-county region

of Pennsylvania. From Abbottstown in the east to North Huntingdon in the west, the two-hundred-mile-long corridor has been transformed into a linear roadside museum featuring Lincoln Highway signage, interpretive exhibits, and murals. The LHHC office in Ligonier, fifty miles east of downtown Pittsburgh, is a source of road information and sells a useful driving guide.

Just west of New Oxford—"The Antiques Capital of Central Pennsylvania"—with its traffic circle and vibrant downtown, is a business located in what appears to be a former residence. A sign near the highway says, "Escape Reality Massage and Tanning." The notion of a rural tanning salon is not surprising, since such enterprises can be found in almost every small American town. This one is bound to attract farm wives and daughters eager to spend their off-time during a long Pennsylvania winter on a cozy tanning bed, or getting a spray tan and a deep

ABOVE
"Muscletown
USA," mural,
painted by Max
Mason, York, PA.

massage to boot. It's fitting that this salon is on the Lincoln—also known here as Route 30 or the York Road. Appropriately, customers whose skin color resembles the copper shade of a penny after too much time in the salon are referred to as "Lincolns."

Adjacent to the tanning salon is Hubcap City, a field covered with hubcaps. It is an astonishing sight—thousands and thousands of hubcaps of all styles and types. There are spinning hubcaps, custom hubcaps, classic hubcaps, baby moon hubcaps, truck hubcaps, and chrome hubcaps. All of the hubcaps—Plymouth, Chevrolet, Ford, Toyota, Pontiac, and the rest—are neatly stacked in formation, facing the highway. Some are rusted and some are pristine. It is a hubcap orphanage, and each one of them is up for adoption. In the morning light, the dew-covered hubcaps gleam like shiny headstones.

Beyond lies Gettysburg, a Lincoln Highway town where the living come in great numbers to view graves and walk on hallowed ground where thousands of men and boys perished during those terrible July days of 1863 when no one could escape reality. Gettysburg has benefited economically from the Lincoln name and the devastating war that raged while he was president.

Besides hosting the best-known battle of the Civil War, the town was the site of President Lincoln's most famous speech. Visitors have been drawn to the battlefield and the various Lincoln-related sites since not too long after

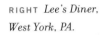

RIGHT *Lee's Diner, West York, PA.*

LOWER RIGHT *Jerry Cusack, owner of Lee's Diner, West York, PA.*

LEFT *Hubcap City, New Oxford, PA.*

the smoke cleared. Lincoln Highway travelers were no exception during the road's heyday, and they still join the throngs arriving in Gettysburg each year. Following a tour of the Gettysburg National Military Park and a stop at the visitor center, travelers return to the town circle to see the refurbished Gettysburg Hotel and the Wills House, where Lincoln polished his memorable

speech—which was criticized for being too brief the day he gave it. These days, a bronze statue of Lincoln giving directions to a tourist provides the best photo op.

The Lincoln Diner, just off the circle, stands across the street from the Majestic Theater, with a renovated marquee thanks to Heritage Corridor grant money. Chocolate-chip pancakes and the "He-Man" French toast served with ham, bacon, sausage, and two eggs are among the diner's breakfast favorites. A roast beef sandwich and lentil soup do the trick at lunch but allow little room for the strawberry shortcake, lemon meringue pie, or the Lincoln's legendary dessert called "The Thing"—eight scoops of ice cream, three toppings, an entire banana, chopped nuts, whipped cream, and of course a cherry.

All that is needed after that is a toothpick to resume the journey on U.S. 30 to the west, a route that closely follows the old Pittsburgh and Philadelphia Turnpike, a well-used stagecoach road in the early nineteenth century.

Not far out of Gettysburg is a worthwhile side trip just off U.S. 30 to Round Barn Farm, surrounded by orchards. At one of the LHHC interpretive sites, a talking gas pump explains the history of the round barn built by the Noah Sheely family in 1914, just as the Lincoln Highway was gearing up. Customers turned off the Lincoln to buy sacks and bushels of apples and peaches. John Fritz, who was hired to erect the barn, bicycled five miles from

THIS PAGE
A 1920s photo of Round Barn farm.

OPPOSITE *Round Barn Farm, west of Gettysburg, PA.*

his home in Cashtown. The barn—built of hemlock, chestnut, oak, and pine—required 250 barrels of cement just to form the foundation for the first floor. Nowadays, people hunting autumn scenery or antiques still come to the barn to buy fruit, pumpkins, or jars of honey.

If some honey is not enough to satisfy a sweet tooth, it may be necessary to return to the route and pay a call on Mister Ed's Elephant Museum, where Ed Gotwalt has assembled a massive collection of thousands of pachyderms of all sorts and sizes from around the world. Elephant fans are in heaven when they step into the museum, but so are candy lovers. Every kind of candy imaginable is for sale—cream fudge, caramels, double-dipped peanuts, candy bars, peanut-butter cups, jellybeans, gumdrops, chewing gum, jawbreakers, rock candy, candy corn, licorice, and on and on. A sign warns, "Shoplifters Will Be Trampled."

By the time travelers reach Chambersburg, where the U.S. 30 bypass is Lincoln Way, it's time to quench that powerful thirst brought on by consuming a bag full of Ed Gotwalt's candy. Dodie's, a local place that featured one of the first drive-up windows in the state, has cold beverages galore to wash away all remnants of fudge. It also serves good food—especially broasted chicken—at honest prices. Travelers can down rounds of iced tea or enjoy some of the soft-serve ice cream, good enough at Dodie's to make even the most faithful dieter jump off the wagon.

While in Chambersburg, some travelers may pop in at Elite Tattoo, the domain of Eric Von Dar. Born in Allentown, Pennsylvania, in 1960, Eric takes his work as a tattoo artist very seriously. Eric keeps the place immaculate—almost like a doctor's office but with much more interesting art on the walls. He does custom work, touch-ups, and cosmetic tattooing and accepts all major credit cards. Walk-ins are allowed, but most of his clients come by appointment and are quite diverse, ranging from bikers and construction workers to physicians and judges. No matter who comes in, Eric always points out the words

emblazoned on the back of his business card: "Remember: A tattoo is forever."

After passing St. Thomas, the birthplace of Jacob Nelson "Nellie" Fox, a major-league star inducted into the Baseball Hall of Fame in 1997, the road reaches Fort Loudon, where a 1928 Lincoln Highway cement marker stands guard in a front yard. Old and new routes come together here, and for the first time in the westward journey, travelers experience some mountain driving. Old people harbor memories of this road and its ups and downs. They recall passing hay wagons in small towns and reaching out the car window to grab the traditional wisp of hay for making a secret wish. They have recollections of cars creeping carefully down the steep hills, the smell of burning brakes, and cars pulled over to the side of the road to cool off.

"Glancing ahead from this level stretch, the tourist will see Tuscarora or Cove Mountain looming up tremendously in the distance, and may wonder how enjoy refreshments and the view of the Cumberland and Cove Valleys before descending into McConnellsburg, the Fulton County seat, and continuing on to Breezewood.

Once a small town on the Lincoln Highway, the bustling crossroads of Breezewood, called "The Town of Motels," changed with the opening of the Pennsylvania Turnpike and then years later when Interstate 70 came along. Little remains from the early days before Breezewood was all fast food, big rigs, and enough motel rooms to house a legion of truckers. The mammoth Gateway Travel Plaza was erected in 1994 to replace the original business built by Merle and Marian Snyder in 1940. For many years, the Snyders made it a practice to swap a meal, a bed in the "bunkhouse," or a tank of gas for a soldier's shoulder patch. Neat rows of all those patches in frames adorn the walls of the big truck stop to this day. Grab a coffee and take a look at the patches before rolling on. In Breezewood, the Lincoln Highway gets lost in the shuffle.

But this is Bedford County, and from this point forward it only gets better on the Lincoln, starting in the town of Bedford itself. The twenty-two-block downtown National Historic District itself has a wealth of landmarks

difficult the crossing of it will be," wrote Robert Bruce in *The Lincoln Highway in Pennsylvania*, a guidebook published in 1920. "One only needs to be sure that the car is in good condition, especially the brakes, strictly observe the rules of the road, and keep a sharp lookout for vehicles coming from the opposite direction, particularly under full headway, perhaps carelessly driven." Not bad advice for travelers today. The payoff comes at the summit of Tuscarora Mountain, elevation 2,240 feet. On clear days from the Mountain House Bar and Grill—originally called Doc Seylar's Rest House—it is a good idea to take time to

dating back to before George Washington came to Bedford to review troops during the Whiskey Rebellion. Road history here is superb. There is much to see along Pitt Street, the original Lincoln Highway in Bedford. A block off the route, the former Fort Bedford Inn, built in 1916, no longer takes in traveling guests, but it remains a comfortable apartment residence. Dunkle's Gulf Service Station—a stunning art deco gem featuring colorful terra-cotta tiles—is still the best place to get a fill-up, just as it was in 1933, when William "Dick" Dunkle opened the station and kept it open seven days a week. Dick's son Jack eventually took over the station where he started working long before he could drive. He and his wife, Sue, are on the job just like his father, but now they close on

Sundays. They provide full service, so customers get their car's tires and engine checked and the windows washed.

A short distance down the road is another Lincoln Highway icon—the Bedford Coffee Pot. Perched near the entrance of the Bedford County Fairgrounds, the former Coffee Pot Cafe opened in the 1920s and became a favorite stop for traveling salesmen and families making their way along the Lincoln. Over the decades after the big pot closed, it fell into disrepair and became an eyesore. Then in 2003, with assistance from the Lincoln Highway Heritage Corridor forces, the Coffee Pot was fully restored and moved to its present site.

Leaving Bedford, travelers on this final leg of the Lincoln Highway over the Allegheny Mountains and across western Pennsylvania come across all sorts of road treasure. Just four miles west of Bedford, the Jean Bonnet Tavern offers food and lodging, as it has since it was licensed as a public house in 1780. A mile farther is the Lincoln Motor Court, built in 1944 and considerably younger than the old tavern—but just as important because of the era of road travel it represents. The dozen cabins, still clad in the original composite shingles, form a horseshoe beneath a stand of pines. "It would have been easier to strip these cabins, gut them, and start all over, but we didn't do that—it would have been wrong," says Bob Altizer, who, with his wife Debbie, painstakingly restored each cabin over the course of twenty years. "It's all worth it when we get customers going back three generations in a family. One man came here and asked to be checked into a specific cabin. He told me that many years before, it was where he spent the very first night with his wife."

High in the Alleghenies on the road to Pittsburgh, travelers pay their respects at the site of one of the Lincoln Highway's best-known attractions—the S.S. Grand View Point Hotel, later known as the Ship Hotel. Located fourteen miles west of Bedford at the top of Mount Ararat, the hotel burned to the ground in October 2001. Scorched ruins remind travelers of the magnificent roadside haven that served guests well for many years and became a true icon of the Lincoln Highway.

At an elevation of 2,464 feet, the site still offers those who stop to pay their respects a dramatic view of three states and seven counties. Across the highway, in the ruins of the old Esso filling station

that used to serve the hotel guests, the fading words "One hundred percent pure Pennsylvania Oil" are painted on the wall. Joan Crawford, Thomas Edison, Henry Ford, Greta Garbo, and Tom Mix, among a host of luminaries, stayed at the hotel in its heyday. All that's left today are the charred wood remains—the ship's burnt bones—and the remarkable view.

A few miles away lies the village of Buckstown, where Duptstadt's Country Store boasts its "old-fashioned hospitality." The store sells western wear, steel-toed work shoes, hunting and fishing licenses, locally made bread, and candy by the piece. Many travelers stop here,

ABOVE *The Coffee Pot, newly remodeled.*

ABOVE *Vintage postcard, circa 1940, S.S. Grand View Point Hotel (later the Ship Hotel) in Bedford County, PA, at one time the most famous landmark on the Lincoln Highway.*

RIGHT *Vintage photo of the S.S. Grand View Point Hotel, Bedford County, PA.*

as do hunters and local residents. The store's owner, Carol Duptstadt, says that a lot of people in this part of the country still call the route the Lincoln Highway.

Next to Carol Duptstadt's store is a winding road that leads to the memorial for United Airlines flight 93, which crashed here on September 11, 2001. Like Gettysburg, this crash site has become, in only a few years, a historic and hallowed place that memorializes tragedy and death. A more formal memorial will mark this place, but initially personal messages, tributes, teddy bears, ribbons, little American flags, and "gimme caps" of all kinds abound. It is clear that people leave a little piece of themselves here. In fact, a guard in a truck has been stationed at the site to prevent the public from going down into the gorged "wound" itself.

Continuing westward, travelers arrive in Stoystown. Here the yellow-brick Hite House, dating back to the 1850s and a popular stop during the peak years of the Lincoln Highway, has been converted into comfortable senior-citizen housing. The Hite House is listed on the National Register, and Stoystown itself has been designated a National Register Historic District. Today, one of the most popular Lincoln Highway food and lodging stops in Stoystown is the Kings and Queens Hotel and Restaurant, a faux castle perched on a highway hilltop.

On the road between Stoystown and Pittsburgh are several vintage "mom and pop" businesses and roadside attractions. Eight miles west of Stoystown, in Ferrellton, a seven-foot-tall praying mantis standing

in front of a secondhand store has drawn the attention of passing gawkers since the mid-1960s. In nearby Jennerstown, named for Edward Jenner, discoverer of the smallpox vaccine, is Our Coal Miner's Cafe, a busy eatery displaying local mining artifacts and memorabilia from the successful 2002 Quecreek Mine rescue. On a sharp turn just beyond Jennerstown and the Wishing Well Motel at the western edge of town, travelers can visit the site where automobile manufacturer Frederick S. Duesenberg on July 2, 1932, crashed his supercharged Model J into the mountainside. He died twenty-four days later in a Johnstown hospital.

Although the Lincoln Highway at this point is nearing the end of its run in Pennsylvania, several

ABOVE *The site of the Ship Hotel on Mount Ararat, PA. The hotel burned to the ground in October 2001.*

interesting destinations lie ahead. At Laughlintown,
the Compass Inn, built as a stagecoach stop in 1799, has
been restored as a museum. A short distance to the west,
U.S. 30 passes Ligonier Beach, the largest swimming
pool in the state when it opened in 1925. Still a summer
oasis, Ligonier Beach's nightclub featured big bands
and such songsters as Perry Como and Dean Martin,
an Ohio native who started as a towel boy at the beach.

The town of Ligonier, fifty miles east of downtown
Pittsburgh, has been called "motion-picture perfect,"
thanks to its charming town square (called a "diamond")
with a copper-roofed bandstand, as well as an array of
antiques shops and restaurants. Three generations of
the Lincoln, a 1928 concrete highway marker, and the
Lincoln Highway Heritage Corridor headquarters office
are located in Ligonier. In fact, the LHHC is responsible
for the Lincoln Highway kiddie-car rides at nearby
Idlewild Park, the nation's third-oldest amusement park.

After traversing the scenic Loyalhanna Gorge,
the highway divides around Loyalhanna Creek. From
this point, the original route reaches a string of small
towns and communities, including Youngstown,
Greensburg, Grapeville, Adamsburg, Irwin, East
McKeesport, and Turtle Creek, before coming to the
city of Pittsburgh. Just east of the city limits, U.S. 30
(the Lincoln Highway) enters East Pittsburgh on the
George Westinghouse Memorial Bridge. Named for
the famous entrepreneur and engineer who founded
Westinghouse Electric Corporation, the majestic bridge

ABOVE *Memorial for United Airlines flight 93, which crashed at this site on September 11, 2001, near Shanksville, PA.*

OPPOSITE *The Duquesne Incline, Pittsburgh, PA.*

Situated at the junction of the Allegheny and Monongahela Rivers, where they join to form the Ohio, this once-polluted city is now considered one of America's most livable and scenic communities. Much of the original route passing through Pittsburgh is now freeway, but glimpses of old highway are still possible along Bigelow Boulevard and other places. Pittsburgh offers many attractions, ranging from a museum for hometown boy Andy Warhol to the Carnegie Museum of Art. Every visit also should include a ride on either the Monongahela or the Duquesne Incline, the two surviving historic tramways that since the 1870s have transported sightseers to the top of Mount Washington for spectacular views of the city and the rivers.

was the world's largest reinforced-concrete arched span when it opened in 1932. Although it was completed after the disbanding of the original Lincoln Highway Association, die-hard proponents of the Lincoln have always considered the bridge important. Not only did it provide a bypass to a dangerous bottleneck that had plagued drivers for many years, but the bridge also came to symbolize the spirit of the Lincoln Highway. It fits the image of the spunky "City of Bridges"—as Pittsburgh is often called because of the more than two thousand bridges in the metropolitan area.

After exploring the second-largest city in the state, travelers using the original pre-1927 Lincoln Highway faced a twenty-five-mile drive along the north bank of the Ohio River through congested railroad and river towns before reaching the Ohio state line. The roads were crowded and in poor shape. Motorists filled the small-town coffers, thanks to speed traps set up by local cops. In 1927, the routing improved when the Lincoln alignment shifted. Instead of crossing directly into Ohio, travelers first entered West Virginia. It remains the best way to go.

WELCOME to WEST VIRGINIA

Chapter Four

WEST VIRGINIA

John Denver nearly got it right when he sang that West Virginia was "almost heaven." Almost, however, just doesn't cut it. Too bad the songster didn't leave the Rockies and go to a junk shop in the Lincoln Highway town of Chester, West

Virginia, nestled on the banks of the Ohio River. That's where he would have found true heaven on earth—that is, if he came on a Friday, and the earlier the better. Friday is the one and only day of the entire week that Gene Amos—"The Chester Pie Man"—dispenses freshly baked pies to a grateful public. One bite—not even a big one—and anybody with even a couple of taste buds knows he or she has died and gone to heaven. No *almost* about it.

Humorist Jack Handey said it best: "If when you die you get a choice between pie heaven and regular heaven, choose pie heaven. It might be a trick, but if not, mmmboy."

By lovingly baking pies, Amos carries on a West Virginia pie tradition that most states would envy and too few people know about. Created as a result of decades-long bickering between the eastern and western counties of Virginia, West Virginia was

LEFT

1928 Lincoln Highway marker, Chester, WV.

loyal to the Union, which it joined on June 20, 1863, when President Lincoln signed the bill making it the thirty-fifth state. Years before that, apple orchards began to sprout in the land that would become West Virginia when a young man from Ohio named John Chapman traveled the northern region planting apple seeds. Hard work and vision paid off for the fellow better known as "Johnny Appleseed," and by 1889, West Virginia was producing five million bushels of apples a year. Some juicy apples became cider, vinegar, or apple butter,

but many of them ended up as the prime ingredient for the all-American apple pie—which is appropriate, because West Virginia, unbeknownst to tens of millions of people who've celebrated it year after year, is the birthplace of Mother's Day as well as Father's Day. And what could be more American than Mom and apple pie?

Over the years, all varieties of pie have remained a staple on West Virginia tables, becoming part of the state's culinary heritage. The Golden Delicious—one of the best apples for pie—is the official state fruit. There is even a West Virginia town that was named Pie in the nineteenth century by the local postmaster because he liked pies so much. When someone says that they live in Pie, it usually brings smiles all around. The little burg of Pie is in Mingo County, down in the southwestern corner of the state. Johnny Appleseed roamed the northwest panhandle, a sixty-mile spindle ranging from five to sixteen miles wide. That was where the commercial fruit industry evolved in West Virginia, and where Gene Amos resides and bakes his pies.

"People come in here from all over the United States in order to get one of my pies," says Amos. "I have had customers from Oregon, Georgia, Indiana, New York, and everywhere else. I really enjoy having them come to the shop and choosing their pie. I get to meet so many people this way, and if I didn't have this, I honestly don't know what I'd do."

It would be foolhardy to proclaim that Gene's pies are the best on the Lincoln Highway. There are simply far too many pie palaces on the old road turning out killer pies of every flavor. From New York City to San Francisco, through all thirteen states, are diners and cafes renowned for serving scrumptious pies. A traveler can sit at a lunch counter and enjoy a slice of pie baked that very morning by the person serving it. That does not mean, however, the pie is homemade—a term that is constantly misused and abused. Veteran travelers have been known to have some fun when they spy the word *homemade* on a menu or sign by asking the waitress whose home the dish was made in. The pies that Gene Amos creates irrefutably are homemade. Every Thursday night, he bakes them at home in his kitchen. If that's the case, then road logic suggests that his pies are among the best *homemade* pies on the Lincoln Highway.

Amos did not always bake pies. He was born in 1935, during the Depression, about 100 miles south of Chester in a "wee little place" named Porter's Falls. In 1960, he and his wife moved to Chester in Hancock County, the northernmost and smallest county in the state, and raised their three children. Amos was only forty-six years old when he was stricken with Guillain-Barré syndrome, a rare inflammatory disorder of the immune system. There is no known cure, and some cases are fatal. He spent two months in intensive care, ate through a feeding tube for four months, and was told he would never walk again. True to the West Virginia motto—*Montani semper liberi*, Mountaineers are always free—Amos found a way to remain mobile. By removing the blade from a riding lawn tractor and making a few modifications, he had all the wheels he needed to get around.

His passion for baking pies began in the mid-1990s, when he decided to try his hand at making a pie for one of the church fund-raisers he and his wife attended. That first pie was a success, and more followed. Eventually Amos set up a pie stand on the sidewalk in front of a secondhand store at the corner of 5th Street and Carolina Avenue, on the original alignment of the Lincoln Highway in downtown Chester. In 2000, he moved his pie operation inside the store. "Actually, I never intended to have a secondhand store and I never intended to sell pies, but here I am," says Amos, whose wife died in 2003.

Each Thursday evening, Amos bakes as many as thirty or forty pies to sell at the shop the next morning. He bakes some with sugar on the crust and others he calls no-sugar-crust pies. "I make seventeen different kinds—apple, pumpkin, pineapple, blueberry, peach, you name it. The only pies I won't make are cream pies. The health department is squeamish about me making cream pies and say they're 'hazardous,' but they say my fruit pies are just fine. They're 'nonhazardous' pies."

Other than regular customers, two restaurants from across the river in Ohio get all their pies from the Chester Pie Man. Lincoln Highway travelers also find their way to the corner building that started out as a hardware store in 1900. They know the shop is open if a gussied-up tractor is parked outside. Whether or not they buy any of the thousands of items—used furniture, carpets, clothing, glassware, and bric-a-brac—does not faze Amos in the least. Even if they don't get a pie, it is all right with him. His pleasure comes from holding forth

THIS PAGE

*Downtown
Chester, WV, then
and now.*

Corner of Carolina and Third Street
Chester, West Virginia

with cronies and strangers as he sits in a wheelchair in his cluttered shop. The exchange of conversation and the gift of stories well told are more important than anything else, including selling pies. Besides, by late morning on Fridays, most of the pies are long gone—especially if he has put out any black raspberry pies.

"One of those pies sells for seven bucks and it costs me five dollars to make it," says Amos. "That is just fine with me. This handicap has helped me more than it hurt me. All the fund-raisers and helping out folks and students, and meeting people from all over who come here, why I couldn't have done any of that if my life didn't take certain turns. I'm a lucky guy."

Travelers fortunate enough to spend time with Gene Amos and snag one of those pies count their blessings as they take in the sights of the Lincoln Highway in West Virginia. It shouldn't take too long. After all, there are only five miles of Lincoln Highway in the entire state—rather like Route 66, which nibbles its way through a few towns in Kansas. Yet that short stretch of two-lane road proves that the oft-quoted phrase, "Less is more," is really true.

For starters, West Virginia's snippet of the Lincoln features the World's Largest Teapot, scenic views of the Ohio River, the world's largest pottery plant (where Fiesta ware is made), and a major thoroughbred racetrack. If that's not enough, there are ghost tales and UFO sightings, a large-scale replica of a Boeing B-52 bomber, and, of course, those nonhazardous *homemade* pies. No superhighway or turnpike anywhere can beat all that.

West Virginia became the last of the thirteen Lincoln Highway states in late 1927, when the highway was rerouted between Pittsburgh and Ohio. Original travelers had three choices when headed westward to Ohio on the Lincoln out of Pittsburgh, but none were satisfactory because the routes through the remainder of Pennsylvania were not state but local roads, and poorly maintained ones at that.

After years of complaining and lobbying, the Lincoln Highway Association was finally able to steer travelers away from the congested river towns on the north shore of the Ohio River and have a new southerly route via West Virginia designated as a state highway. From the Pennsylvania line, the newer route enters the northern tip of West Virginia and Hancock County—named for John Hancock, the enthusiastic first signer of the Declaration of Independence.

The highway then descends a curvy hill notorious for frequent vehicular crashes and makes its way into the town of Chester. Between May and October, today's travelers may wish to deviate from the route in order to take in a flick at the Hilltop Drive-In, opened in 1950 and, despite closures through the years, still in operation. The original route to Chester turned southwest at the bottom of the hill and followed Carolina Avenue to Third Street to Virginia Avenue and then north on First Street to the Chester Bridge, built across the river in 1897, and East Liverpool, Ohio, waiting on the other side.

In 1928, Boy Scouts marked the route through Chester—as they did the rest of the highway—with

RIGHT *Vintage postcard, Chester Bridge, Chester, WV.*

BELOW *Lincoln Highway marker, Chester, WV.*

the distinctive cement posts memorializing Abraham Lincoln. Three of those posts can still be seen in Chester; according to the Lincoln Highway Association, they represent the highest density of the remaining historic markers on the entire route.

The Chester Bridge, a 705-foot suspension span, served the Lincoln Highway and U.S. 30 as the river crossing for motor vehicles and, for a time, a local trolley. Through its long years of service, many people also walked across the bridge, including kids and families headed to the Saturday matinees at the movie houses in East Liverpool. The bridge closed in the spring of 1969 and was dismantled the following year. The site where the bridge once was anchored became the Dr. David S. Pugh Memorial Overlook, in memory of a revered hometown physician who for a half century made countless house calls, delivered an untold number of babies, and also acted as a community leader before his death in 2001.

For seven years after the Chester Bridge's removal, traffic was diverted a mile downstream over the Newell Bridge, until the 1977 opening of the Jennings Randolph Bridge, named in honor of a West Virginia senator. The pylons for the new bridge stand on Babb's Island, where George Washington and his surveying party reportedly buried a barrel of biscuits. It is unknown whether they ever came back for them.

Today U.S. 30 crosses the river on the Jennings Randolph Bridge and bypasses the old Lincoln route through Chester. Wise travelers exit and check out Chester and nearby Newell. Before jumping onto Carolina Avenue and passing beneath the ramps leading to the bridge, there is an important stop to make. Adjacent to the bridge ramp, at the busy intersection of U.S. 30 and Carolina Avenue, stands the World's Largest Teapot, in all its restored glory, on a concrete pad surrounded by a cyclone fence.

Constructed in 1938 by William "Babe" Devon, the Teapot actually was a giant hogshead barrel that had served as a Hires Root Beer stand in Oakdale, Pennsylvania. After buying the barrel and shipping it to Chester, Devon proceeded to attach a handle and spout and place a lid with a large ball on top. Since Chester and nearby Newell (and East Liverpool across the river) had long dominated the pottery market, Devon thought a huge teapot not only honored the area's heritage but would attract passing customers. He placed it in front of his own pottery outlet shop near the corner of Carolina Avenue and First Street, a prime spot for catching the attention of Lincoln Highway traffic. Local teens ran the souvenir and concession stand inside the pot except for a couple of years during World War II, when Devon was forced to close because of the decrease in traffic due to gas and tire rationing. Eventually Devon sold his business, and by the late 1960s the Teapot was used to sell pottery items as well as everything from cigarettes, hot dogs, and fireworks to postcards and lawn and garden supplies.

The Teapot changed hands several times, fell into disrepair, and was shut down. It sat abandoned and was on the verge of being demolished in 1984, when the local telephone company purchased the property and donated the Teapot to the citizens of Chester. After a few years of fund-raising, the Teapot was completely refurbished. It was given a new spout, covered with new

tin, and repainted with its original red and white colors. In 1990, townspeople turned out for the rededication ceremony, when the Chester Teapot was moved to a cloverleaf near the Jennings Randolph Bridge, where it could be seen by travelers on both the Lincoln Highway and U.S. 30.

In 2005, there was talk of moving the Teapot yet again to make room for a fifty-year-old B-52 bomber that the Chester Veterans of Foreign Wars Post 6450 planned to buy in Oklahoma and bring to Chester. The VFW members believed that the old airship would serve as a fitting veterans' memorial, but because it was so huge—reportedly taller than the Great Wall of China—the best place for it was exactly

where the Teapot sat. The VFW pointed out that the Teapot could be easily moved to a nearby plot of ground that was too small for the airplane. Those plans quickly changed when the Federal Highway Administration refused to issue a permit for the VFW project. Giving up their dream was not an option for the stalwart VFW members, so they scaled down their project and found a new site. The Teapot stayed put.

On July 4, 2006, the Ohio Valley Veterans Memorial—a fiberglass one-eighth-scale replica of a B-52 bomber, which appears to be in flight over a waterfall—was unveiled beside the Chester VFW Hall on Carolina Avenue. There also is a black granite wall, and granite blocks with the engraved images and names of veterans and their loved ones, including those who have died. It seems the folks of Chester—whose donations lovingly built the memorial—do not neglect their dead

Leap the Dips, Rock Springs Park, Chester, W. Va.

LEAP THE DIPS

RIGHT *Vintage flyer for Rock Springs Park, Chester, WV.*

or forget their past. Travelers find that out from local folks who remember the old days—not just the good old days but the rowdy ones, too. There are tales of the wide-open days of slot machines and payday bar fights and of raucous nights at the Club 30 on top of Chester Hill, where Joey Bishop and Vegas-style entertainers brought in droves of customers. Some of the best memories involve the famous Rock Springs Park.

This amusement center opened in 1897 and continued to operate well into the twentieth century on land where George Washington had camped and sipped water from the natural springs, probably about the same time he buried those biscuits on Babb's Island. Great crowds came to Rock Springs to jam the floor of the dance pavilion, shoot the chutes, and fill the dining hall and cafes. People flocked to the shooting gallery and the bowling alley, swam in the pool, and rode all the rides until they ran out of money or courage. Couples walked the shady paths or watched ball games. Rock Springs always drew Lincoln Highway travelers. It was the perfect spot to unwind while traveling cross-country. Attendance remained good even in the face of tragedy. In June 1915, during the annual outing of public and parochial schools from towns on both sides of the river, a fire broke out at the entrance of an attraction called the Old Mill. Many were injured and at least six teenagers—between twelve and seventeen years old—tragically died in the blaze.

Through both world wars and even the Depression, when it was difficult to come up with carfare, much less money for amusements, Rock Springs was a place of refuge where people could forget their troubles, if only for a while. A wooden roller coaster named The Cyclone, installed in 1927, became an instant sensation. At any time of day or early night, blood-curdling screams reverberated across the park from riders who promised God never to tempt fate again if they could just get off the coaster alive. Big bands led by Ray Anthony, Stan Kenton, and others showed up to play the dance pavilion. Kids from towns on both sides of the Ohio met beneath a mirrored ball spinning above the dance floor, and many of them married. It was said that dwindling attendance due to the introduction of theme parks brought about the park's closure in 1970. Others disagree, claiming the amusement park was still prospering and not in decline. They believe Rock Springs was a victim of progress and the coming of the new Jennings Randolph Bridge. What is known is that the state of West Virginia used the right of eminent domain to purchase and then condemn the park property. The carousel was auctioned off, and so was that scary roller coaster. The dismantled Cyclone sold for a mere buck. Demolition crews and bulldozers took over from there, and today the park and the springs where Washington drank cold water lie beneath the four southbound lanes of the bypass highway. Nearby, a historic marker telling the stories of Rock Springs and the restored World's Largest Teapot remind travelers of the way things used to be in Chester.

There are yet other reminders of the area's past. Unadorned but tasty meals are served along Carolina Avenue, the old Lincoln route through town, at the Let's Say Cafe, Tom's Country Kitchen, Mary's Cafe, Bruno's Pizza, and Taco Huey's Restaurant & Lounge. Sophia Rae's Cafe—"More fun than you can handle"—rates high marks from locals and travelers alike. The sentimental favorite for Lincoln Highway enthusiasts is Connie's Corner

LEFT *All that remains today of Rock Springs Park, Chester, WV.*

Restaurant, owned and operated by Connie and Bob Hissom, featuring specials seven days a week. Breakfast is served all day, and the sausage gravy over biscuits might have done the trick for George Washington had Connie's been open when he was around. At noontime most any day, Connie's is packed. Diners tangle with liver and onions, tuna melts, roast beef sandwiches, beef noodle soup, and grilled pork chops. The Thursday night spaghetti dinner at the Chester American Legion Hall and the Friday night early-bird supper special and bingo games at the Moose Lodge give Connie's and the other eating houses some stiff competition. Moose Lodge members count themselves especially lucky if they have a Gene Amos berry pie waiting for them at home.

There are more dining choices and a couple of major attractions a few miles west of Chester, along Route 2 toward Newell. The northernmost city in West Virginia, Newell is the home of the Homer Laughlin China Company, the world's largest manufacturer of dinnerware, including Fiesta ware. The factory offers two tours each weekday, and a retail outlet shop is open daily.

Farther down the highway is the Mountaineer Park Race Track & Gaming Resort, formerly known as Waterford Park. Those hoping to strike it rich come from great distances in buses and cars to try their hands at the 3,500 slot machines in six casinos, to bet on Thoroughbred horses racing on the one-mile oval dirt track, or to dine in one of ten restaurants. Although Homer Laughlin and the nearby gambling resort are closer to the unincorporated community of Newell than to Chester, they often are more associated with the latter. Bitter rivals of Chester in sports, Newell residents still find comfort knowing that their "Big Green" roundballers were West Virginia's high school basketball champs in 1951–52.

When the time comes to bid West Virginia farewell and take the old road to Ohio, instead of driving all the way back to the newer crossing in Chester, travelers can take the Newell Bridge, even though it was on the Lincoln route a relatively short period of time.

Built in 1905, the Newell Bridge closely resembles the old Chester Bridge. It is historically important if for no other reason than that it was one of the first all-steel suspension bridges. Gamblers departing Mountaineer Park at Newell need to save some pocket change if they cross the Ohio at this point: Homer Laughlin owns the bridge and charges a nominal toll. Periodic reports of unidentified flying objects hovering in the area are no cause for alarm—unless a UFO ever lands on the bridge and exceeds the ten-ton weight limit. Instead of mysterious flying objects, travelers usually see barge traffic and, in the rear-view mirror, a sign saying, "Welcome to wild, wonderful West Virginia."

The fifty-cent toll is collected near the north end of the bridge. Then, with a soft push on the gas pedal, travelers glide into Ohio—just as easy as pie.

Welcome to OHIO

Chapter Five

OHIO

Like a blue-ribbon pie, the Lincoln Highway town of East Liverpool, Ohio, was made from scratch. First settled in the late 1700s, but not incorporated as East Liverpool until 1834, the town had a recipe for success concocted in large

part by James Bennett, an English émigré who was a skilled potter. High on the bluffs over the Ohio River, East Liverpool had the ideal combination of basic ingredients to sustain a thriving pottery industry: an abundance of natural clay, deposits of salt for glazing, a navigable river, plenty of entrepreneurial spirit, and a workforce of immigrant craftsmen willing to sweat for a living. After Bennett built the first kiln, many others quickly followed. Before long, the town of hills and kilns was well on its way to earning the nickname "America's Crockery City."

East Liverpool became to the American ceramics industry what Detroit was to automobiles and Pittsburgh to steel. As potteries expanded and more firms opened, the city grew. For many years, much of America ate dinner from plates made in East Liverpool. Between 1870 and 1910, the population of the town swelled from two thousand to more than twenty thousand, with at least ninety percent of the wage earners working in the potteries along the river. But East Liverpool was a one-industry town, and 1910 was when the pottery boom

LEFT
Highway sign on the road between Convoy and Van Wert, OH.

peaked. Instead of buying ceramic products, the public started turning to cheaper and more durable materials, such as glass and tin.

The first town today's travelers reach when headed west on Ohio's portion of the Lincoln Highway, East Liverpool was still riding high from the volume of pottery produced there when it became part of the road's original alignment in 1913. Two years later, a motion-picture crew arrived in town while making a promotional film about the Lincoln to show at the Panama Pacific International Exposition in San Francisco. Out of deference to East Liverpool's role as pottery center of the nation, an old kiln covered with pottery donated by local manufacturers was blown up to give the filmmakers some unusual action footage. Celebrants cheered when the kiln was detonated, sending a shower of debris into the sky.

Following World War I and through the 1920s, there was little to cheer about. The Depression delivered another hard blow, and East Liverpool's importance steadily declined, along with the local economy. The ceramics industry never bounced back from the impact of mass-produced products from overseas manufacturers flooding the market. By the close of the twentieth century, only a few pottery companies remained from the scores of manufacturers that at one time had produced more than half of the annual ceramics output for America.

Despite the devastation of its primary industry, East Liverpool did not wither and die. In fact, old-road towns are used to the changes brought about by shifts in the economy, technological advances, and, of course, the impact of being bypassed by newer and supposedly better highways.

"The time is now for those who cling to the hope that East Liverpool can survive," says Frank "Digger" Dawson, today one of the town's most vocal cheerleaders. "The challenge is here and the present is all we have. Enough has been said about the past, and tomorrow is filled with question marks. We have no alternative but to charge forward but at the same time not neglect our heritage."

Dawson led that charge starting in 1986, when community leaders recruited him to spearhead a drive to restore the 126-foot-tall clock tower in the downtown business district. The antique clock had been taken down and placed in storage in 1969, when the old high school building was demolished. To accomplish the task, Dawson helped establish the East Liverpool High School Alumni Association. Before long, the members raised more than $2 million to restore the old clock, build an impressive office and museum complex, and develop a scholarship program. Dedicated on July 4, 1992, the clock tower—on its original site by the Lincoln Highway—promptly became a symbol of the town's spirit and its new moniker, "America's Hometown." Dawson did not stop there. Next he founded and served as the first president of the Lou Holtz/Upper Ohio Valley Hall of Fame, named after the East Liverpool native and famed football coach and established to showcase individuals and communities from throughout the region.

Other citizens and community leaders did their part to keep East Liverpool alive. Thanks to the hard work of Tim Brookes—an attorney with a passion for preserving history—and his many cohorts, the restored Thompson House, a mansion built near the river's edge in 1876 by pottery magnate C. C. Thompson, is listed on the National Register of Historic Places. Nearby, the Broadway Wharf, part of the Ohio River Scenic Byway, attracts picnickers and travelers pausing to feed the ducks and watch barge traffic before returning to the old road.

Frank Dawson remains a true son of the Lincoln Highway. After all, he was born, bred, and baptized on West Fifth Street, one of the road's alignments in East Liverpool. It is also where he works at the only job he has ever held—embalmer and funeral director. He may be an undertaker, but he acquired the nickname "Digger" when he was a teenager. The story of how he earned that name actually begins at the eastern terminus of the Lincoln Highway, Times Square.

In the summer of 1948, on his first trip to New York, Dawson and his mother were lunching at a busy Automat restaurant near Times Square. There they bumped into Sara Ostermann, a member of a prominent East Liverpool family and the widow of Henry Charles Ostermann, the original field secretary of the Lincoln Highway Association. In 1920, Ostermann, had been killed in an automobile accident while driving the Lincoln west of Tama, Iowa. He was buried in the Riverview Cemetery in his wife's hometown, and Sara lived comfortably in a downtown mansion that eventually was leveled to become a parking lot for a branch of Kent State University.

During their lunch, the threesome from East Liverpool discovered that the world premiere of *The Babe Ruth Story*, starring William Bendix, was occurring at a nearby theater. Mrs. Ostermann suggested that they wade into the crowd of onlookers to catch a glimpse of some of the movie stars and perhaps even Babe Ruth himself. They scrambled for the door.

"We got to see 'The Babe,' but we never did locate William Bendix in that mass of humanity," laments Dawson. "I was a big fan because Bendix also was Riley in the original radio version of *The Life of Riley*. I loved that show, and it gave rise to a character named Digby O'Dell, the local mortician nicknamed 'Digger.' Back in East Liverpool, it didn't take long for my pals to hang the name 'Digger' on me because of our family's funeral business. The name not only stuck, but to this day I get mail addressed to Digger."

Digger learned the mortician's trade firsthand from his father, Frank A. Dawson. The son of an East Liverpool cop, the elder Dawson was only sixteen when he dropped out of school and hired on with undertaker E. G. Sturgis. Dawson had learned every aspect of the business by the time the Sturgis Funeral Home moved into a rambling, Victorian-style residence built in 1905 at 122 West Fifth Street. In 1934, as the Depression raged and old man Sturgis battled terminal cancer, Dawson embalmed a young man still remembered not only in East Liverpool but also throughout the Midwest and along stretches of the Lincoln Highway, Route 66, and country backroads that crisscross the land.

"It was October 22, 1934. I was six weeks old and, obviously, have no recollection, but it was the day my father took care of the body of Charles Arthur 'Pretty Boy' Floyd," says Frank Dawson. "My father fashioned himself as a Rudolph Valentino look-alike, and that autumn afternoon he walked across Fifth Street to get his hair cut. He told the barber: 'Do a good job because G-men are going to shoot Pretty Boy Floyd today and bring him to our funeral home and I'm going to be in all the photographs and stories.' And that was just what happened."

Tagged by J. Edgar Hoover as "Public Enemy Number One," and trying to get back to his beloved Oklahoma hills, Floyd had been the subject of an intensive three-day manhunt in the countryside outside East Liverpool. Old-timers said there had not been so much excitement in Columbiana County since the summer of 1863, seventy-one years earlier, when John Hunt Morgan, a dashing cavalry officer, had surrendered his exhausted raiders there after making

the Confederacy's deepest thrust into Union territory. Charley Floyd, often called "The Sagebrush Robin Hood," was not about to surrender either, and late in the afternoon of October 22, local police and federal agents gunned him down as he dashed for freedom across a cornfield. Leading the posse was Melvin Purvis, one of Hoover's crackerjack crime fighters, who exactly two months earlier had disposed of John Dillinger, another well-known criminal operating in Lincoln Highway territory.

After Floyd's body was transported to town, the dapper Frank Dawson and law officers posed for photographs behind the outlaw in repose on an embalming table. Then the mortician shaved Floyd, combed his hair, and took note of the dead man's manicured nails and neatly plucked eyebrows. Dawson summoned a potter—out of work because of the Depression—to the basement room to make a death-mask mold of Floyd's face. A number of the cream-colored plaster casts were later distributed like hunting trophies.

Later that evening, crowds of curiosity seekers jammed the Sturgis Funeral Home to see the man who helped take their minds off of the Depression, if only for a while. Dawson rouged Floyd's cheeks and laid out the corpse on a small cot in the front parlor with a blanket

of crushed velvet pulled up to his chin. An estimated twenty thousand people—most likely an exaggerated number—filed through the room for several hours. Finally, Dawson had to summon police when the crowd got out of hand, trampled bushes, and even tried to gain entry through a coal chute. On the Sturgis record book, Floyd's occupation was listed as "bandit." The body was shipped to Oklahoma for what some sources claim was the largest funeral in that state's history.

Two months after Floyd's death, Sturgis succumbed to cancer. The twenty-eight-year-old Dawson took control of the business and gave it his name. By 1939, the Dawson Funeral Home had moved into new quarters just down the street, where the younger Frank Dawson took over the business in 1960, when his father's health began failing. But the passage of time did not sever the Dawson family's connection to Pretty Boy Floyd. In the early 1990s, the family acquired the old Sturgis Funeral Home property and began restoring the Victorian mansion to its original luster. When that was accomplished in 1998, the Dawsons opened the doors to Sturgis House, a six-bedroom bed-and-breakfast.

"We get business guests, wedding parties, family reunions, and visitors from as far as Switzerland, France, Germany, and Africa," says Susie Anderson, the Sturgis House manager. "And we get our share of Lincoln Highway travelers, too, including some who arrive in vintage cars."

Relatives of Pretty Boy have even booked rooms at Sturgis House. After a tasty breakfast in the first-floor parlor where Floyd's body was displayed, guests often tour the basement, where one of the Pretty Boy death masks and other memorabilia from that era are displayed. On the walls are photos of a handsome young funeral director with a fresh haircut standing next to the infamous decedent.

"Our town is trying to make a comeback, and I really think it will continue to improve," says Dawson. At Sturgis House, some of his guests return from lunch at the Hot Dog Shoppe followed by dessert from L&B Donuts—two local favorites on the Lincoln Highway.

Before continuing their journey, travelers can tour the magnificent Carnegie Library, built in 1912, and the Museum of Ceramics, a tribute to the industry that served the town for so long. Formerly the post office, the museum is operated by the Ohio Historical Society and contains samples from the various potteries, including the Hall China Company, founded in 1903 and still in business at the east end of town. Near the corner of Fifth and Broadway, where the museum stands, a relocated concrete Lincoln Highway marker from the 1928 routing reminds everyone that East Liverpool is still proud of its past even as it grapples with its future.

Departing "America's Hometown," travelers face about 240 miles of Lincoln Highway before reaching the Indiana line. There were four generations of the old road in Ohio, and East Liverpool had at least two different Lincoln Highway alignments between 1913 and 1928. The Ohio Lincoln Highway Historic Byway,

LEFT *The Museum of Ceramics, East Liverpool, OH.*

headquartered in Canton, provides detailed information about the various routings and realignments travelers can take. The Ohio Lincoln Highway History Primer Tour suggests starting east of East Liverpool on the original pre-1928 alignment near the Pennsylvania border, at a place appropriately called the Point of Beginning. An obelisk indicates the spot where, in 1785, geographer Thomas Hutchins marked the beginning location for the surveying of all public lands in the United States.

From there, many travelers backtrack to the north end of the Chester Bridge, the newer 1928 route through town that eventually became Lisbon Street or State Route 267, one of the steepest climbs in Ohio. This route takes travelers through sixteen miles of hilly country to Lisbon, second oldest town in Ohio and the

RIGHT *Vintage postcard depicting the Chester Bridge over the Ohio River, which connects Chester, WV, with East Liverpool, OH.*

BELOW *Minerva Cheese Factory, Minerva, OH.*

CHEESE and BUTTER
MADE WITH LOVE... ...FROM MOO TO YOU!
MINERVA DAIRY Inc.

seat of Columbiana County. Prior to 1928, the Lincoln in these parts was widely thought of as "one of the worst stretches in the East," according to the official 1924 highway guide. However, the guide went on to point out that thanks to improvements, such as a million-dollar paving job, that same stretch "represents one of the finest and longest continuous stretches of hard surfaced Lincoln Way between the two coasts."

Those making the drive today move through open, rolling countryside sprinkled with farmhouses, and barns with old advertisements such as "Chew Mail Pouch" painted on the side. Farther up the road, on an old alignment, another barn is adorned with the words "Kentucky Club Pipe Tobacco." Before entering the town of Hanoverton, home of the restored Spread Eagle Tavern, offering food and lodging since 1837, a handmade sign in a field promotes "Doctor Boom's Lightning Rods."

Travelers on U.S. 30 go through Hanoverton and then Kensington, both of them long-ago stops on the historic Sandy and Beaver Canal. At Minerva, on the Lincoln since 1920, travelers can pull in at the Minerva Cheese Factory, family owned and operated since 1935. Every vat of cheese and batch of butter is "made with love from moo to you"—using milk from free-range cows pastured on local dairy farms. A sack filled with slices of their sharp Cheddar and pepper jack, a hunk of summer sausage, and some crackers ought to tide over anyone until lunch.

Between Minerva and East Canton to the west, the original route of the Lincoln was a narrow and twisty farm road, and segments of the 1913 dirt alignment and the 1919 brick improvement can still be found. At East Canton, travelers wishing to supplement their cheese snacks may dine at Nicole's Family Restaurant, a 1950s-style malt shop with good vittles and lots of Lincoln Highway souvenirs—or else wait to eat in Canton just five miles ahead on U.S. 30. Bender's Restaurant, a Canton favorite since 1902, serves prime aged beef and seafood shipped from Boston.

To walk off a big meal, consider visiting the Pro Football Hall of Fame, Canton Classic Car Museum, or the William McKinley Presidential Library and Museum. There are also several Frank Lloyd Wright homes as well as the First Ladies National Historic Site, where visitors can learn all they need to know about the wives of the nation's presidents—or, at least, whatever they were willing to share.

Football reigns mightily in Ohio, especially on the portion of the Lincoln Highway between Canton and Massillon, to the west. Mention Massillon and some people may think of Lillian and Dorothy Gish, famous actress sisters who came from this town. Sports fans, however, equate Massillon with football and nothing else.

The Massillon Tigers are reputed to be one of the winningest high-school football teams in the nation, second only to the Valdosta High School Wildcats, in Valdosta, Georgia. Many sports authorities consider the annual competition between the Tigers and the Canton McKinley High School Bulldogs the greatest high-school football rivalry in the United States. In fact, the annual meeting of the two teams is the only high-school contest in the nation to carry odds in Las Vegas. Massillon has produced such talented football stars as Paul Brown, who went on to coach championship teams at Ohio State and the Cleveland Browns, and Harry Stuhldreher, one of the famed Four Horsemen from Notre Dame. While Massillon's population hovers at about 30,000, the school stadium holds more than 20,000. Every boy born at the local hospital is presented with a miniature football. Ron Maly, reporting for the *Des Moines Sunday Register*, summed up football in Massillon this way:

In the beginning, when the Great Creator was drawing plans for this world of ours, He decided there should be something for everyone. He gave us mountains that reach to the sky, deep blue seas, green forests, dry deserts, gorgeous flowers and gigantic trees.

Then He decided there should be football, and He gave us Massillon.

He created only one Massillon; He knew that would be enough.

After torturous late-summer football practices, untold numbers of weary Tigers have made their way to a Lincoln Highway oasis called Twistee Treat. Its twenty-four flavors of soft-serve ice cream end up in cones, shakes, floats, malts, sundaes, and splits—all intended to revive dehydrated football players and their fans as well as sweat-drenched travelers.

Refreshed and ready for more of the road, travelers can take a sweet side trip just off the 1928 Lincoln route between Massillon and Wooster and head north to the Wayne County community of Orrville, headquarters of the J. M. Smucker Company.

It was 1897 when Jerome Monroe Smucker started pressing locally grown apples into cider and apple butter and sold them from the back of his wagon. Many of those apples came from trees grown by John Chapman, the famous Johnny Appleseed, who wandered the Ohio countryside as he had done elsewhere. Four generations later, and with more than 3,500 employees worldwide, the name Smucker's is still associated with jams and jellies.

Back on the Lincoln, several small towns do their best to get travelers to stop for food, gas, and a bed for the night, or just to look around. There is Dalton, the first Ohio town to be bypassed by the newer U.S. 30, followed by Wooster, site of a former Lincoln Highway campground, and then several smaller crossroads communities before getting to Mansfield, a city founded in 1807 that is cognizant of its highway heritage.

Mansfield was located on a major highway corridor that in the early 1900s was called Ohio Market Route 3. This was the original route chosen in 1913 to become part of the Lincoln Highway, but alignment changes in 1928 moved the new route to the center of the city. The Richland Carousel District, just two blocks off the route in downtown Mansfield, was a popular stop even before Ohio's Lincoln Highway Historic Byway was created in 2004. The district's centerpiece, a park at the corner of 4th and Main Streets, features a hand-carved carousel, the first one to be built in the United States since the 1930s.

Speaking of the 1930s, just down Main Street from the handsome carousel is the Coney Island Diner, in business since 1936. This is the kind of place where regulars just come in, sit on a counter stool, and say, "Bring me the usual" to a waitress who is already headed back to give the fry cook the order. Breakfast is busy at the diner, but lunch is crowded too. In summer, the booths are usually filled all the time, and friendly gossip is served all day. The specialty, of course, is hot dogs smothered in chili, and some diners order thirteen at once—the "baker's dozen special." Fried bologna and meat-loaf sandwiches are big hits. The pea salad is famous up and down the Lincoln Highway, as is the jukebox with tunes ranging from the likes of Kate Smith, Glenn Miller, and Nat King Cole to Elvis, Patsy Cline, and Chuck Berry.

After inhaling a pile of Coney dogs, movie buffs traveling the Lincoln can go just north of downtown Mansfield to take a guided tour of the historic Ohio State Reformatory, built in 1886 and used until 1990. The old prison resembles a Gothic castle and has been the location for several motion pictures, including *The Shawshank Redemption* and *Air Force One*. Every Halloween season, the prison—listed on the National Register of Historic Places—draws large crowds when it becomes the "Haunted Reformatory." If literature holds more appeal than a dank dungeon, bookish travelers can go south of town to Malabar Farm, the 914-acre estate of Pulitzer Prize–winning author and noted conservationist Louis Bromfield. Now a state park, the thirty-two-room residence is open for guided tours, which include the site where Bromfield's friend Humphrey Bogart wed Lauren Bacall in 1945, the famous couple's honeymoon suite, and the piano that played their wedding music.

Leaving Mansfield, travelers once more have to make routing choices. The old alignment loop goes to towns such as Ontario and Galion, which were original Lincoln towns until 1921. Most travelers today prefer to rejoin U.S. 30 just a few miles west of Mansfield and head straight into Crestline, on the route since 1921. The 1924 guidebook warned travelers about "poor dirt"

roadway between the two towns that made driving treacherous in wet weather. In Bucyrus, where two different paths of the Lincoln enter from the east, it is worth stopping for a look at the huge "Great American Crossroads" mural on the town square, depicting the business district in the 1890s. Upper Sandusky, seat of Wyandot County on the Sandusky River, has a short piece of original brick Lincoln Highway as well as some lip-smacking curly fries at the Dairy Snack Drive-In.

Travelers driving the thirty-seven miles of the 1928 alignment between Upper Sandusky and Beaverdam find themselves on one of the straightest stretches of the Lincoln. Occasionally, newer Lincoln Highway signs are tacked on trees standing between the highway and the cornfields. A long-deserted farmhouse looks as though it had come from an Andrew Wyeth painting. No Trespassing signs are posted, and a great gnarled tree with a tire swing hanging from a bough stands guard. The paint has disappeared from the wooden building where families once lived. Rust creeps up a corrugated tin shed. The bushes and flowers have gone feral and the chimney is cold. Windows with no glass stare blankly at the highway. Farther west, travelers pay their respects at the derelict Bon-Air Motel, where a sign indicates that truckers once may have been welcome but now have no place to stay. Another sign on a tree says it all: "Silence Is Forever." This is a ghostly place being devoured by vines and weeds and musty old nightmares. Inside, swallows build their mud nests on the walls and atop a shower spigot. It is their place now.

Sometimes it's good to visit such "ghost places." They remind travelers of what can happen when the chain businesses clustered at freeway ramps and interstate exits strangle the independent motels and cafes trying to turn a buck. Thankfully, signs of life remain across the western route of Ohio's Lincoln Highway—in places such as Williamstown, New Stark, and Beaverdam, where the Dixie Highway crosses the Lincoln Highway and a plaque honors Carl Fisher, the man who conceived both roads. The 1928 straight alignment proceeds through Cairo; west of town, it meets the original route coming up from Lima and follows it to Gomer. In 1939, Gomer enjoyed fleeting fame when Admiral Richard Byrd's Snow Cruiser—a fifty-five-foot-long, thirty-seven-ton behemoth designed for polar exploration—went out of control on the Lincoln Highway en route from Chicago to Boston and crashed into a cow pasture just outside of town. The four crew members and their six guests escaped unharmed, but traffic had to be rerouted for several days while workmen struggled to remove the cruiser. An estimated 125,000 spectators, from as far away as Wisconsin, rushed to Gomer to see the unique vehicle—half truck and half tank. Boys made good money hawking hundreds of hot dogs at a dime each. The cruiser was finally removed and continued on to Boston, but Gomer enjoyed its brief time in the limelight.

After passing through Gomer, travelers realize that their time in Ohio is coming to a close. In Delphos, a front-porch kind of town trapped in time, locals enjoy pointing out a modest house where they claim the famous Western author Zane Grey briefly resided in the 1890s, when he played baseball for the Delphos Reds. If it is anywhere close to mealtime, however, tales about old ball teams have to wait. The town of Van Wert may be a fair piece down the highway, but the chance to feast on fried chicken at Balyeat's Coffee Shop might make a preacher desert his flock. Located on Main Street in the heart of Van Wert, a solid Lincoln Highway town from the start, the famous neon sign outside Balyeat's

BELOW

Downtown Delphos, OH.

reminds diners that just inside they may partake of "Young Fried Chicken Day and Night"—just as avid fans have done since 1924.

Founded by the Balyeat brothers, the restaurant had various owners until 1964, when another pair of brothers—Dale and Don Davies—bought the place. Don had worked for the previous owner for ten years and remains the restaurant's hands-on manager and chief cook. On any given day, Dale in his white cap and apron can be seen dishing up spuds or noodles, carving turkeys, or busing tables. It is a family business with an unbroken chain of command of three generations, including Dale's son Clark, daughter-in-law Lorie, and granddaughter Emilee, who works at the coffee shop when she's not going to school. Dale's wife, Marcia, handles the cash registers and Lorie's mother, Barbara Silance, has baked pies for Balyeat's for decades. Together they have made their restaurant one of the finest places in the state to enjoy real food prepared with love and care.

Across Main Street, the onetime Marsh Hotel—now a community center—opened for business in 1915 when the Lincoln was getting started. Just down from Balyeat's, a pocket park occupies an empty spot where a building once stood. There are flowers, a wall mural, and an old Lincoln Highway marker. A few blocks to the west, the first public library in Ohio has catered to readers since 1903. The majestic county courthouse looks like a wedding cake.

"It has been almost eighty-one years since I was a five-year-old boy living on a farm on the Lincoln Highway, about five miles east of Van Wert," recalls Alfred J. Baxter, a retired county agricultural agent now living in Wilmington, Ohio. He continues:

We realized that U.S. 30 was a direct route from New York City and San Francisco. The local people called the road the Ridge Road, since the highway was located on a sandy ridge, which long ago was the southern beach of Lake Erie. As a small boy in the mid-1920s, it was fun to watch the cars speeding by. Every now and then a large touring car with New York or California license plates would go whizzing by. Most of those out-of-state cars—normally big, expensive touring cars—would have three or four spare tires on the back. I would wave at the drivers and they would wave back, or blow their horns. Since it was a busy highway, we would often have hoboes and tramps, who would stop and beg for food. My mother was afraid of them and usually would have nothing to do with them.

The Highway was also a popular place for groups we called gypsies. There would be four or five families in horse-drawn covered wagons that would be looking for a place to camp. Dad would allow them to use the orchard beside our house. The men would work for local people—painting buildings, building fences, and other such work. They would stay for a few weeks and then move on. My parents told me the gypsies would like to steal little boys like me, so I was afraid of them.

The Lincoln Highway was one of the best roads in the area. We never went very far on it—thirty miles or so to the east to Lima and thirty miles to the west to Fort Wayne. Years later, when my son moved to Clinton, Iowa, it was always a warm feeling to see road signs indicating that U.S. 30 or the Lincoln Highway still existed. Even now, so many years later, I can still picture the old touring cars. It's nice to know that I can still go on the same highway that they were on.

It is hard to leave a place so unscathed by the passage of time, but the desire to head west prevails. There are no towns between Van Wert and the Indiana state line—just fifteen miles of the Lincoln Highway and time to reflect. And that is exactly how it should be.

Welcome to INDIANA

Steel Mills

Dunes

Chapter Six

INDIANA

There are 163 miles of Lincoln Highway in Indiana, but the road running northwestward from the Ohio border to the outskirts of Fort Wayne is among the most memorable. This original route takes travelers through the small settlements

of Townley and Zulu, site of a bar and a combination general store, filling station, and post office. Another landmark is the Zulu Garage, at least ten times older than most of the vehicles its wrecker trucks haul in for fixing.

Next up is Besancon, settled long ago by French immigrants when there was no highway but only a dirt farm-to-market trail. Named for a town in France, Besancon is dominated by St. Louis Catholic Church, built in 1846 of white stones, plus a rectory and a cemetery. Masses are said on Saturday and Sunday, and the faithful with appetites come from afar for Friday fish dinners in the parish hall. The entire complex is listed on the National Register of Historic Places.

A one-room brick schoolhouse erected in 1892 stands idle. So does its replacement—the forlorn WPA-era Jefferson Township Centralized School, built of buff-colored bricks in 1938. Between the two buildings in the shaded cemetery are graves of war veterans, stillborn infants, victims of influenza

LEFT

Vintage Chevy, Osceola, IN.

and polio, farm families, and men and women who were baptized, wed, and eulogized in the old rock church. Many of them attended one of the schools, and some may have played on the baseball team that won the 1951 district championship. All of them rest on the edge of the Lincoln Highway, where the living pass and remember the dead of Besancon beneath the chiseled tombstones.

Even directionally challenged travelers will know they are on the right path in these parts. In 2006, the Allen County Highway Department and the Indiana chapter of the Lincoln Highway Association placed Historic Lincoln Highway signs and 1928 posts on a nine-mile section of the route. Soon the old road hooks up with U.S. 30 and acts as a series of frontage roads that go by the name Old Lincoln Highway. Instead of bypassing Fort Wayne, travelers can take State Road 930 into New Haven, a suburb along the Maumee River. From New Haven, they can follow their guidebooks into Fort Wayne—where the St. Joseph River and the St. Mary's River join to form the Maumee. The city is the birthplace of actress Carole Lombard and fashion designer Bill Blass, and author Edith Hamilton grew up here.

Fort Wayne is worth a stop if for no other reason than to experience Cindy's Diner on the downtown corner of Harrison (the Lincoln Highway) and Wayne Streets. Valentine, the revered Wichita, Kansas, manufacturer, built the diner in 1954, twenty years before it stopped diner production. Noah Clauss bought the diner in 1954 for $6,000 and opened it as Noah's Ark. In 1990, John and Cindy Scheele bought the diner. The couple, married since 1957, totally refurbished the interior and returned the luster to the white porcelain enamel exterior trimmed in red neon. They moved it to its present location, dubbed it Cindy's, and started cooking. Since then, the Scheeles have never stopped trying to fulfill the mission printed on their menu: "We serve the Whole World . . . fifteen at a time!" Not coincidentally, fifteen swivel stools line the counter.

Four bird feeders hang outside the diner windows, and the jukebox is as good as any on the open road. John is a time-proven griddle master and Cindy—with her droll sense of humor, charming banter, and speedy service—entertains and satisfies customers. The lunch

LEFT *John and Cindy Scheele, owners of Cindy's Diner, Fort Wayne, IN.*

crowd mostly order burgers, but there's a tempting list of sandwiches, soups, and sides. As it should be, breakfast is served anytime. Of all the menu items, by far the most popular choice remains one listed simply as "Garbage." It is described as a blend of eggs, potatoes, cheese, onions, and bits of ham "prepared our special way." The recipe for Garbage has appeared in print, but when folks try to duplicate it at home, it never tastes the same as it does at Cindy's. Maybe it's that well-seasoned grill. No amount of bribe money can coax the Scheeles into revealing what "our special way" means, but countless customers order the Garbage just as they did in the 1960s, when a previous incarnation of the diner started making the dish for hungry cops on the beat.

In 1997, Cindy and John perked up the breakfast crowd by adding the vintage machine that had churned out doughnuts at nearby Murphy's Dime Store until it fell victim to the big retail chains and closed in the late 1980s. "Every morning at 5 a.m., we fire up that old doughnut machine and start making cake doughnuts," says Cindy between shuttling food orders. "People start lining up and pretty soon ten dozen hot doughnuts come out. The doughnuts go pretty fast. By 6 a.m., this place is jammed and there's a bunch of people waiting outside."

In 2006, the shoebox-shaped diner survived a scare when plans were scrapped to build a new hotel on its site. When the deal fell through and an alternative site became available, preservationists and highway advocates breathed a sigh of relief. So did a bunch of people addicted to Garbage, hot doughnuts, and Cindy's wisecracks.

RIGHT Jukebox on the counter at Cindy's Diner, Fort Wayne, IN.

"We feed people from all over the place," says Cindy. "They come here from across this country and from Canada, England, Mexico, Spain, Romania, Egypt, and other countries. I've served the Righteous Brothers, Doc Severinsen, Jack Jones, and the Beach Boys at this counter." Maybe, if Cindy's is allowed to stay put and the antique doughnut machine doesn't break down, the diner will end up feeding the world . . . fifteen at a time.

Fort Wayne has rarely been considered a major tourist destination, and perhaps part of that problem stems from a mind-set that new is always better. For a long time, the prevailing attitude in the city was that if a historic or culturally important structure stood in the way of progress, it had to be torn down. That way of thinking now has shifted somewhat, thanks to the efforts of preservationists and concerned citizens who understand the value of architectural treasures.

After lunch at Cindy's or Powers Hamburgers—also on Harrison Street and an outstanding supplier of fresh burgers and chili since 1940—travelers may decide to stop at the downtown public library and pick up a self-guided tour booklet of the city's architecture. Although much has been lost, significant sites survive, such as the Embassy Theatre, a movie palace opened in 1928 and fully renovated in the 1990s. The Embassy reopened in 1996 as a performing arts center, which accounts for some of the famous customers who have dined at Cindy's. Another first-rate downtown stop is the Lincoln Museum, home of the world's largest collection of Abraham Lincoln memorabilia.

Fort Wayne is another one of the places where Lincoln Highway travelers have to make a decision about which alignment to take. They can follow the original 1913 route—a northwesterly drive that bends to the west at Elkhart and makes its way across northern Indiana to the Illinois line—or pursue the 1928 rerouting of the Lincoln. The newer path bypassed most of the original highway and shaved off twenty miles by leaving Fort Wayne on U.S. 30 through Columbia City, Warsaw, and Plymouth before merging with the 1913 alignment at Valparaiso. Neither route is a poor choice, and some travelers even do some backtracking and take both. Of course, many people speculated in 1913 that Carl Fisher, the man who dreamed up the Lincoln Highway, would make sure it went right through his hometown of Indianapolis. Fisher made a fortune in that city with his business dealings and inaugurated the Indianapolis 500 at his famed speedway.

But because of the poor conditions of the existing state roads—many of which were disconnected—the highway planners decided on the long-used continuous route northwest of Fort Wayne. This route was officially the Lincoln until the new alignment was designated in 1928, but even then many people still took the original path.

Travelers who take the newer 1928 version of the Lincoln may notice some blank spots. Long gone are various road treasures, as well as the tourist camps and cabins outside of Columbia City that at one time served people going to and fro on the busy highway. Students of Hoosier politics may remember that this crossroads town was once home to Thomas Marshall, a highly regarded Democratic political leader who served as governor of Indiana from 1909 to 1913 before becoming Woodrow Wilson's vice president. Once described as "a liberal with brakes on," Marshall is credited with making the famous observation, "What this country needs is a good five-cent cigar."

Warsaw, the next Lincoln Highway town of any size, takes great pride in its historic marker in Funk Park on North Lake Street. The only Lincoln Highway marker in the entire state in its original location, it also is one of the few remaining markers on the twenty-three miles of the Lincoln in Kosciusko County, named for the Polish hero of the American Revolution. The county is well known for its 103 lakes—including Lake Wawasee, largest in the state, covering more than 3,000 acres, and, at 120 feet, the deepest lake—Tippecanoe, just north of Warsaw and one of three lakes within the city limits.

Warsaw, one of the largest orthopedic-device producers in the world, is also headquarters for the largest manufacturer of projection screens in the world, and has put CoCo Wheats on America's breakfast tables since 1930. If travelers aren't in the mood for cereal before heading out of town, they might go to Dig's Diner on North Buffalo Street for some "inferno hot" chili. A brimming bowl of Dig's fiery ambrosia ought to get travelers through Atwood, Etna Green, Bourbon, Inwood, and Plymouth, site of the restored Marshall County Courthouse and the Hemminger Travel Lodge, a Colonial Revival classic built in 1937 for Lincoln Highway motorists and now listed on the National Register of Historic Places.

From Plymouth, the 1928 Lincoln route touches a few more small towns, such as Grovertown, Hamlet, Hanna, and finally Wanatah. From here, U.S. 30 gets travelers speedily to Valparaiso, where this version of the Lincoln joins with the original alignment.

If travelers can only take one of the two alignments in Indiana, there is little question that the original route is the one to choose. The endorsement of this particular length of the Lincoln in the 1924 official road guide is still accurate: "The Lincoln Highway drive across Indiana is delightful. The country through which it passes is practically level, richly agricultural and offers many pleasing scenic attractions."

Leaving Fort Wayne for the west, travelers cross the St. Mary's River on the Lincoln Highway Bridge, erected for $200,000 in 1915 and completely rebuilt in 1987. At this point of the journey, New York is 724 miles to the east and San Francisco lies 2,260 miles to the west. Northwest from Fort Wayne, with only a few jogs and merges, the old alignment goes by U.S. 33 all the way to Elkhart.

Just fifteen miles after leaving Cindy's Diner appears the town of Churubusco—allegedly named for a site where U.S. forces were victorious in 1847 during the Mexican War. Although tracking down details of how the town got its name might be an interesting pursuit, most travelers tend to be more curious about a sign at the city limits that says, "Turtle Town U.S.A." The chronically inquisitive can seek answers at the Magic Wand, a drive-in restaurant where there usually are at least three times more cars in the parking lot than at the fast-food franchise joint across the highway. All three meals are served at the Magic Wand. Besides daily specials such as beef and noodles, or ham and scalloped potatoes, Magic Burgers and every imaginable kind of ice cream concoction are big sellers. Everywhere in the dining room are paintings and sculptures of clowns.

The clown collection belongs to Judy Myers, the daughter of turkey farmers. She and her husband, Max, took over the restaurant in 1964. A grandson and Judy's sister are cooks; another grandson and a niece wait tables. "We get recreational travelers, vacationers just passing through, and, of course, our local trade, including some who eat here three times a day," says Judy.

As for the town's turtle connection, apparently it started in 1898, when a local farmer named Oscar Fulk announced that he had spotted a gigantic turtle in his lake. Nobody thought much of it, but as the years went by, Oscar sold his place and the new owners said they thought they had seen a huge turtle. When their story drew some guffaws, they said perhaps it was a cow swimming in the lake. Subsequent owners and their friends who fished in the lake—which by then had become known as Fulk Lake—had their own stories of the mysterious turtle. Some reported that the turtle came out of the water and snatched away their fishing poles. They said the turtle's back was as large as a dining table. In 1949, some fellows finally trapped the big turtle with some chicken wire, but when they tried to lift it from the water, it broke free. Local newspapers wrote up the various turtle sightings and incidents, and soon the national press caught wind of the story. One newspaper dubbed the turtle Oscar, after old man Fulk. Another paper gave the turtle a more ominous handle—"The Beast of 'Busco."

When more and more sightseers showed up with hopes of seeing the big turtle—Indiana's version of "Bigfoot"—a professional trapper was summoned, but he had no luck. A female turtle was brought to the lake in hopes she might entice Oscar, but when that didn't work, it was pointed out that no one knew whether Oscar was male or female. People started referring to Churubusco as "Turtle Town," and some mail was addressed to Turtle Town, U.S.A. A halfhearted attempt to drain the lake failed and there were a few more sightings, but eventually the sightseers went away and apparently so did the turtle.

No matter the truth, the town ended up with a memorable nickname, and every summer it holds the

ABOVE *Judy Myers, owner of the Magic Wand in Churubusco, IN.*

LEFT *Dig's Diner, Warsaw, IN.*

barrels of meat, Wilson had his crews stamp "U.S.," which he jokingly suggested stood for "Uncle Sam" Wilson. From then on, soldiers used "Uncle Sam" to refer to anything government issued, and eventually the name came to symbolize the federal government.

Almost every credible source—and some not so credible, including the U.S. Congress—concluded that the genuine Samuel Wilson was born in Massachusetts in 1766 and in 1854 died in Troy, New York, where he was buried in the Oakwood Cemetery. Still, it is interesting to hypothesize that the experts and Congress made a mistake. Maybe the grave along the Lincoln Highway in Merriam contains the remains of the real Uncle Sam. If that won't convince passersby to stop and have a look, then nothing will. It takes some searching to find the grave; there are no flags, no patriotic mausoleum, nothing to remotely indicate that this is the resting place of Uncle Sam. All that is inscribed on the face of the stone is:

SOLDIER OF 1812

SAMUEL WILSON

DIED

MAY 7, 1865

AGED

100 YEARS AND 3 DAYS

Turtle Days festival, complete with a parade, carnival rides, cotton candy, and, naturally, turtle races.

Not many miles up the highway, the town of Merriam has no monster turtle lurking in murky waters but it does claim to be the burial site of none other than America's own Uncle Sam. Most historians who have traced the origins of the legendary character believe he was named after Samuel Wilson, a successful meat packer who shipped great quantities of meat to the U.S. Army during the War of 1812. On every one of the

When travelers succeed in finding the grave, that alone is satisfying. Let Troy, New York, keep its Uncle Sam. To stand in rural Indiana over the plot where an old soldier who probably ate beef from barrels stamped "U.S." and died as a centenarian when the Civil War still raged is more than enough reward.

Continuing on U.S. 33, the old route winds through Wolf Lake and Kimmell. Many travelers stop at the Elkhart River town of Ligonier, founded in 1835 by Isaac Cavin in an area known as Strawberry Valley because of its abundance of wild strawberries. Cavin named the settlement after his Pennsylvania hometown that many years later would also become a Lincoln Highway town. Indiana's Ligonier started to grow when the railroad arrived in 1852, along with a large number of Jewish immigrants. After the Civil War, the town thrived as a regional banking center with dozens of new businesses. Of the 2,000 residents in Ligonier in 1900, at least ten percent were Jewish, and the town was known as "Little Jerusalem." That changed, however, when the next generation of Jewish residents moved to larger cities. By the time of World War II, the economy began to sour. There was a rally in the early 1950s, when area business leaders banded together and created a large industrial park.

In the late 1990s and into the 2000s, town leaders recognized the need to preserve Ligonier's history and culture as a means of attracting tourist dollars. Large numbers of visitors now tour the Indiana Historic Radio Museum, housed in a 1920s filling station on Lincoln Way. Besides the more than four hundred vintage radios and other broadcast paraphernalia, the collection includes the first all-transistor radio,

which was made in Indiana in 1954. Ligonier hosts several festivals tied to its ethnic and pioneer past. One of the most popular is the Ligonier Marshmallow Festival, an annual shindig that acknowledges the millions of marshmallows that were produced over many years by Kidd & Company in its local plant.

When the old road enters Elkhart County and gets to Benton and Goshen, travelers are reminded of the Pennsylvania Dutch Country when they see the horse-drawn buggies of the Amish and Mennonites, whose ancestors settled this area in the 1830s. The name *Goshen* comes from a region of ancient Egypt on the Nile River delta that was described in the Bible as "The Land of Goshen." About a hundred miles east of Chicago and

RIGHT *Motor inn,*
Goshen, IN.

FAR RIGHT
Maple City Bowl,
Goshen, IN.

only twenty-five miles east of South Bend, Goshen is known as "Maple City" for the many maple trees lining its streets. Film director Howard Hawks—remembered for such notable motion pictures as the original *Scarface*, *To Have and Have Not*, *The Big Sleep*, *Red River*, and *Gentlemen Prefer Blondes*—was born in Goshen in 1896. Another native is former Notre Dame and NFL quarterback Rick Mirer, who, during his playing years in nearby South Bend, was referred to as "The Goshen Motion."

In the heyday of the Lincoln Highway, travelers enjoyed seeing the majestic courthouse on Main Street and, on the southeast corner of the courthouse square, the intriguing police booth, a WPA art deco gem complete with thick glass windows and gun ports. According to the local historical society, the limestone structure was erected in 1939 "to protect the Maple City from gangsters who might travel along this, the old transcontinental Lincoln Highway." Perhaps no one told the city fathers that John Dillinger, Pretty Boy Floyd, and Baby Face Nelson had passed on by that time. A number of travelers overnighting in Goshen in those years stayed on the town square at the Alderman Hotel, "Known for its Table" and with running water in every room. Rates started at $3.50 per night. The Hattle Hotel, with steam heat, attracted others. The adventurous stopped just west of the city limits on the Lincoln at Ulrey's Triangle, a camping ground and tourist headquarters that touted its filling station and ladies' restroom.

Only a dozen miles north of Goshen is Elkhart, where, according to local legend, Indians thought that

LEFT *Police booth in Goshen, IN, erected in 1939 "to protect the Maple City from gangsters who might travel along this, the old transcontinental Lincoln Highway."*

a small island—near what was to become the Elkhart River, which emptied into the St. Joseph River—was shaped like an elk's heart. Whether the story is true or apocryphal, neither elk nor Indians have been spotted in these parts for a mighty long time. What *are* spotted here quite frequently are recreational vehicles and motor homes: Elkhart has long reigned as the RV manufacturing capital of the world. Whether

Turning due west out of Elkhart, travelers pass
through Osceola and find that old U.S. 33 becomes
Lincoln Way as they enter the town of Mishawaka, a
Potawatomi Indian word that is believed to mean "dead
trees place." Just ahead in South Bend, on the St. Joseph
River, the golden dome of the University of Notre Dame
shines like a beacon. Every autumn, throngs of Notre
Dame football fans show up on game days to root for the
Irish in a stadium that holds more than 80,000. Looming
over the stadium is a large mural of Jesus Christ with
arms raised—lovingly referred to as "Touchdown Jesus."

Notre Dame may have put South Bend on the map,
but so does the Studebaker National Museum and
Archives, chronicling the carmaker's rich history
from horse-and-buggy days until the last Studebaker
rolled off the line in 1966. West of South Bend, in
New Carlisle, is what some consider the world's
largest "living sign" at the old Studebaker proving
grounds, where white pines were planted to spell out
the company name. The former racetrack and test
grounds eventually became a county park, and the trees
planted in 1938 have grown so tall that the only way to
see the Studebaker name is from an aircraft. Lincoln
Highway travelers not wishing to rent an airplane or
helicopter can cruise on through Rolling Prairie, La
Porte, and Westville before reaching Valparaiso.

Anyone entering "Valpo" (as even the locals call
the city) on the original Lincoln passes a large
Frostop Root Beer mug sign next to what used to be
Hannon's, a roadside eatery that was converted to a bank.

or not travelers are riding the Lincoln in an RV, they
will be welcome at the RV/MH Heritage Foundation
Hall of Fame and Museum in downtown Elkhart.
Besides making RVs, the town produces most of the
brass band instruments made in America. Miles
Laboratories, the pharmaceutical firm, was founded
in Elkhart in 1884 and maintains a major presence.

Although the restaurant is gone, the spinning neon sign was such an important community landmark that it was left intact. Travelers looking for nourishment need not worry. Valpo still has plenty of roadside dining, including Culver's Frozen Custard, where walleye (fish) sandwiches are served, or the Big Wheel Restaurant, founded in 1963.

Valparaiso is home of Valparaiso University, founded in 1859 and, just like the town, is referred to as Valpo by the four thousand students from around the world who call the 310-acre campus home. Valpo students start off the school year right every September when the town holds a festival to honor a Purdue grad named Orville Redenbacher.

ABOVE *Mural, La Porte, IN.*

RIGHT *The intersection of Franklin Avenue and the Lincoln Highway in downtown Valparaiso, IN, in the 1920s.*

FAR RIGHT *John and Billie Pappas, owners of B. J.'s American Cafe in La Porte, IN. The restaurant has been in the Pappas family for eight decades.*

Born in Indiana in 1907, just six years before the Lincoln Highway's birth, Redenbacher earned a degree in agronomy. He went on to become a prosperous farmer and developed several hybrid strains of corn to be consumed as popcorn packaged in his Valparaiso plant. Not only was the company named for him successful, Orville became a familiar figure in homes across America. Appearing in television commercials with his eyeglasses and wearing a bowtie, the popcorn king charmed viewers by telling them, "My gourmet popping corn pops up lighter and fluffier than ordinary popping corn. Eats better, too." Orville's days as a popcorn booster ended with his death in 1995, but his popcorn remains a top seller and he is remembered at the popcorn festival, held on the first Saturday after Labor Day.

At Valparaiso, both the original and the newer alignments of the Lincoln Highway meet and continue as one on U.S. 30, or the Joliet Road, through Deep River, Merrillville, Schererville, and Dyer on the border of Illinois. Although this final leg of the old road in Indiana is no more than twenty-five miles long, it is a critical link in Lincoln Highway history.

Anyone who fancies himself or herself a Lincoln Highway traveler must stop at Teibel's, a restaurant at the intersection of U.S. 30, the Lincoln, and U.S. 41 in Schererville. That is an unwritten rule of the road. Founded in 1929 by brothers Stephen and Martin Teibel, this restaurant has evolved from a simple twelve-seat

highway diner, which sold halves of chicken for fifty cents, into a Midwest institution that turns out three thousand pounds of fried chicken every week. The tourist court that formerly comforted stuffed travelers is gone, and the dining rooms have greatly expanded, but the Teibel family still runs the place, using the same fried-chicken recipe that Grandma Teibel brought from her native Austria. The family guards the recipe closely but admits the secret to good fried chicken is freshness, and all the chicken they serve is processed and delivered daily. Besides ordering chicken—served family style with heaping bowls of side dishes—customers clamor for Teibel's famed lake

ABOVE

Interior of Teibel's Family Restaurant, Schererville, IN.

Vintage photo of Teibel's Family Restaurant, Schererville, IN. Note tourist court in inset.

FAR RIGHT

The Henry C. Ostermann Memorial Bench on the Lincoln Highway Ideal Section in Dyer, IN. Ostermann was killed in an automobile accident in Iowa in 1920.

perch dinners or perhaps frog legs, steaks, or roast turkey. Plate flippers who turn over cleaned-off dishes will find the stamp of Homer Laughlin, whose pottery is made on the Lincoln Highway in West Virginia. Teibel's is the kind of establishment where a young man proposes marriage after the strawberry shortcake and then returns every anniversary with his wife and all the kids. Teibel's is a Mother's Day kind of place.

Between Schererville and Dyer on today's U.S. 30 lies a special 1.3-mile stretch of roadway built by the Lincoln Highway Association in 1922 and unveiled in 1923. Called the "Ideal Section," this segment of the Lincoln—funded by U.S. Rubber as well as county and state funds—was highlighted as an example of the safest and best road possible. It was forty paved feet wide and featured a one-hundred-foot right-of-way, steel-reinforced concrete, underground drainage, a lighted and landscaped bridge, and pedestrian pathways. The section, alas, is no longer ideal, as it has been greatly altered through the years.

Near the eastern end of the Ideal Section, on the south side of the highway, is a stone bench monument to Henry Charles Ostermann, the Lincoln Highway Association field secretary who died in a 1920 car crash on the road in Iowa and was buried in East Liverpool, Ohio. Travelers may choose to sit on the Ostermann bench and, if they can ignore the traffic buzzing by, try to conjure up the past. They should imagine what it was like before concrete or even dirt roads existed—when the highway before them was the Sauk Trail, traversed by Indians and early settlers. With those thoughts in mind, they can leave and proceed to Dyer, the last town on the old highway in Indiana.

The Lincoln passes St. Joseph's Church—its red bricks still as solid as when they were laid in 1878—and crosses Plum Creek, via a bridge restored in 1994 that was built in 1913, when the Lincoln Highway was the talk of the town. Up ahead is Illinois—the Land of Lincoln awaits.

Chapter Seven

ILLINOIS

It is appropriate that Illinois, the state most associated with the man who provided the name for the Lincoln Highway, exposes travelers to an exceptionally interesting share of the storied road. Every one of the Lincoln Highway's 179 miles

spanning the width of northern Illinois is ripe with the promise of discovery experienced by open-road travelers.

The excursion begins where the Lincoln Highway slides across the Indiana border into Illinois on U.S. 30, managing to avoid Chicago to the north. Travelers pass Lynwood and soon come upon Chicago Heights, an old community thirty miles south of Chicago that was settled in the 1830s by Scots-Irish families near the crossing of the Sauk Trail and the Vincennes Trail. First

known as Thorn Grove, the name was changed to Bloom in 1849, after an influx of Germans moved into the area. Finally, in the 1890s, the village became Chicago Heights and grew into a significant industrial center with a steel mill and other large manufacturers. By the time the Lincoln Highway was created, the city supported a lively downtown shopping district. Chicago Heights earned a somewhat shady reputation during Prohibition, suffered during the Depression, and recovered with the

LEFT *Highway sign painted on a telephone pole near Franklin Grove, IL.*

industrial boom brought on by World War II. In the postwar period, however, the city started its decline. New superhighways led to suburban growth and the introduction of regional shopping centers and, later, gigantic malls. Rail service decreased and the city's industrial base weakened. Chicago Heights lost its identity and soon became a shadow of what was once a bustling city.

Life was much better in Chicago Heights when it was known as a flourishing crossroads where Carl Fisher's two highways—the Lincoln and the Dixie— intersected. At this point, the Dixie also provided one of three feeders allowing motorists to turn northward

BELOW Lincoln memorial at the crossroads of the Dixie and Lincoln Highways, Chicago Heights, IL.

On the Road to Greatness

to reach Chicago. In 1916, to commemorate the two famous roads, the Arche Memorial Fountain was installed in Arche Park at the intersection of the Lincoln—U.S. 30—and the Dixie—Illinois Route 1.

Today, travelers willing to brave traffic sometimes stop to grab a quick photo or rub for luck the big Lincoln penny mounted on top of the fountain. From the park, the Lincoln Highway heads west on U.S. 30 toward Olympia Fields, Matteson, Frankfort, and New Lenox. Just brushing the southern bulge of sprawling Chicago, the route breaks free into the countryside, allowing for plenty of pauses in the necklace of farm towns and highway communities dotting its path to the eastern bank of the Mississippi River. Lincoln Highway advocates had cause to celebrate in 2000, when the entire route of the Lincoln in Illinois—mostly made up of U.S. 30 and State Road 38—was designated a National Scenic Byway. It was a good choice. That becomes apparent in every one of the eight counties and thirty-one towns and cities through which the byway passes.

It is certainly evident in Joliet, settled in the 1830s on the Des Plaines River. Historically, Joliet always prided itself on being economically independent of Chicago, thirty-five miles to the northeast. Almost from its beginning, this city paid its own way with its paper mills, factories, shipping canal, railroads, blast furnaces, quarries, and processing plants.

Carl Sandburg, the poet of Abraham Lincoln and the heartland, was inspired to write of Joliet:

On the one hand the steel works.
On the other hand the penitentiary.
Santa Fe tracks and Alton trains
Between smokestacks on the west.
And gray walls on the east. . . .

The penitentiary Sandburg mentioned is a big part of the city's story. Incarceration is another long-time Joliet industry. Convicted criminals have been coming to this city to do hard time since before the Civil War, when Abe Lincoln and Stephen A. Douglas engaged in heated political debate, gathering great crowds in towns across Illinois. The fact that Joliet is a prison town does not dominate daily life or conversation. Yet it is another lure for some travelers and offers reason enough to investigate the city and find that the Joliet area has not just one but two state prisons.

The newest—Stateville State Prison—was built in nearby Crest Hill in the early 1920s. Considered state-of-the-art at the time, it has been expanded and updated through the years and is now called the Stateville Correctional Center, housing 2,800 inmates. Outside the building where visitors check in, a solitary gravestone bears the inscription "Duke, A Real Police Dog, 1943–1956."

Near downtown Joliet on Collins Street, travelers can find the more photogenic of the two prisons—Joliet Correctional Center. Known locally as Joliet Prison, the limestone walls twenty-five feet high and five feet

ABOVE *Joliet Prison, built in 1858, Joliet, IL.*

thick at the base were hand-hewn from a quarry by the inmates. Built just outside the city limits in 1858 for $75,000, Joliet Prison was the design of William T. Boyington, the man who also designed the landmark Chicago Water Tower and the Capitol building in Springfield. At the time it opened, it was the largest prison in the country. Life was brutal and cheap inside the walls, and some of the toughest inmates chose suicide or were killed in brawls and buried in Monkey Hill, the prison graveyard. A prison for females, built across the street in 1896, was closed in 1932.

By early 2002, the Joliet Correctional Center closed as a working prison and holding center due to budget cuts and the obsolete facilities. It continued as an intake center until 2004. The old place earned a brief reprieve when Hollywood came back to town. Motion-picture companies had used the prison with its stone walls and Victorian guard towers as a setting as far back as the silent-picture era. Many years later, scenes from the cult classic *The Blues Brothers* were filmed at Joliet, as were episodes of the television series *Prison Break*.

A hiking trail with interpretive signage winds through the site of the first ironmaking blast furnaces, across the railroad tracks running by the old prison. Constructed in the 1870s, by the turn of the century the four furnaces employed more than 3,000 workers and, along with the limestone quarries, formed the backbone of the local economy. Now only ruins remain from the time when Joliet was "The City of Steel and Stone." The historic site is a good vantage point for seeing the old prison. Sometimes white-tailed deer peer out from the trees, and passing trains moan greetings and farewells.

Although Joliet Prison is closed and the old blast furnaces are distant memories, Joliet does more than survive—it prospers. As in other midwestern cities that suffered economically, Joliet's unemployment rate skyrocketed as high as twenty-five percent in the 1980s. That turned around when the city realized it could tap into Chicago and other markets for jobs and still retain its own identity. More recently, the city experienced a tremendous growth spurt as thousands bought homes in Joliet and began commuting to work in greater Chicagoland. By 2006, Joliet was ranked as the fastest-growing city in the Midwest and the fourteenth-fastest-growing city in the nation among cities larger than 100,000. The city clearly became an *exurb*—a term that stands for "extra-urban," first used in 1950 to describe the band of communities beyond the suburbs that became the primary places to live and raise families.

Joliet may be both an exurb and a prison town, but it is also a highway town. Besides the Lincoln Highway, two other important American roadways run through the city: the Grand Army of the Republic Highway, or U.S. 6, a transcontinental route connecting Cape Cod, Massachusetts, with Long Beach, California; and U.S. Route 66, considered by many the most famous highway in the world.

Created in 1926 and stretching more than 2,400 miles between Chicago and Santa Monica, California, U.S. 66

OPPOSITE
Knock-out sale at South Oak Dodge, Matteson, IL.

LEFT *Abe Lincoln Motel, Frankfort, IL.*

traverses eight states and three time zones. Despite the 1956 federal legislation creating a new interstate highway system, Route 66, just like the Lincoln Highway, did not wither away. As much as eighty-five percent of Route 66 is enjoyed today by a growing number of travelers who have become shunpikers, going back to the old pathways. Also, just as is occurring on the Lincoln, associations were formed to preserve the highway, historic signage was restored, and sections were designated National Scenic Byways, including the route in Illinois. Older and longer than Route 66, the Lincoln offers travelers the same allure but with altogether different settings.

If Route 66 is "The Mother Road"—as John Steinbeck wrote in his classic novel *The Grapes of Wrath*—then the Lincoln Highway is this country's "Father Road." In Joliet, these two linear American icons intersect downtown with no fanfare and share some of the same road treasure, most notably the historic and beautifully restored Rialto Square Theatre. Opened in 1926, this stunning entertainment palace, listed on the National Register of Historic Places, has been called one of the ten most beautiful theaters in the United States. Visitors from both major highways came to the Rialto in its glory days and still do today.

Originally, Route 66 passed right through Joliet. In 1940, an alternative route was built and travelers had a choice of either going to Joliet or taking a new road just a little farther to the west. Either way, they'd still be on Route 66. If travelers opted for the newer routing, however, they went northwest to Plainfield, where they happened upon the Lincoln Highway coming into town on what was then called the Joliet Road. In Plainfield, the Mother and Father Roads actually unite for three blocks, embracing like a pair of aging but still glamorous celebrities. Signs posted side by side for both highways mark this historic road alignment, and twin banners honoring the two roads line the brief joint passage down the main drag.

In downtown Plainfield, the last of five filling stations that provided top-notch service to motorists has been saved from demolition and restored. Built in 1928, the white stucco building with a red tile roof had several owners who pumped various gasoline products, including Texaco and Standard. Die-hard travelers might want to linger here over egg and pepper sandwiches at Whitey's Hot Dogs on West Lincoln Highway. If it's the Sabbath and Whitey's is closed, there is always Gruben's Uptown Tap & Grill—a great place for doing battle with a hot dog. The dogs served at Gruben's are deep fried and charbroiled, loaded in buns, and smothered with kraut, scallions, jalapeños, tomatoes, relish, and mustard. A person who eats one never forgets it.

Before the Lincoln starts its westward turn toward Iowa, travelers who think of a Gruben's loaded hot dog as an appetizer may need to stop in Aurora, northwest of Plainfield. If they are in luck, there might be some fiery food waiting at a Mexican restaurant on Hill Avenue, one of the names for the Lincoln in this city. Originally a

LEFT *Downtown Plainfield, IL.*

LOWER LEFT

The alignment of Route 66 and the Lincoln Highway, which run on the same road for three blocks through Plainfield, IL.

Wadham's Service Station when it opened in the 1920s, the building with a pagoda-style roof has housed a variety of culinary enterprises, especially Mexican eateries.

Travelers should not be surprised that genuine Mexican food, not bland franchise fare, can be found in a midwestern city so far north of the Mexican border. As early as 1910, large numbers of Mexican families moved into the area to escape the upheaval of violence and religious persecution during the Mexican Revolution and the ensuing civil war. Drawn by the promise of employment, most of the refugees took menial jobs with the railroad or a local manufacturer of earthmoving equipment.

The immigrants lived in a boxcar camp on the eastern edge of Aurora and labored hard to improve their families' lives. These urban pioneers inspired the next generations, as well as Mexican migrant workers who left the harvest trail to settle in Aurora. By the turn of the twenty-first century, Aurora's population was thirty-two percent Hispanic and growing. Hispanics hold political office, teach school, work on dairy farms, manage businesses, operate groceries, and run restaurants.

Across Hill Avenue from the old gas station is Phillips Park, where in the 1920s and 1930s Mexican brass bands would serenade picnickers enjoying deviled eggs and fried chicken. Some of those listening to the music were travelers off the Lincoln Highway, camping overnight in the park beneath a sturdy shelter. One of many "auto camps" built along the original highway, the shelter was a free place to stay for travelers on a tight budget. Unfortunately, the shelter hadn't yet been built in 1919, when Aurora city fathers welcomed the U.S. Army's first Transcontinental Motor Convoy, which was driving the Lincoln to demonstrate the advantage of improved roads. Instead of an overnight in Aurora, the convoy stopped only for an hour-long lunchtime reception sponsored by the Red Cross at McCarty Park. Thousands of onlookers turned out to watch the enlisted men and officers—including a young Dwight Eisenhower—gobble down sandwiches, cake, and ice cream before chugging westward.

In 1923, the Aurora Automobile Club built the shelter in Phillips Park. It was highly touted the following year in the Lincoln Highway road guide for its "two fireplaces, two ovens and a sink" and "a good well with plenty of drinking water just outside the building." Besides boosting their city's image with travelers, the auto club knew the free shelter would cut down on "auto hoboing," the common practice of camping in a farmer's pasture or squatting on private property. The Aurora shelter mostly served highway travelers until the 1940s, when it became a popular camp for traveling gypsies, who made a bit of money by telling fortunes. During World War II, the shelter was enclosed and became an air-raid shelter staffed by volunteers. In subsequent years, the shelter fell into disrepair and was seldom used. By 2001, it was about to be torn down to allow expansion of the golf course when the city came to its senses and saved this important piece of road history. With state grant funds, the Lincoln Highway Shelter received a new roof, refurbished stucco and bricks, operable fireplaces, and a new water pump. As part of the total restoration, Lincoln Highway visitor information is available and interpretive plaques tell the Lincoln story.

Built in part as an alternative to expensive hotel lodging, the park shelter once again serves the traveling

public. At least two of the hotels with which the shelter competed for many years—the eight-story Aurora Hotel, built in 1917, and the Leland Tower, erected in 1928—also have been restored, albeit as apartment buildings. Keenly aware of the need to preserve its historical, cultural, and ethnic heritage, Aurora—hailed as "The City of Lights"—has become a leader in architectural preservation. This becomes evident during a drive through the city's many historic districts and neighborhoods, which include the work of such noted architects as Bruce Goff and Frank Lloyd Wright. It also shows in the scores of restored homes, churches, and commercial buildings, and in the preservation of downtown landmarks, such as the magnificent Paramount Theatre and the LaSalle Street Historic District, where fifteen auto-related businesses once operated. The iconic 1950s neon sign at Northgate Shopping Center also has been recognized as a valuable example from the more recent past.

Departing Aurora, travelers cross the Fox River and turn north on Illinois 31 through North Aurora, where the road becomes the Lincolnway and leads to Mooseheart, a community with an important place in Lincoln Highway history. The name comes from the Mooseheart Child

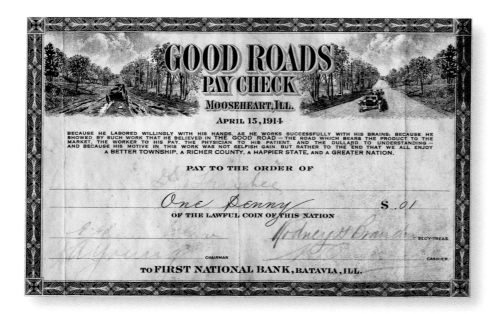

ABOVE *Good Roads Pay Check, one penny earned for participating in Good Roads Day, April 15, 1914, "because he labored willingly with his hands . . . because he showed by such work that he believed in THE GOOD ROAD . . . and because his motive in this work was not selfish gain, but rather to the end that we all enjoy a BETTER TOWNSHIP, A RICHER COUNTY, A HAPPIER STATE, and a GREATER NATION," Mooseheart, IL.*

City and School, established in 1913 as a home and vocational school for the orphans of deceased members of the Loyal Order of Moose. That same year, the fraternal organization agreed to pave their two-mile stretch of the newly unveiled Lincoln Highway—if the state provided the equipment. On April 15, 1914—coincidentally, the forty-ninth anniversary of Abraham Lincoln's death—1,500 Moose members showed up in coats and ties to

pave the highway. Illinois Governor Edward Fitzsimmons Dunne, a former mayor of Chicago, was there to declare it Good Roads Day and oversee the project. Anyone who put in at least fifteen minutes of work was handed a check for one Lincoln penny as a memento of the auspicious occasion. The paving cost $12,000 and was the first stretch of road paved in rural Illinois.

Up the road, travelers who stop in the towns of Batavia and Geneva along the picturesque Fox River are not disappointed. Both towns are vibrant yet have retained the flavor of the past. Settled in the late 1830s after the Blackhawk Indian War, Batavia became known for its limestone deposits and earned the moniker "Quarry City." The town's ten quarries rebuilt Chicago following the Great Fire of 1871. Only four years after the fire scorched Chicago, and a decade following the assassination of President Lincoln, the slain president's widow briefly took up residence in Batavia—against her will. It occurred in 1875, when fifty-six-year-old Mary Todd Lincoln was declared insane by a Chicago court after a competency trial instigated by her sole surviving son, Robert Todd Lincoln. Instead of going to the state hospital for the insane, the former first lady was taken to Batavia to stay at Bellevue Place, a private sanatorium for well-to-do mental patients. Four months later, Mrs. Lincoln was declared sane and released to the care of her sister in Springfield. Eventually, Bellevue Place was converted into apartments, but the bed and dresser from Mary Todd Lincoln's room are on display at a local museum.

Back on Illinois 31 just outside Geneva, travelers pass Riverbank, the villa occupied for many years by George Fabyan, a charter member of the original Lincoln Highway Association and a man of many pursuits. Fabyan, a millionaire textile dealer, and his wife, Nelle, came to the Fox River Valley in 1905 and bought a farmhouse on ten acres not far from Geneva. Two years later, they hired Frank Lloyd Wright to redesign their residence into a palatial home as they expanded their property holdings to more than six hundred acres. On this estate, upwards of one hundred servants, groundskeepers, animal handlers, and others looked after a zoo, an antique Dutch windmill, stone sculptures, 18,000 chickens, a Roman-style swimming pool, a lighthouse, a boathouse, extensive formal gardens, and much more.

The eccentric Fabyan had an abiding interest in science and research. In 1912, just before the advent of the Lincoln Highway that he always supported, Fabyan established the Riverbank Laboratories, considered one of the world's first think tanks. Fabyan staffed the laboratories with the brightest cryptologists, geneticists, and acoustic engineers he could find and turned them loose on a variety of projects, such as deciphering a secret code that allegedly proved the works of Shakespeare were actually penned by Sir Francis Bacon. Riverbank researchers and cryptologists were credited with cracking German secret codes during World War I, and they helped Scotland Yard expose secret agents operating abroad. When the U.S. Army finally developed cipher experts, the first batch of officers trained at Riverbank.

Fabyan died in 1936, but much of the work he inspired continues at the Riverbank Acoustic Laboratories in Geneva, where a plaque reads: "To the memory of George Fabyan from a grateful government." The National Security Agency presented the plaque years ago, prompting some to point out that perhaps Riverbank was the prototype for both the NSA (the federal government's largest intelligence-gathering agency) and the Central Intelligence Agency.

Geneva offers plenty of vintage road culture and period architecture, including the former Geneva Theater on State Street. Downtown looks like a movie set—which it was in 2002, when filmmakers used Geneva to shoot some of *Road to Perdition*, the 1930s-era gangster film starring Tom Hanks and

Paul Newman. Today travelers can make their own getaways by exiting town to the west on Route 38.

Although the Lincoln Highway has made its way through open countryside and prairie, it is at this point that the old road finally breaks free of Chicago's clutches. Instead of circling the mammoth city, the Lincoln bravely, even resolutely, turns westward and stays on this course the rest of the way across the state. Unadulterated Main Street America is there to be experienced along the road from Geneva all the way to Dixon—through DeKalb, Malta, Creston, Rochelle, Ashton, and Franklin Grove.

Long before the high-flying years of the Lincoln Highway, DeKalb was proudly known as "The Barbed Wire Capital of the World." It was here in 1874 that Joseph Glidden patented his improved barbed wire and forever changed the face of the American West. Then, in 1938, the barbed wire folks packed up and moved out of town. Over the years, other key businesses and industries left, too. Even hometown girl Cindy Crawford— apparently known for brains as well as beauty—left after graduating as valedictorian from DeKalb High School in 1984 and launched her supermodel career.

The Lincoln Highway, however, didn't leave. The Lincoln had been an old cow trail that became Main Street, just as it did in so many other towns. The old road through DeKalb still has a presence and is highly regarded. Pride in the Lincoln and the town it serves shows in the fully restored art deco Egyptian Theatre, built in 1929—one of only six such theaters in the United States and the only one in the Midwest. This national-

RIGHT *The art deco Egyptian Theatre, built in 1929, DeKalb, IL.*

landmark movie palace dazzles visitors and supports almost twenty performing-arts groups. After matinees, folks walk over to Lothson's Karry-Out Chicken, as customers have done since 1949. Or, if they want to sit, they find a spot next door at Rosita's, a longtime-favorite Mexican restaurant. Afterward, there might be time to buy a lottery ticket, magazine, cigar, or joke gift at Ralph's Newsstand, in continuous operation on the downtown Lincoln since the end of World War II.

After leaving DeKalb, travelers soon approach Malta, where west of town is the site of the first of four "Seedling Miles," a brainstorm of the Lincoln Highway Association. These one-mile sections of smooth concrete roadway were inserted into stretches of unimproved dirt or gravel highway to show the advantages of cement for smoother driving. A historic marker in Malta, on the campus of Kishwaukee Community College, tells the story of the November 1914 unveiling of the ten-foot-wide Seedling Mile—the first in the nation. The following year, two more Seedling Miles were paved in Illinois—one at Morrison, west of Malta, and the other at Chicago Heights to the east.

At both Creston and Rochelle, banners mark the original route of the Lincoln. Called the "Hub City," Rochelle is where the Lincoln Highway intersected with the Meridian Highway, a predecessor to U.S. 81 and the first major north–south road connecting Canada to the Gulf of Mexico. In 1916, residents of Rochelle formed the Meridian Highway Association to promote the highway's construction. They were aware of the Meridian's

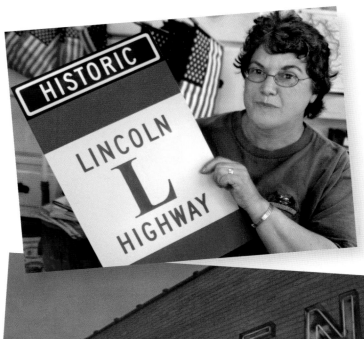

LEFT *Lynn Asp, director of the Lincoln Highway Association National Headquarters, Franklin Grove, IL.*

BELOW *Janet Lothson in front of Lothson's Karry-Out Chicken, DeKalb, IL.*

RIGHT

Dixon Arch, spanning the Lincoln Highway in downtown Dixon, IL.

BELOW *A six-foot portrait of Ronald Reagan, made from 14,000 jellybeans by Peter Rocha, on display in the lobby of the Dixon Historic Center, Dixon, IL.*

importance because of the positive impact the Lincoln already had had on their community. Rochelle remains a staunch highway town, and travelers are warmly greeted at the Welcome Center, located in a restored brick canopy filling station with vintage gas pumps at the corner of the Lincoln Highway and Lincoln Avenue. From there, they can stop at the Beacon Restaurant, crowned with a neon sign shaped like a lighthouse; take a peek at the 1930s-era Hub Theatre; or seek out the pair of 1928 Lincoln Highway concrete markers still in place on private property south of downtown.

Sharp-eyed motorists can spot four more of the 1928 markers, each about a mile apart, on the old road between Ashton and Franklin Grove, where the original Lincoln turned right up Main Street. Franklin Grove is the home of the National Headquarters of the Lincoln Highway Association. The office is located inside the historic H. I. Lincoln Store, built in 1860 by Henry Isaac Lincoln, a distant relative of Abraham Lincoln. The limestone block building originally housed Henry Lincoln's dry-goods store and later was used as a post office and newspaper office. When the newspaper ceased publication in the 1950s, the building sat vacant—except for a brief period in the 1970s, when it was used as an arcade and dance studio. In the 1990s, ten local men banded together to preserve the history and heritage of their community. One of the first properties they purchased was the old Lincoln Store. With volunteer labor, they began to restore the historic site. When members of the Lincoln Highway Association—which had been reactivated in 1992—learned

about the building restoration, they became interested. They knew they had found the ideal home for their organization when the citizens of Franklin Grove agreed to keep the headquarters open every day, year round. In March 1999, the doors opened and remain that way today.

Pilgrims striking out on the Lincoln from Franklin Grove are a thousand miles west of New York City and about fifty miles east of the Iowa state line. In Dixon, the Lee County seat, travelers can pay homage to President Lincoln at a site between two bridges spanning the Rock River. Here stands a large bronze statue of young Lincoln as a volunteer soldier in the Blackhawk Indian War of 1832. It is thought to be the only statue

ABOVE *Ronald Reagan at his desk, where he kept a fully stocked jar of jellybeans.*

of Honest Abe in uniform. Another locale worthy of a visit is the Dixon Theatre, deemed the most beautiful theater between Chicago and Des Moines when it opened in 1922, on the exact spot where the opera house had burned in 1920. Most of the other recommended visitation sites in Dixon are in some way connected to another American head of state—Ronald Reagan.

Although Reagan—fortieth president of the United States—was born in nearby Tampico, his family soon moved to Dixon, where he raised rabbits, played football, and delivered the local paper. Local lore has it that the notches on a log displayed at a museum represent the seventy-seven people "Dutch" Reagan saved from drowning while working as a lifeguard at Lowell Park. Besides the log, there are many other Reagan points of interest, including one of the homes where he lived for three years, a life-size statue of Reagan holding what appear to be kernels of corn in his outstretched palm, and the church where Reagan and his brother were baptized. The high school that both Reagan boys attended has been restored as the Dixon Historic Center. In the lobby is a large portrait of President Reagan created from hundreds of jellybeans, his favorite snack.

In downtown Dixon, the Wings of Peace and Freedom Park features a full-size replica of a section of the Berlin Wall, in recognition of President Reagan's efforts to crush Communism. After seeing all the Reagan sites, time has come for the final leg of the trek through the Land of Lincoln. After passing through Sterling on

the Rock River, the route through Morrison features a highway mural, fluttering Lincoln Highway banners, Fat Boy's Bar and Grill, and a rebuilt plank-deck covered wooden bridge. There is farmland galore all the way to Fulton, the last town on the Lincoln Highway in Illinois.

In 1876, eleven years after Abraham Lincoln's death, Ben Boyd, a master engraver for a ring of counterfeiters, was captured in his Fulton workshop. Boyd was convicted and sentenced to ten years behind the limestone prison walls at Joliet. Unable to replace the skilled engraver, the rest of the gang plotted to steal the body of President Lincoln, stash it in the Indiana sand dunes, and use it to win Boyd's freedom. When the Secret Service learned of the scheme, they staked out Lincoln's tomb in Springfield. On the night of November 7, 1876, the ghoulish gang had already removed the coffin when an agent accidentally discharged his pistol. In the confusion that ensued, the agents started shooting at each other, and the body snatchers made their getaway. Two of them were later captured and given the maximum sentence for grave robbing—a year in prison. They were released from Joliet long before Boyd, who never returned to Fulton and who vanished in the mists of time.

Named for the inventor of the steamboat, Fulton owes its existence to both the paved highway and the commerce generated from the Mississippi River. The Great River Road, the longest National Scenic Byway, travels through Fulton along Highway 84. Proud

of its Dutch heritage, Fulton's welcome center is a ninety-foot-tall working windmill shipped from the Netherlands in 2001 and assembled near the flood-control dike in the heart of the city. The windmill sits where the Lincoln originally crossed the Mississippi via a bridge that charged vehicles a toll of twenty cents for the driver and a nickel for each passenger. U.S. 30 now crosses "The Father of Waters" about a mile south of that original span. No tolls are charged. In only a few minutes, travelers are in Iowa, free and clear.

Welcome to IOWA

Chapter Eight

IOWA

Every morning when Steve Smith unlocks the door at Smith Brothers General Store in Clinton, Iowa, there is a smile on his face. It's there for good reason. Unlike so many other people, Smith earns a living doing exactly what he wants to do.

This Clinton native operates a special business inside a two-story brick building that was standing on 4th Street long before the Lincoln Highway came to town.

Fading words painted on an outside wall say, "Emporium of Unusual Items." That is an understatement. People come to the store to buy "stuff," the all-inclusive word used to cover a diverse range of miscellaneous materials, products, merchandise, equipment, and supplies. The stuff that Smith sells includes every imaginable type of tool and hardware—baskets, cookie jars, bread boxes, kitchen utensils (most of which folks have never heard of), washboards, coffee grinders, chains, work gloves, ropes, cleaning supplies, brooms and mops, postcards, and pocket knives. *Mad Magazine* is in the periodicals rack next to *Field and Stream*. There is a ton of candy. Anyone in need of handcuffs, galvanized washtubs, cast-iron cookware, canning jars, or a kerosene lamp can find them here. Steve cheerfully makes keys while the waiting customers browse the big

LEFT
Lincoln Cafe,
Belle Plaine, IA.

store that actually feels snug because of the potpourri of paraphernalia that's everywhere.

"I do love my work," says Smith. "We sell old and new stuff alike, including things you just won't find anywhere else. Also, we keep special items in stock for our regulars who come back again and again. But regulars or not, we try our best to take care of everybody that comes through that door."

Born in 1959, Smith picked up his business savvy as a kid, when he and his two older brothers stocked shelves and swept the floor for the store's original owners—their father, Millard Smith, and his brother, Eugene Smith. "When folks joked around and asked my dad if he and my uncle were the cough-drop Smiths, my dad always replied, 'Nope, they're dead millionaires and we're still here.'"

Sons of a used-car salesman, Eugene Smith was in kindergarten and Millard barely walking on July 22, 1919, when the Transcontinental Motor Convoy, put together by the U.S. Army and the Lincoln Highway Association, crossed the Mississippi at Clinton. After setting up camp at Riverfront Park, the troops enjoyed slices of watermelon and fired machine guns across the river, to the delight of the cheering crowd. Besides a band concert, a ball game, and speeches, all of Clinton—including the Smith clan—turned out for a dance at the Coliseum. Jeff, the convoy's raccoon mascot, watched the dancers sway to the music of Shea's Jazz Orchestra until the wee hours. Reveille sounded all too early, and the convoy took to the muddy path across Iowa and pushed on to Cedar Rapids.

A few years later, the Smith brothers dropped out of grammar school and entered the workforce. They hawked candy bars, apples, and tobacco to passengers riding the old interurban train that ran between Clinton and Davenport, another river town forty miles downstream. Still only youngsters when the Depression began, Millard hired on as a freight bill collector and Eugene took a job with a grocer. In 1933, their lives changed. The youngsters saw a For Rent sign hanging in the window of a grocery going out of business on 4th Street, not far from the river and the Chicago & North Western Railroad depot. They pooled their stashed-away savings and leased the store. Eugene was nineteen years old, Millard only fifteen.

"They started from scratch," says Steve. "No bank loans, no help at all from anybody, just the two of them working as hard as they could." For the first twenty-five years of their partnership, the Smiths only sold groceries. Both of them married and at different times lived above the store. They put in long hours, bought fresh produce from area farmers, and ran a good butcher shop. Despite the country's bleak economic condition, they kept their heads above water and built up a solid base of

La Fayette Hotel, Clinton, Iowa.
On the Lincoln Highway.
Horton & Warden.

First Trans-Continental
Sign erected on the
Lincoln Highway.

ABOVE *Vintage postcard of the La Fayette Hotel, "On the Lincoln Highway," in downtown Clinton, IA.*

RIGHT *Bridge in Clinton, IA.*

customers. In addition, highway travelers stopped to buy sandwich fixings and fruit to eat while on the road.

When World War II erupted, business stayed steady, despite food rationing and the decline of civilian highway traffic. During the war, more than forty-four million military personnel rode trains, keeping the nation's depots busy—including the one in Clinton near the Smiths' grocery. Wounded GIs arrived by train to recuperate in the veterans' hospital; toward the end of the war, other personnel came to Clinton when a German prisoner-of-war camp was established near town. Most of the trains, however, transported troops between training bases and debarkation points. For them, Clinton was a brief but popular stop—especially if any young ladies happened to be walking on the platform. If so, there was a rush of uniformed passengers to one side of the train car to get a better look. Even young women clad in grimy overalls and headscarves, who helped the war effort by cleaning the giant locomotives, rated wolf whistles.

In the 1950s, the Smiths added hardware and other retail products to the grocery store, and they maintained a coin-operated laundry on the premises for many years. By the early 1970s, they had totally closed out the grocery business and focused on selling their stuff. To make more room for the vast and ever-expanding inventory, the brothers bought the neighboring tobacco shop and combined the two spaces. Steve started working full-time in 1977, when he was eighteen. The next year, following years of leasing, the Smiths finally bought the original property. After his uncle died and then his father passed away in 1985, Steve took over the business.

"I am so proud of our history," says Steve. "I've always been aware that the Lincoln Highway runs close to our store, and I think that is one reason so many folks hear about us. We get people coming in here from the Netherlands, Germany, Japan, France, Poland, Indonesia, Africa, South America, and every state in the Union."

Across the way, the old brick train depot looks forlorn. Other than a picture-framing business, the building is used mostly for storage. Not far away, eagles soar over the Mississippi. The low rumble and screech of trains rolling down steel rails can be heard, but none of them stop at the depot. Down the block from the store, a bearded man sweeps the sidewalk and gutter in front of Just One More, a neighborhood tavern. Next door, at Gary's Barbershop, a five-dollar bill buys a haircut if the customer is a senior. If not, the price goes up another fifty cents.

Steve and his life partner, Kathy, have a daughter, Allison, born in 2002. "I have another daughter," says Steve. "Her name is Stacey. She was born in 1984 but she contracted cystic fibrosis and left us when she was eleven. She's gone. Stacey is an angel now." He speaks in the present tense of his little girl who would be a grown woman. There are no tears. There is just that trademark smile, the same one Steve has everyday when he unlocks the front door of the store and sells stuff to the world.

Steve Smith is just one reason why people should take the Lincoln Highway if they really want to experience Iowa. Those who choose to cross the state on Interstate 80 miss so much. They hear no stories of boy brothers and GIs going off to war. They don't learn that Clinton was the hometown of Lillian Russell, a legendary actress and singer at the turn of the twentieth century and the companion of Diamond Jim Brady. They never find out that Felix Adler, one of the nation's most beloved circus clowns, who performed for three U.S. presidents, was born in Clinton. They don't see the Clinton LumberKings play minor-league hardball under the lights or hear the town's fifty-member symphony orchestra perform a classical concert. They can't tour the museum on the ground floor of an old four-story department store designed by renowned Chicago architect Louis Sullivan. Worst of all, they don't get to see Steve's smile and buy some of his stuff.

LEFT

Ghost sign, Clinton, IA.

Daniel Baxter, a physician who lived and practiced in Clinton for seven years in the 1980s, has fond memories of the river community and the devoted patients who still send him Christmas and birthday cards. "They're straight down-the-middle people," the physician says fondly. "In their hearts they are liberals, and in their pocketbooks they are conservative."

Folks in this quintessential border town consider themselves Iowans. They root for the Hawkeyes in Iowa City and, given their midwestern tenacity, they steel themselves for the Iowa snowstorms that often begin right after Christmas and continue until spring.

Many stately homes in Clinton date from the 1800s. Eagle Point Park, at the northern edge of the city, once was part of Lyons, a separate town now absorbed into Clinton. From here, travelers can enjoy a panoramic view of the bluffs lining the Mississippi before continuing along the rest of the 360 miles of Lincoln Highway in Iowa, through towns such as Wheatland, Mechanicsville, Tama, Marshalltown, Boone, Ralston, Dunlap, and so many others.

From the Mississippi River in the east to the Missouri River forming the Nebraska state line in the west, travelers find themselves landlocked on a road that allows them to slow down and forget about time. They also find that the Lincoln in Iowa is much easier to navigate now than it was when travelers first used it.

For many years, Iowa was notorious for its poorly maintained roads that needed just a little rainfall before turning into a sticky mud called gumbo. Gumbo was

to be avoided at all costs. One early traveler described gumbo as having "the consistency of stale mucilage and when dry is as hard as flint." Out West, settlers used gumbo to chink the crevices in log houses. There was no mud like it anywhere. Drivers reported that gumbo was worse than driving through sand. Those who tried pushing a trapped vehicle out of the heavy ooze usually had their shoes sucked right off. Anyone walking in a pasture with just a little bit of gumbo on his or her soles uprooted the grass with every step. A 1920 Lincoln Highway Association publication declared Iowa's gumbo "a particularly vicious and viscous and generally impassable brand of mud peculiar to the state."

Iowa had 102,000 miles of road in 1912, but few were paved, graveled, or even graded. By 1920, not much had changed. Iowa still had only twenty-five miles of paved roads outside its major cities, which made any improvements on the Lincoln Highway eagerly welcomed. Yet so precarious were the roads that the 1924 Lincoln Highway Association guidebook warned motorists: "It is folly to drive on Iowa dirt roads, during or immediately after a rain." Association officials bluntly recommended, "When it rains in Iowa or Nebraska, the tourist should stop if he wishes to save his car, his time, his tires, and his temper." The guidebook also pointed out that the state was making a concerted effort to provide a permanent road grade and install badly needed drainage systems—two key steps before permanent paving. "In the process of providing this grade, Iowa has eliminated many of the curves and unnecessary jogs and railroad crossings originally existing on the route, and is rapidly moving into a position where the permanent paving of the route will be possible. A great deal of the mileage across Iowa has been gravelled, removing the terrors of gumbo mud in wet weather, and a little paving has been laid, notably in Clinton County. . . ."

The original alignment of the Lincoln Highway across Iowa—from Clinton west to Council Bluffs on the Missouri River border—paralleled the tracks of the Chicago & North Western Railroad, which in 1995 was taken over by the Union Pacific Railroad. Through the years, much of the Lincoln Highway was bypassed in Iowa, as happened elsewhere. A major reroute of the highway took place in 1930, when the Abraham Lincoln Bridge opened over the Missouri River and U.S. 30 was realigned to the new bridge. Instead of taking the south loop down to Council Bluffs, travelers used the more direct route to the north. The new Lincoln no longer crossed the river into Omaha but entered Nebraska at the town of Fremont. Additional sections of the highway changed with the creation of U.S. 30 and again in 1966, when Interstate 80 came along and plowed through Iowa like a delinquent John Deere tractor.

Although the old highway frequently changes course in Iowa, it is estimated that at least eighty-five percent of the original highway can still be driven and enjoyed. Much of the driving pleasure comes from the efforts of people who were born at least half a century after the Lincoln's demise. Iowa, in fact, has the distinction of having hosted the October 31, 1992, meeting that resulted

ABOVE *Paving the Lincoln Highway in Iowa, 1922.*

in the reactivation of the long-defunct Lincoln Highway Association. The meeting had been called to save from destruction an original stretch of highway in Greene County. Although this first effort proved unsuccessful in the short run, the gathering resulted in the reincarnation of the national association. When that committed band of preservationists and concerned citizens from across the nation came together in the highway town of Ogden, Iowa, it was exactly seventy-nine years to the day since the original association had been formed. The one-line mission statement that they drafted is straightforward and to the point: "Dedicated to preserving and promoting America's first transcontinental highway for the automobile." Not only has the national association lived up to its mission, so have the state chapters, including the conscientious Iowa Lincoln Highway Association, based in Ogden. Some of the best of the Lincoln is in this state—running through farmland and fields and the many towns and cities that the highway either skirts or passes through. It is an ideal state for nostalgia buffs to rediscover the hidden charms of the Lincoln Highway.

Between Clinton and Cedar Rapids—a stretch at least partly paved by 1923—the highway westward takes travelers to Low Moor, Elvira, Malone, and De Witt— the "Crossroads to Opportunity." East of De Witt, at the point where the new highway leaves the old road, a directional sign hangs on a wooden pole. As in other old-road towns, some of the businesses in De Witt carry the first name of the owner or are named for the town itself. There is Murf's, selling "Cold Beer, Good Booze, Lousy Service," and next door, Art's Barbershop, with two chairs, stacks of magazines, and a stainless-steel coffee urn that's usually perking. Martha's Cafe is handy for a meal and, if it's not closed for the winter, De Witt Dairy Treats is easily located by its large ice cream cone sign.

The highway makes its way westward to Grand Mound, well into Iowa's corn belt. Prizewinning seed corn was grown here by Descartes Pascal, a Clinton County farmer with the unlikely names of two world-famous seventeenth-century French philosophers and scientists. Pascal became interested in corn breeding in 1902 and won a silo full of awards and honors, including a single perfect ear named Champion of the World at the 1908 National Corn Exposition, held annually in Omaha. The event motto was "Prosperity moves on crutches when crops go wrong," and its symbol was the Corn

Show Mermaid, with a corncob tail and a cloak made of husks. Besides farming, Pascal also experimented with photography. At Iowa State University in Ames—a Lincoln Highway town—is a collection of several hundred of Pascal's gelatin glass-plate negatives depicting family, farm life, and the Pascal homestead east of Grand Mound.

Iowa usually produces the largest corn crop in the nation, and the stalks are tall in the summertime along the old Lincoln. Farmers mostly harvest field corn for animal feed and commercial products, but they grow enough sweet corn to guarantee plenty of good eating come July. Travelers ride through rich farmland as they near Calamus, guardian of a concrete Lincoln Highway marker and a vintage gas station with a canopy. Just a few miles farther, Wheatland is a good spot for picking up live bait after grabbing a bite at the Harvest Cafe or Mac's Triangle on Lincoln Way. Not far from town, the Wapsipinicon River, sometimes called Wapsi by locals, makes its way to the Mississippi. It has always been a pretty good stream for snagging crappie, catfish, and smallmouth bass, and there is nothing to match a skillet of fried fish, vine-ripened tomatoes, and a platter of that Iowa sweet corn drenched with butter.

Moving into Cedar County and the town of Lowden, travelers who have not caught the fishing bug should cruise by the Lincoln Hotel, built in 1915 and lovingly restored in 1995 as apartments with a few overnight rentals. The two-story stucco-clad hotel, with an inviting front-porch swing, is listed on the National Register of Historic Places. Across the street, trucks and tractors surround the Arrow Cafe; the historic Chevrolet dealership building and sign is a favorite of photographers. The town's high-noon whistle is so loud that newcomers unaccustomed to the shrill blast might end up on the ground in a duck-and-cover position. The Herbert Hoover Highway—a forty-two-mile series of local, state, and county roads—begins in Lowden and ends in Iowa City, southwest of the Lincoln. Hoover, the thirty-first president of the United States, was born in 1874 in West Branch, ten miles outside of Iowa City. The Hoover family's small cabin is now part of the Herbert Hoover National Historic Site—a worthwhile side trip for Lincoln Highway travelers.

Much like Lowden, the other three Lincoln Highway towns in Cedar County—Clarence, Stanwood, and Mechanicsville—provide their share of abandoned alignments, vintage gas stations, and ghost signs on old brick walls. Almost every small hamlet along the way has a towering grain elevator, usually between the highway and the railroad tracks. These prairie cathedrals mark the way and can be seen from great distances, growing larger with each passing mile.

After going into Linn County, U.S. 30 curves just south of Lisbon and Mount Vernon and totally bypasses both Marion and downtown Cedar Rapids. All four deserve a visit. At Mount Vernon, federal funding was wisely used in the late 1990s for the restoration of a wooden-decked pony-truss bridge that carried Lincoln Highway traffic over the old Chicago & North Western rails. Electrified faux gas lamps were installed on the brick section of the Lincoln leading up to the bridge. Cornell College—unrelated to Cornell University in Ithaca, New York—has turned out scholars since its founding in 1853. Five years after that, Cornell became the first college west of the Mississippi to accept women in all its degree programs. Today's Cornell students study one course at a time and cover in three and a half weeks what would normally be taught in a full semester at most universities. Some of Cornell's best and brightest are usually seen at the Lincoln Cafe, best known for its "small-town feel" and dinner specials prepared from local and regional meats, vegetables, and fruits. Four miles west of Mount Vernon is the site of Iowa's Seedling Mile, completed in 1919 on a section of the highway that had been an old wagon-and-stagecoach route.

On the edge of Cedar Rapids, the original gravel-surfaced Lincoln headed north to the town of Marion and through Squaw Creek Park. The old route then used a series of streets to loop south again to Cedar Rapids, the Linn County seat. In Cedar Rapids, both the city hall and the county courthouse are located on May's Island in the Cedar River, which runs through the city and provides its name. For many years, the Lincoln used to run down Second Avenue, and a six-block-long stretch of the street became known as "Automobile Row" because of all the car dealers, gas stations, and repair shops. Among the city's best-known residents was Grant Wood, the internationally acclaimed artist who painted *American Gothic* and many of his other works in a studio near downtown. The loft

Back on U.S. 30, to the west is the Youngville Station, a one-stop gas station and cafe built in 1921 at the junction of the Lincoln and U.S. 218. Like other places on the old road impacted by the newer superhighways and a public who wanted everything fast and could not wait twenty minutes for a properly prepared meal, the station closed and fell into serious decay. That came to a halt in the mid-1990s, thanks to a grassroots restoration campaign. Federal funding was sought and found, and the Youngville Station was brought back to life.

When travelers take a short back road and reach Belle Plaine, they have more reason to smile. This history-minded town, just like little Chelsea up the road, was on a segment of the Lincoln Highway that was bypassed in 1937. Belle Plaine remains a stronghold of highway legend and lore. Much of that is due to the late George Preston, a guardian of the old road whose old filling station—covered with every oil-company sign he could get his hands on—is a colorful tribute to the highway. The station moved to its present site in 1921, when the route changed. That was just a few years before Preston started working there at the age of thirteen. Immediately, the youngster began the collection that adorns the station he ultimately owned.

Preston also became a masterful storyteller—so well known that word reached Iowa native Johnny Carson, the late-night TV host. In 1990, Carson flew Preston to California to share some of his best yarns on *The Tonight Show*, an appearance that not only doubled Carson over in fits of laughter but also made Preston

studio—open to the public for tours—is owned and operated by the nearby Cedar Rapids Museum of Art, where the largest collection of Wood's art is housed.

The straight path of highway west of Cedar Rapids passes just north of the famed Amana Colonies—seven villages settled in the 1850s by a Protestant religious sect with German roots. Residents lived a communal life until the early 1930s. Since then, the community has become widely known for Amana Refrigeration, Inc., a national leader in refrigerator production. Amana also has evolved into a major tourist attraction and draws visitors year-round to its brewery and many craft shops and restaurants. The colonies are listed as a National Historic Landmark and make an interesting detour off the Lincoln.

LEFT *Ron Preston,*
George's son,
inside Preston
Station in Belle
Plaine, IA.

and Belle Plaine even better known. Preston died three years after his national television debut, but his gas station is visited more than ever by a growing number of shunpikers. George and his wife, Blanche, who passed away in 1998, rest side by side in the Oakhill Cemetery on the edge of town. Their tombstone bears the logo of George's favorite highway, and often travelers leave Lincoln-head pennies on top of the stone out of respect.

The F. L. Sankot Garage, in Belle Plaine since 1914 and on the National Register of Historic Places, is still

Oat-processing
plant, Chelsea, IA.

Some storefronts are boarded up, but Chelsea's city hall and library are in a well-kept old bank building. A schoolyard is filled with kids at play. The brick Catholic church erected in 1867 appears sound. Across from the Silver Dollar Bar and Grill, a burly man in overalls and a little boy who has to be his grandson emerge from a dusty pickup. The man's gray flattop was probably cut in the last forty-eight hours at the local barbershop. As the pair heads for the front door of the Silver Dollar, the man notices travelers watching them. Without breaking stride or waiting for an answer, he breaks out in a big grin and yells, "Hello there, isn't this a great day?" As the man and the boy disappear inside, it is a safe wager that in a heartbeat both will be on stools with a bottle of ice-cold pop and a frosty beer before them.

The old road out of Chelsea rejoins U.S. 30 and continues westward to Tama. On the east side of town, the two-story King Tower Cafe, with a dazzling neon Indian-chief sign, looks much as it must have when it first opened in 1937. Tama is the town with the most famous bridge on the entire length of the Lincoln Highway. Built in 1915, it has the words *Lincoln Highway* spelled out in concrete letters on the balusters, and handsome lights adorn both ends of the bridge. The original construction was financed by the local citizens, who were bursting with pride about being included on the Lincoln Highway. Even though Tama was completely bypassed in 1926, the town has never neglected the bridge. In 1976, it was listed on the National Register of Historic Places; in 1987, the descendants of the people

in the Sankot family. West of the garage, yet another Lincoln Cafe, established in 1928 and famous for great coffee and broasted chicken, stays busy. Back on the old segment into Tama County and continuing to Chelsea, travelers may find the past and present gently colliding.

In Chelsea, where the route goes via Irish Street, pigeons coo from the tops of the prairie cathedral, and lines of rolling freight thunder by. The words *Vatos Locos*—Spanish slang for "crazy rascal boys"—are spray-painted on an open metal door atop a grain elevator. In the ruins of a gutted building is a broken lamp with a pair of stuffed squirrels in boxing poses mounted on the base. The town's one-chair barbershop looks like it may sometimes be open. A window decal says, "Get Wild Root Cream Oil, Charlie," there is a wood-burning stove, and a huge lobster is mounted on a board. A black-and-white snapshot of a sailor in uniform is taped to the mirror.

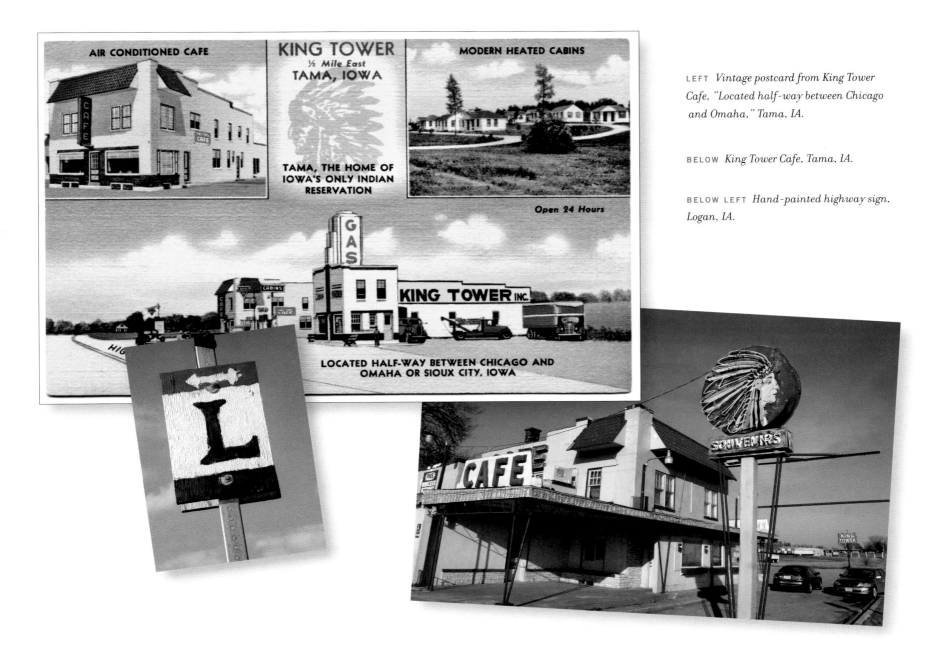

AIR CONDITIONED CAFE

KING TOWER
½ Mile East
TAMA, IOWA

MODERN HEATED CABINS

TAMA, THE HOME OF
IOWA'S ONLY INDIAN
RESERVATION

Open 24 Hours

GAS

KING TOWER INC.

LOCATED HALF-WAY BETWEEN CHICAGO AND
OMAHA OR SIOUX CITY, IOWA

LEFT *Vintage postcard from King Tower Cafe, "Located half-way between Chicago and Omaha," Tama, IA.*

BELOW *King Tower Cafe, Tama, IA.*

BELOW LEFT *Hand-painted highway sign, Logan, IA.*

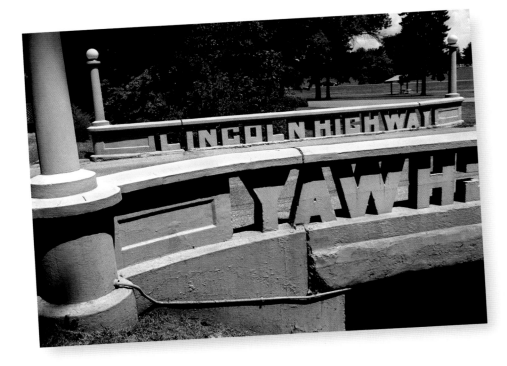

who first paid for the bridge raised the funds to restore it. The town hosts an annual Lincoln Highway Bridge Festival, and on summer afternoons, kids catch frogs beneath the bridge, just as their predecessors always did.

West of Tama, the Lincoln passes the Mesquakie Settlement—originally a reservation for Sac and Fox Indians from Oklahoma—and crosses the Iowa River. In the days before paving, this river bottom yielded some of the thickest gumbo in the universe. Then, just before the route rejoins U.S. 30, is the place where the Lincoln Highway Association's field secretary, Henry Ostermann, was killed on June 8, 1920. (Just

seven months earlier, Ostermann had wed his bride from East Liverpool, the Lincoln Highway town on the eastern border of Ohio.) After a dinner party in Tama, Ostermann's wife felt ill and stayed with friends while her husband departed for a conference in Marshalltown in his bone-white 1918 Packard Twin Six touring car. On a hilly section of old road, less than a mile east of Montour, Ostermann drove up behind a Model T straining to make the grade. When he pulled out to pass, the tires of the big Packard slipped on the wet grass along the left shoulder. Ostermann lost control of the vehicle and it turned over twice before landing upright. His head had been crushed against the steering wheel and he died instantly. The congenial and well-liked Ostermann was forty-three years old. It was his twenty-first transcontinental journey over the Lincoln.

Travelers often seek out the place where Ostermann perished. On that gentle curve next to a cornfield, a small wooden cross stands on the shoulder, but it is not for Ostermann. His memorial is back in Illinois and his grave lies in Ohio. The cross is in memory of a sixteen-year-old Mexican boy who died at this spot in a car crash in 2001. His name was Eduardo and, like Ostermann so long ago, he also was far from home.

On the road ahead, a home-away-from-home since 1925 continues to serve highway travelers only a few miles west of Le Grand. The Shady Oaks Campground along Brush Creek in Marshall County is regarded by many as the first cabin camp opened on the Lincoln Highway in Iowa. That was in 1925, when the campsite—

including eighteen cabins, gas station, restaurant, and grocery—opened in a grove of ancient bur oaks. The stand of trees had been a resting place for Indians, trappers, and early settlers. A wagon road ran past the grove in the mid-1800s, and later it was part of a stagecoach route. The oaks provided a shady and cool place for revivals, community meetings, and the site of an early school. In 1996, the state of Iowa added the oaks to its Register of Famous and Historical Trees.

By the late 1940s, when traffic dwindled on the old road and business fell off at Shady Oaks, many of the cabins were sold and moved off the property. Robert and Mary Gift, who now own the property, have restored some of the buildings remaining from the old highway era, including an original cabin. There is still life in the old place. The Gifts' grandson, Mick Jurgensen, has lived at Shady Oaks since he was a toddler. In 1983, he began building a magnificent treehouse with more than five thousand square feet of floor space on twelve levels. The Big Treehouse, as Jurgensen calls the structure, is equipped with electricity, running water, and telephone service. It has a music system, a full kitchen, and more than a dozen porch swings. A guided tour can be arranged by appointment if the weather is cooperating.

Three miles west of Shady Oaks at Marshalltown, no reservations are required at two celebrated pie palaces—Stone's Restaurant, with its trademark lemon chiffon pie, and Zeno's, making acclaimed pizza pies since 1957. Marshalltown, which was home to actress Jean Seberg, who was selected from thousands of aspirants to star in Otto Preminger's *Joan of Arc*, also houses Taylors Maid-Rite, which has fed tens of thousands of special "loose meat" sandwiches to local patrons and highway travelers since 1928. The third-oldest franchise in the restaurant chain that was started in Iowa in 1926,

RIGHT *Taylors Maid-Rite, Marshalltown, IA.*

Taylors remains family operated and is arguably the finest of the Maid-Rites remaining in the state.

West of Marshalltown, the route takes travelers through Lamoille and State Center—known as Iowa's rose capital—to Colo, where the Lincoln crossed the Jefferson Highway, organized in 1915 and running in a north–south direction between New Orleans and Winnipeg. In Colo in the early 1920s, Charles Reed opened the L & J Service Station, named in honor of the two highways. Soon after Reed started pumping gas, his cousins, Florence and Reed Niland, opened a cafe next to the filling station. Business boomed and Reed built Colo Cabin Camp—eventually twelve cabins with showerhouses—on the other side of the cafe. Reed / Niland Corner, or simply Niland's Corner, prospered for many years—until U.S. 30 was rerouted to the south in the early 1960s and Interstate 80 came along. The gas station closed in 1967 and the cafe hung on until 1991. Fortunately, none of the buildings were destroyed, and by the late 1990s, the city of Colo formed a development group with dreams of restoring the complex as a tourist attraction. That dream was realized after the property was acquired and Lyell Henry, a member of the Iowa chapter of the Lincoln Highway Association, devoted five years to reviving Reed/Niland Corner. By 2003, Niland's cafe opened once again and the gas station had been transformed into a period museum.

Following a jukebox concert at the resurrected Niland's, travelers proceeding west enter the town of Nevada. If there were any doubt about Nevada's awareness of its highway heritage, all folks need to do is stand before a stone monument on the edge of town: "You are traveling on the original Lincoln Highway." To back up that statement, Nevada hosts an annual celebration known as Lincoln Highway Days, featuring a rodeo, dances, and, of course, parades down the old road.

Many of the celebrants in Nevada come from Ames, the home of Iowa State University and also a town where the celebrated graphic artist R. Crumb lived during part of his childhood. In this pleasant college town, Billy Sunday, a well-known pro baseball-player-turned-evangelist, was born in 1863, just four months before his soldier father died in the Civil War. Sunday bounced around as a boy and for a time tended Shetland ponies and played sandlot ball in Nevada, where the local baseball field bears his name. Cap Anson, a future Baseball Hall of Fame member from Marshalltown, heard about young Sunday's baseball prowess and signed him to a major-league contract with the Chicago White Stockings. After several years of playing ball for various teams,

LEFT
Flamingo Motel, Marshalltown, IA.

LOWER LEFT
A recollection from graphic artist R. Crumb, who grew up on the Lincoln Highway in the early 1950s.

Sunday got religion and became a strict fundamentalist preacher, delivering fire-and-brimstone sermons across the nation. "Whiskey and beer are all right in their place, but their place is in hell," became one of Sunday's famous quotes. Sunday ranted and raved throughout the heyday of the Lincoln Highway, and he died a wealthy man in 1935 at the height of the Depression.

Out of Ames, travelers come to Boone, the Lincoln Highway town where Mamie Doud was born in 1896. She grew up to become the bride of a young army tank officer named Dwight David Eisenhower. During the famous Transcontinental Motor Convoy trip on the Lincoln in 1919, Ike was welcomed to Boone like an adopted son, but his wife and the couple's infant son were in Denver, where Mamie was tending to a dying sister. During the convoy's brief stop, Eisenhower visited with Mamie's aunt and uncle, Joel and Eda Carlson. After trekking through many miles of Iowa gumbo, Eisenhower displayed diplomacy when reporters asked what he thought of the path through Iowa: "I can't say too much on the condition of the Lincoln Highway." Visitors coming to Boone can tour the former first lady's girlhood residence on Mamie Eisenhower Avenue.

Besides the Eisenhower connection and close ties to the Lincoln Highway, Boone has always been known as a railroad town. That is why the story is still told of Kate Shelley, a fifteen-year-old Irish immigrant who saved a train filled with passengers in 1881. It happened one July night when a horrific storm broke over the Des Moines River Valley. Not far from where Kate and her widowed mother lived, the bridge over Honey Creek gave way, and a pusher train searching for washouts along the tracks fell into the swirling waters. Kate heard the crash and knew that an express passenger train was due to pass over the fallen trestle within the hour. Grabbing a lantern, she ran to help, first assuring the two survivors from the four-man crew at the crash site that she would return. Kate crawled over the broken bridge to the depot in Moingona, where she sounded the alarm. After the station agent stopped the express train, Kate

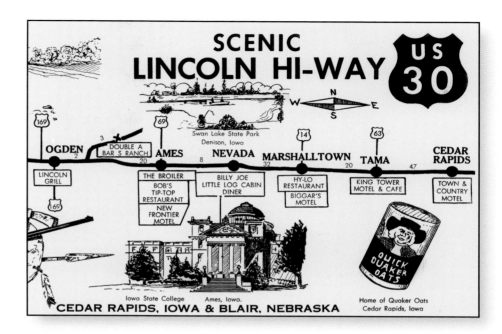

led rescuers to the two grateful survivors. Hundreds of articles about the young heroine appeared around the world, and the state of Iowa presented Kate with a gold medal made by Tiffany's. The money she received from generous donors put her through college, but she chose to work as a railroad agent. Kate Shelley was only forty-six when she died of Bright's Disease in 1912. At her grave in the Sacred Heart Cemetery in Boone, a plaque is inscribed "Hers is a deed bound for legend . . . a story to be told until the last order fades and the last rail rusts."

U.S. 30 runs south of Boone and below Ogden, but most Lincoln travelers follow the old route into town. Visitors to Ogden often search out the piece of road where someone left footprints in wet cement

ABOVE

Vintage placemat advertising the "Scenic Lincoln Hi-Way" in Iowa.

RIGHT *Pair of liar's tables in the Ogden Diner, Ogden, IA.*

in 1929. Not far from "the scene of the crime," the Ogden Diner is a former Maid-Rite franchise that has attracted townspeople, farmers, and travelers since 1930. Sue Nelson turns out marvelous bootleg versions of the loose-meat sandwich that often fool even die-hard Maid-Rite addicts. Sue calls her creation the Nellie—from her last name and her son's nickname. Besides ordering Nellies, diners go for such specials as pork loin with baked potatoes and scalloped corn followed by a slice of "pumkin" pie.

Every morning, Sue turns out biscuits and gravy and cinnamon rolls, but the majority of customers are there to drink coffee and visit. They do lots of both. If a traveler's timing is right, the door of the Ogden Diner opens to reveal the place packed with local gents, mostly in their sixties and up. Sometimes all four of the tables

are filled. Although these Formica-topped tables may not look like much, they are special. They are "liar's tables."

Every self-respecting small town cafe and roadside diner has to have at least one liar's table—a specific roost where the local storytellers and wisdom keepers gather faithfully every morning to sip coffee and solve the world's problems. At a liar's table, everything gets discussed, chewed over, and settled. Sometimes gossip is tossed in and the truth gets stretched, but the name *liar's table* implies no disrespect to those who occupy the seats.

Sue Preston must brew up some pretty good coffee to rate not one but four liar's tables in her snug establishment. On an early weekday morning—especially in winter when the crop fields are dormant—travelers who find an empty stool at the counter are indeed fortunate. Not only will they enjoy a good meal, they will catch snatches of conversation, jokes, and perhaps a lie or two—all priceless. Conversations might cover where the best morel mushrooms grow, why so-and-so deserves to be elected, and the need to at least start thinking about putting in a vegetable garden. There is plenty of talk about trucks and tractors. Some men use the latest issue of the *Ogden Reporter* to spur discussions—a neighbor's grandson who enlisted in the army, the passing of a friend who served in World War II and came home to farm, and plans for a high-school class reunion.

One fellow regales his table with stories of bloody car wrecks. The words, ". . . then I unfastened the seat belt and pulled the dead man from his car," reach eavesdropping travelers. Their ears turn like radar screens to hear the rest: "That fellow was deader than a witch. He had a seat belt on but it sure did him no good." A heated discussion of the pros and cons of seat belts follows, but finally the man who started the row turns the conversation from auto safety and back to car wrecks. "Another time, I heard a crash right outside my place and I found this woman in her smashed-up car and she was hurting real bad." The man sees that he has everyone's attention. "So I eased her out of that mess and carried her to my house. I laid her down on the davenport and comforted her. She was there all night long." The man goes back to his coffee, and finally somebody prods him and wants to know what happened to the woman. "Oh, I called her folks in Iowa City and they drove up the next morning and took her home." An anticlimactic ending to his tale earns the man a chorus of well-deserved guffaws. Then a latecomer strides into the cafe and heads directly to a table. "You didn't wave at me the other day," he informs a startled man, who replies that he did not see his friend. "Well, I saw you, and I waved," says the jilted man, as he turns away and joins another table. Waving at all oncoming vehicles, or at least lifting a couple of fingers from the steering wheel, is one of the unwritten laws of rural America, and violators must be chastised.

Nourishment for mind and body supplied at the Ogden Diner sustains travelers for many miles through a string of Lincoln Highway towns such as Beaver, the first one in the state bypassed by the newer Lincoln. A dirt section of the old road remains just north of town, as well as a forlorn 1915 bridge with a distinctive letter "L" cut into each end. The bridge, now marooned in a field, is at the border of Greene County, which has many miles of Lincoln Highway, including multiple routes and stretches of dirt road and original pavement. The trio of highway towns in this county—Grand Junction, Jefferson, and Scranton, site of Iowa's oldest working water tower—give travelers a close look at canopied gas stations, tourist camps and motels, working roadside cafes, Lincoln Highway markers, and historic bridges.

Just south of U.S. 30 in Jefferson, the Uptown Cafe—with hot daily specials and breakfast served all day—draws crowds. The 162-foot-tall Mahanay Memorial Carillon Tower—resembling a grain elevator—dominates the courthouse square. The tower features fourteen cast bells and an electronic carillon that chimes mostly patriotic and religious music. Visitors can ride an elevator 120 feet to an observation deck, a popular activity every June when the town hosts the Bell Tower Festival. A bronze statue of Abraham Lincoln, dedicated in 1918, still stands facing the old Lincoln Highway alignment in the shadow of the bell tower. Just

Lincoln Highway Trading Company, Carroll, IA.

To the west in Carroll County, the old road skirts the northern edge of Ralston and heads to Glidden, named for the barbed-wire inventor, who came from the Lincoln Highway town of DeKalb, Illinois. Glidden has always touted itself as a fine rest stop for tourists. Early travelers were told to halt in Glidden because it had "plenty of shade, excellent drinking water, refreshment parlors, cafes and a hotel whose home cooking, chicken dinners, rich cream, fresh butter and eggs have made it famous all over the west." Glidden still has plenty of shade, most people drink water from the tap, and travelers now get plenty of broasted chicken at the Dairy Mart, a longtime local hangout marked by a smiling plastic rooster larger than a man. The closest thing to a liar's table in Glidden is at an immaculate garage owned by Cal Hughes, where coffee drinkers with plenty of news and stories have gathered each weekday morning for many years. In the heart of the downtown business district, plenty of good stories make the rounds at the Merle Hay American Legion Post, named for a young Iowa farmhand who was twenty-one when he went off to serve and perish in World War I.

Half a mile west of Glidden, on U.S. 30, many travelers pause at a granite monument to Merle Hay, who was killed during hand-to-hand fighting in France the night of November 2, 1917. Hay was one of the first three U.S. soldiers, and the first from Iowa, to die in the war. Of the eight local boys who went to war, six did not make it home alive. In 1919, the Transcontinental Motor

west of the square, the former 5 Spot Cafe houses the headquarters of the local chapter of the Lincoln Highway Association. The numerous highway segments, markers, and bridges in Greene County were combined into the nation's first Lincoln Highway multiple-properties listing on the National Register of Historic Places.

PARK MOTEL

ON U.S. 30 AND 59 AND IOWA 4 AND 141 AT THE CROSSROADS OF WESTERN IOWA.

Park Motel

CRONK'S CAFE

DENISON · IOWA

90 Very Modern Rooms
Unexcelled Beds
Rates $1.25 and Up
Fireproof Addition and Garage
HOTEL DENISON
"On the Lincoln Hiway"

Another noted Iowa soldier was Ralph G. Neppel, who left Glidden when he was twenty-one to fight in World War II. He survived and was one of five Iowans from that war who received the Congressional Medal of Honor, the nation's highest military tribute. Leader of a machine-gun squad during fighting in Germany in late 1944, Neppel inflicted heavy casualties on the enemy and stopped a determined counterattack, despite having one leg severed and suffering severe wounds that eventually led to the amputation of his other leg. On August 23, 1945, during a White House ceremony, President Harry Truman pinned the Medal of Honor on Neppel, who sat in a wheelchair. "I really didn't do much," Neppel said years later. "It was just a question of fighting on and doing what a fellow could or get killed." After the war, Neppel graduated from college and worked for the Veterans Administration and also served on the Governor's Committee for Employment of the Handicapped. Neppel, who died of cancer in 1987, was laid to rest in the town of Lidderdale, north of the Lincoln Highway.

Convoy of Army vehicles and soldiers made a point of stopping in Glidden to pay homage to Hay. Officers visited with his parents and a movie crew filmed the occasion. Hay's body was not returned to Iowa until 1921, when the largest funeral ever held in Iowa up to that time took place on July 24—as many as 20,000 mourners turned out to pay last respects. Hay and his parents are buried side by side behind the monument, erected in 1929 after legislation was passed funding the memorial.

Down on the old route, only the county seat, marked with Lincoln Highway banners, remains in Carroll County before travelers reach Crawford County. Just a mile east of Arcadia, on U.S. 30, is the point where all water runs either east to the Mississippi River or west to the Missouri River. Now the route begins to bend to the southwest, through Westside, Vail, and Denison—a predominantly Protestant community that over the years slowly became a Hispanic town.

This dramatic demographic shift began when Latinos moved to Denison to take jobs in the meatpacking plants, butchering more than ten thousand hogs daily. Denison retains many of the old Lincoln Highway cafes and motels, but increasingly more signage appears in Spanish, reflecting a vibrant new diversity in Iowa. Travelers are just as likely to find sustenance in a Mexican restaurant, such as El Jimador, just off the town square, or La Santaneca on Main Street, featuring Salvadoran cuisine, including savory octopus dishes.

Cronk's Cafe, built in 1929, and the Park Motel still serve large numbers of old-road wayfarers. The Park, a classic Spanish Colonial Revival constructed in 1940, is listed on the National Register of Historic Places. The list of well-known guests over the years is impressive, including motion-picture and television actress Donna Reed, who was born and raised in Denison. *It's a Wonderful Life*, the name of one of her most beloved films, is scrawled across the town's water tower. The Donna Reed Theatre is located in a restored opera house at Broadway and Main. Even after the passing of Denison's favorite daughter, the Donna Reed Festival for the Performing Arts is still held every June.

As U.S. 30 departs Denison, it bends even more toward the Nebraska border, passing Arion and Dow City and continuing through Dunlap, where, three miles southwest of town, travelers will be startled to come upon pop art on the edge of a cornfield. The work of California artist John Cerney, the tableau depicts a tearful seventeen-foot-tall girl holding the remains of her chewed-up teddy bear. Sitting on its haunches and looking at the distraught girl is the culprit—an eight-foot-tall Dalmatian showing little if any remorse. Located on the farm of Gerald and Lorene Hein, the large-scale artwork makes truckers and travelers smile, no matter how many times they pass it.

Often those smiles are still in place when they reach Woodbine, proud of its restored brick section of the Lincoln lined with picturesque homes. The eleven blocks of Lincoln Way in Woodbine still get plenty of use, and this stretch represents a significant portion of the original Lincoln Highway. A few miles farther, in Logan, more original Lincoln winds through town.

At this point of the Iowa trek, travelers can continue south on the original path, passing Loveland, and drive on to Honey Creek, Crescent, and finally Council Bluffs, the historic Western crossroads where the Lincoln joins U.S. 6 and crosses the Missouri. The other option stays clear of Council Bluffs (and Omaha on the other side) and takes travelers on the newer 1930 route, more than twenty miles north of the original crossing. After reaching Missouri Valley, the last Iowa town on the Lincoln Highway, travelers arrive at a bluff overlooking the Missouri River, where it becomes clear that the old road has come to the place where the East meets the West.

OPPOSITE *Art in a cornfield by John Cerney, Dunlap, IA.*

Iowa (165)

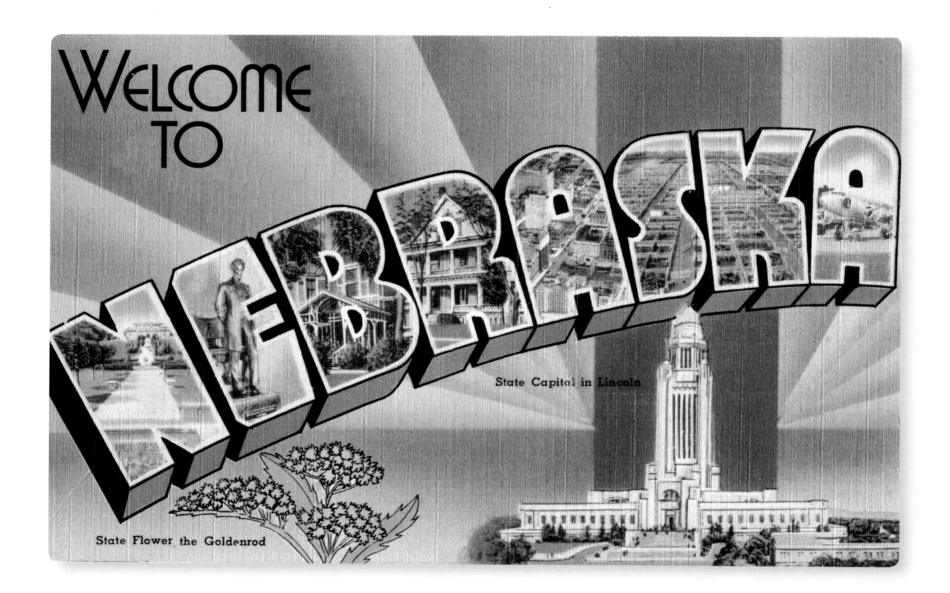

WELCOME TO NEBRASKA

State Capitol in Lincoln

State Flower the Goldenrod

Chapter Nine

NEBRASKA

The mere suggestion that the 462 miles of Lincoln Highway romping their way across Nebraska are not to be missed can be a mighty tough sell. Conventional tourists all too often consider Nebraska a huge pasture to

pass through as quickly as possible in order to arrive at their destination.

Bill Bryson, an engaging and talented travel writer and Iowa expatriate who has spent much of his adult life in England, has little good to say about Nebraska. "I was headed for Nebraska. Now there's a sentence you don't want to have to say too often if you can possibly help it," wrote Bryson in *The Lost Continent: Travels in Small*

Town America. "Nebraska must be the most unexciting of all the states. Compared with it, Iowa must be paradise."

It's a free country. Those looking for Hollywood glitz or a fancy Western dude ranch should clearly glom on to Interstate 80. That's the fastest way to enter and exit Nebraska in a matter of hours. By contrast, travelers who view the drive itself as a major component of

LEFT
Remains of a concrete Lincoln Highway bridge, Overton, NE.

any road trip will find the Lincoln Highway a far more interesting course, and they will be all the better for it.

Anyone driving the old route from the muddy Missouri in the east to the Wyoming border in the west will learn very quickly that all the things they have heard about Nebraska are hackneyed characterizations with little substance. For example, not all Nebraskans live on farms, sport seed-company caps, drive pickups, take their dates to livestock shows, or husk corn. At least one-third of the state's population dwells in Omaha or Lincoln. Like other farm-belt states, Nebraska has experienced its share of "rural flight," and although the production of beef, pork, corn, and soybeans is important, the state earns part of its income from manufacturing, rail and truck transport, technology, and insurance.

On the other hand, one common perception is difficult to deny—the good folks of Nebraska live for their Cornhuskers football. Every University of Nebraska home game has sold out since 1962. When the football team plays in Lincoln, the 80,000 people in the stands—mostly Big Red fans cheering as one voice—make Memorial Stadium larger than any Nebraska city except Omaha and Lincoln.

Yet, there is life after football. Keep in mind that Nebraska has produced all sorts of people willing to try almost anything. Nebraska is where Charles Lindbergh learned to fly, and where "Buffalo Bill" Cody organized the first Wild West show. A native Cornhusker invented the strobe light, and, for true trivia devotees,

the nationwide 911 emergency system originated in Nebraska. So did figures as diverse as investor extraordinaire Warren Buffett, President Gerald Ford, Malcolm Little (better known to the world as Malcolm X), and L. Ron Hubbard, the founder of Scientology. In the early 1900s, James Vincenzo Capone, brother of the notorious Al Capone, moved to Nebraska and earned a reputation as an outstanding law-enforcement officer.

In regard to culinary history—important to every traveler—Nebraska was where Iowa schoolteacher Christian Nelson showed up in 1921 with his newly patented chocolate-covered vanilla ice cream bar wrapped in foil. He partnered with Omaha chocolate manufacturer Russell Stover, and, after changing the name from I-Scream Bar to Eskimo Pie, they mass-produced the delicious treat and sold the first 250,000 pies off the line within twenty-four hours. By the following year, one million Eskimo Pies were sold. Later that year, Stover took his share of the profits to Denver and launched Russell Stover, Inc., the best-selling chocolate brand in the United States.

In the early 1950s, C. A. Swanson & Sons, a poultry and egg supplier in Omaha, developed the frozen TV dinner while looking for a way to use frozen turkey meat left over after Thanksgiving. The original dinners—packaged in tin trays with modest helpings of cornbread dressing, frozen peas, and sweet potatoes—hit grocery stores in 1952 and sold for ninety-eight cents a pop. A little more than a decade later, University of Nebraska research scientists came

WELCOME AND LINCOLN HIGHWAY, BY NIGHT, OMAHA, NEBR.

up with a way to restructure meat into shapes. That technology proved instrumental in the creation of the McRib pork sandwich, a fast-food product that test-marketed quite well in Nebraska and elsewhere.

According to food lore, the Reuben sandwich—rye bread, corned beef, Swiss cheese, Russian dressing, and sauerkraut—first appeared in Nebraska in the 1920s when an Omaha grocer named Reuben Kulakofsky

made batches of them to feed hungry players at an all-night poker game in a downtown hotel. Given a choice, most Nebraskans hankering for a sandwich still go for a runza, a regional favorite consisting of a rectangular yeast-dough pocket bread filled with beef, cabbage or kraut, onions, and seasonings. To wash down all those sandwiches, there is always Kool-Aid, which Nebraskan Edward Perkins first concocted in 1927. Icy pitchers of it have been sold by generations of kids at streetside stands and throughout the world without the slightest inkling that their product originated in Nebraska.

Clearly, a state that has yielded such diverse products and people does not deserve such a bad rap. Even Nebraska critic Bill Bryson admits that he finds no pleasure in an interstate highway system that has "drained the life from thousands of towns." Dispensing with his trademark sarcasm, he also writes: "Today in western Nebraska, the old Lincoln Highway, or Route 30, is so little used that grass grows in its cracks. . . . It has become a fading memory and what a sad loss that is."

Bryson's observation is well put, but not quite correct. The old road is not lost—at least not yet. Members of the Nebraska chapter of the Lincoln Highway Association are confident that their two-lane ribbon of history is holding its own. "The Lincoln Highway across Nebraska is the most important road in the state," according to the Lincoln Highway Association's 1924 guidebook. Regardless of all the new state and federal roads built since then, many Nebraskans still agree with that assessment. The original road shows its age with grass poking up here and there like stray whiskers on an old man, but that did not stop state officials from designating the Nebraska route as the Lincoln Highway Scenic Byway. The old highway has hardly been forgotten by towns such as Fremont, Columbus, Grand Island, Kearney, Cozad, Gothenburg, North Platte, and Ogallala.

Nebraska is a land capable of producing high theater, just as it did in the nineteenth century with its Indian buffalo hunts, outlaw chases, and immigrants tracking dreams across high plains and prairies. The state is a stage for an infinite variety of human drama along the many miles of streams and rivers, the steel tracks of the Union Pacific, and the shoulders of the Lincoln Highway. This sense of drama is revealed, perhaps most acutely, in old-road towns still thriving and others where time seems to have stood still for many decades.

In small Nebraska towns and cities, including several along the Lincoln Highway, the drama of everyday struggles has turned out some of the biggest names in Hollywood. The long list of homegrown entertainers and actors includes Ward Bond, Sandy Dennis, James Coburn, David Janssen, Harold Lloyd, and Robert Taylor. Talk-show host Dick Cavett is a native; although Johnny Carson was born in Iowa, he grew up in Nebraska. Darryl F. Zanuck, the film producer and founder of 20th Century Fox, came from Wahoo.

Many theatrical careers also began in Omaha, the state's only real metropolis, along the banks of the Missouri River. Omaha's impressive list of stars who later made it big in Hollywood includes Marlon Brando, Montgomery Clift, Fred Astaire, and Henry Fonda, who was born in the Lincoln Highway town of Grand Island but made his way to Omaha at the age of twenty. Dorothy McGuire, Nick Nolte, and Swoosie Kurtz are others who also got their start in Omaha.

Much of that raw talent was cultivated at the Omaha Community Playhouse, founded in 1924, when the city was still on the Lincoln Highway. That same year, the

The Blair Bridge connecting Missouri Valley, IA, and Fremont, NE. When it opened in 1930, the Lincoln was rerouted over the bridge's more direct northern route, bypassing Omaha. The bridge advertised: "Save Time, Save Miles, No City Traffic, Lincoln Hiway."

FAR LEFT *Vintage decal from the Cornhusker State.*

ABRAHAM LINCOLN MEMORIAL BRIDGE
Crossing the Missouri River at Blair, Nebraska
Save 30 Miles—Follow Lincoln Highway
BLAIR BRIDGE

LINCOLN L HIGHWAY

NEBRASKA
CHADRON ST. PARK
SCOTTS BLUFF
CHIMNEY ROCK
NORTH PLATTE
HASTINGS
OMAHA
LINCOLN
CAPITOL 126
Corn-Huskers

3729-29

Douglas Street toll bridge over the Missouri on the original route was widened. By 1930, the Lincoln Highway route was moved well north of Omaha to the new U.S. 30 river crossing. Even though the city was bypassed, the spirit of the old road remains in Omaha, as does the Community Playhouse. This nationally recognized launching pad for so many theatrical careers has experienced tremendous growth since that first season when Dodie Brando—baby Marlon's actress mother—recruited Hank Fonda for his first acting role.

Ten miles west of downtown Omaha, on a stretch of U.S. 6 that was formerly the Lincoln Highway, is another launching pad—Boys Town. Established at its present site in 1921 by Father Edward Flanagan, the Irish priest whose famous motto was "There are no bad boys," this 160-acre community is dedicated to housing and educating troubled youth. It was incorporated as a village in 1936 and made famous by the 1938 film *Boys Town*, starring Spencer Tracy and Mickey

Rooney. A few miles west of Girls and Boys Town (as it is now called), the original route turns north.

Just east of the town of Elkhorn, travelers encounter a four-mile segment of original Lincoln Highway that in 1920 was regraded and paved with bricks laid over a base of sand and concrete. One mile of this stretch—perhaps the finest example of rural brick pavement in the nation—survived, as is often common, simply because it was bypassed. The section, including a pony-truss bridge over West Papillion Creek, was added to the

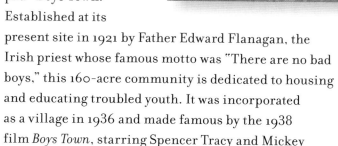

National Register of Historic Places in 1988. From Elkhorn, the original Lincoln heads for Waterloo, a town that lost and then regained much of its charm by revitalizing a sagging downtown; and Valley, where the local speed limit in the mid-1920s was twelve miles per hour, according to the Lincoln Highway guidebook.

To the west and slightly north is Fremont, named for the intrepid John C. Frémont, who explored the area between the Kansas and Platte Rivers in 1842, before proceeding westward to pre-Union California. John C. Fremont Days, with a rough-stock rodeo, music, and a living-history encampment, are still celebrated every July. In Fremont, the original route of the Lincoln snaking up from Omaha joins the new version of U.S. 30, which dates from 1930, when the Abraham Lincoln Memorial Bridge was opened and the route began running west from Blair through Kennard and Arlington to Fremont.

Heading westward from Fremont, the Lincoln cozies up to the tracks of the Union Pacific Railroad and runs along the Platte River. These three historic

paths—of water, steel, and varicose pavement—remain the traveler's allies throughout much of the Nebraska journey. A tributary of the Missouri, the Platte forms in western Nebraska, east of the Lincoln Highway city of North Platte. At that point, the South Platte and the North Platte—rising from the Rocky Mountains near the Continental Divide—merge, and the Platte flows southeast and then northeast across Nebraska. It passes such Lincoln Highway towns as Gothenburg, Cozad, Kearney, and Grand Island and then joins the Loup River near Columbus. From there, it flows east to Fremont before turning south past Omaha to join the Missouri.

The Platte played a key role in the expansion of the United States. It served both Indian tribes and fur trappers and became a clear path for settlers headed westward. The Oregon and Mormon Trails followed the Platte and the North Platte, while both rivers were used as the route for the Pony Express and the Union Pacific's portion of the first transcontinental railroad. It was only fitting that in a new century, the dreamers and planners who envisioned the Lincoln Highway chose this long river valley for their new route.

One of the early Seedling Miles, just outside of Fremont, was started in 1914 to boost the idea of hard-surfaced roads. Delays created by World War I brought work to a standstill, however, and cement shipments did not start again until 1918. But work crews made up for lost time. When the work was completed the next year, a total of six miles of roadway had been paved all the way to Ames. Outside Fremont, travelers pass stone markers erected in 1928 for the Overland Trail, 1813–1867; the Mormon Trail, 1847–1864; and the Military Road to new Fort Kearney, 1856.

At North Bend—"Pride of the Platte"—the Corner Cafe is a safe haven for the weary. The buff-colored brick edifice, clearly built to last when it opened as a bank in 1882, has done just that. It was then one of two banks in town, and everything went smoothly until 1929, when the one-two punch of a bank robbery followed by the stock-market crash exacted a heavy toll. The bank went bust. In the early 1930s, a restaurant opened in the building, and that's what has been here ever since. The kitchen is in the old bank vault and the terrazzo tile floor is original. Darrell and Mary Ritenour bought the cafe in 1996 and feed a large following of soybean and corn farmers, as well as old-road travelers.

"Folks tell us that years ago this town was really humming," says Darrell. "Stores were open until midnight every Saturday and everybody from miles

RIGHT

Kracl & Son Garage, Rogers, NE.

around came to town. They'd shop and visit. They'd have supper at the cafe and stay to see the movie shows."

People still come to town, but not as they did when the Lincoln Highway was the only path to take. Still, Darrell and Mary remain optimistic. Maybe the number of weekend visitors has dwindled, but the town's population has stayed steady. Over biscuits and gravy, Darrell produces a 1909 map of North Bend listing the population at 1,200. "Our town's population at the last census was 1,213," says Darrell. "We're still growing!"

Continuing west on U.S. 30, travelers reach Rogers and pass the old Kracl & Son Garage, a brick landmark that was run for decades by Anton Kracl. A short distance down the highway at Schuyler, a statue of a World War I doughboy stands at the ready in front of the Colfax County Courthouse. Settled about 1870 as a railhead and cattle loading post, the town and its county were named for Schuyler Colfax, vice president of the United States under Ulysses Grant. Over the years, many Czech, German, and Irish immigrants made their homes in Schuyler. By the late 1930s, residents from all over the county gathered at the Oak Ballroom on Saturday nights to dance polkas and listen to the music of Lawrence Welk and other big bands.

The polka music has stopped, but folks now come to Schuyler to hear salsa bands playing at a new downtown dance hall. Since the 1990s, the town has become mostly Latino. As in other small towns on the Lincoln Highway (such as Denison, Iowa), the influx of Hispanics was sparked by the need for workers in the meatpacking industry. These new Nebraskans have reenergized the town by filling jobs, buying new homes, and opening businesses. Their traditional family lifestyle is reminiscent of America in the 1950s.

West of Schuyler and the small town of Richland, more Hispanic influence is evident in Columbus, the seat of Platte County. Lopez Foods, the nation's largest Latino-owned meat-processing company, maintains one of its three plants in Columbus; the other two are in Oklahoma City and Guatemala. By 2006, nearly seventy percent of the more than three hundred employees at the Columbus plant were Hispanic, compared with only three percent when Lopez took over the operation in 1992. Shipments of hamburger and sausage processed in Columbus go to McDonald's, Wal-Mart, and other major chains.

Besides churning out bulk quantities of fast food, Columbus is noted for its inventory of historic buildings. Many of them are located in a thirty-one-acre downtown historic district, which is on the National Register of Historic Places and is the state's largest business district in continuous use. That seems appropriate, since Columbus is home to Glur's Tavern, built in 1876 and thought to be one of the oldest such establishments west of the Mississippi that still serves food and drink. Glur's was a favorite spot for William F. "Buffalo Bill" Cody whenever he came to town,

as he frequently did when rehearsing his Wild West shows. If the old showman were still alive, more than likely he would divide his time between Glur's and the popular Duster's Restaurant and Gottberg Brew Pub. At one time, the brew pub was the Gottberg Auto Company, a car assembly plant, garage, and dealership built in 1920 by entrepreneur and Brooklyn native Max Gottberg. Complete restoration of the building, featuring terra-cotta autos molded into the white stone cornices, began in 1993; two years later, the restaurant and bar opened. Duster's was named for the long protective coats worn by drivers in the days of open-air automobiles. Those who have tried the Sunday brunch and prime-rib buffet swear on their mothers' eyes that Duster's is the finest restaurant between Omaha and Denver. In the connecting Gottberg Brew Pub, travelers and locals pull up tractor-seat barstools and sample freshly brewed lagers and ales or swig root beer and cream soda made on the premises.

Columbus also is where the Lincoln Highway and the Meridian Highway—a predecessor to U.S. 81—briefly connected and then went their separate ways. The Meridian—which started in Canada—continued on its way south to the Gulf of Mexico, and the Lincoln kept going west. At this point of the Nebraska journey, U.S. 30 angles to the southwest, keeping company with Union Pacific rail lines above the Platte River. The route reaches the towns of Duncan and Silver Creek, where early Lincoln travelers cruised through Wooster's Lovers' Lane—or Wooster Lane, as locals called the one-mile stretch of shade trees

forming a canopy over the road. The big cottonwoods are long gone, however, victims of road widening.

Travelers who stop in the village of Clarks just may end up believing the local boast that "There is no better place to live." Named for Union Pacific official Silas Clarks, the town has fewer than 400 residents, some churches, a public swimming pool, a cozy campground, and a decent ballfield. Then there's AJ's Entertainment Emporium. Operated by two sisters, this is where townsfolk come to rent movies, get hot meals, and find out all the news of the day. Best of all, the coffee is free. One of the booths is devoted to coloring books and crayons, and a baby swaddled in blankets might be napping on the pool table. Not far from AJ's is a building with a Lincoln Highway mural painted by some local high-school kids.

Clarks is in Merrick County, the only county in Nebraska named for a woman—Elvira Merrick DePuy, whose husband, Henry, was serving in the Nebraska Territorial Legislature when the county was established. The county seat was going to be named Elvira, to complete the tribute, but that never happened. Instead, it was named Central City, a fairly tranquil town except perhaps when a Union Pacific train roars past. More than a century ago, temperance activist Carrie Nation visited the Schiller Hotel during one of her frequent speaking tours in 1902. The old hotel is now the Lincoln Manor Steak House and Lounge, an establishment with a beverage selection that would have caused the fiery Carrie to brandish her trusty hatchet.

LEFT *Lincoln Highway mural, Clarks, NE.*

Chapman is the last town in Merrick County before the route enters Hall County and approaches Grand Island, the county seat that grew on the Platte at the point where vast herds of buffalo crossed the river during their annual migrations. In a bygone era, the Shady Bend—known as "The Tourist's Haven"—operated on the Lincoln a mile east of Grand Island. Started in 1929, the complex included a gas station, cafe, trailer camp, and thirty-three cabins with private baths. Eventually, eighty-eight clay tennis courts were added near the cabins, but in homage to the past, Shady Bend's main attraction was the herd of bison pastured on both

*Kensinger Service
and Supply,
established in
1933, Grand
Island, NE.*

sides of the road, with a connecting tunnel under the road. Shaggy "monarchs of the prairie" no longer roam at Shady Bend, and the only significant architectural remnant is the filling station converted to a bar. Not far away is the site of Nebraska's first Seedling Mile, paid for with locally sold subscriptions and dedicated in 1915.

In Grand Island, some early Lincoln Highway travelers breezed past Shady Bend in order to stay at the ten-story Hotel Yancey, which opened in 1923 with 185 guest rooms, a dining room, and a coffee shop that never closed. The Yancey, however, did close as a hotel in 1982, when it was converted to private apartments. Kensinger Service and Supply, an honest-to-goodness full-service filling station and garage, has operated since 1933 and is still in the same family. Good eats of all sorts can be had at the Farmer's Daughter Cafe or the folksy Bosselman and Eaton Restaurant, much like the old-time places that satisfied the appetites of the hungriest railroaders and harvest crews.

The 1939 WPA guide to the Cornhusker State points out that Grand Island is the birthplace of Henry Fonda as well as the home of Jake Eaton, the world champion gum chewer who was "capable of chewing 300 sticks at a time." Mr. Fonda is long gone

and so is Jake, but visitors to Grand Island step back in time at the Stuhr Museum of the Prairie Pioneer, a two-hundred-acre living-history complex located between Interstate 80 and the Lincoln Highway.

West of Grand Island, the old road goes through tiny Alda—where for many years Frank Denman serviced vehicles at his garage—and then continues on to Wood River, the site of the Gloe Brothers Service Station, built in 1933 on East 11th Street. Closed long ago and listed on the National Register of Historic Places, it has become a fine example of adaptive reuse since the Bank of Wood River converted it into a handsome drive-through banking facility. There is more to see less than ten miles to the west at Shelton, the town that proudly calls itself "The Lincoln Highway Capital of Nebraska." Shelton is headquarters for the Nebraska chapter of the Lincoln Highway Association and since 1998 has honored the old road with an annual Lincoln Highway Festival and Antique Car Show. The former Meisner Bank Building has been renovated to house a historical interpretive center, complete with vintage Lincoln Highway signage and loads of travel information. About six miles west of Shelton is the town of Gibbon, followed by Kearney, seat of Buffalo County.

LEFT
Randy's Auto Sales, Grand Island, NE.

RIGHT *The Hotel Yancey, Grand Island, NE.*

BELOW *Vintage postcard from the Hotel Yancey, Grand Island, NE.*

Beautiful Scenic Room

Yes Sir

Hotel
YANCEY
GRAND ISLAND,
NEBRASKA

On Lincoln Highway

Like other towns on the Lincoln Highway in Nebraska, Kearney got its start because of its proximity to the Platte River. The town took its name from Fort Kearny, built to protect settlers and named in honor of General Stephen Watts Kearny. It is unclear why the extra "e" was inserted in the town's name, thus misspelling General Kearny's surname. What is clear is that one of Kearney's draws is now the Great Platte River Road Archway Monument, a privately owned eight-story tourist attraction spanning the busy lanes of Interstate 80. Opened with much fanfare in 2000, the Archway Monument was created to transport visitors back in time and show them the many historic trails, paths, and highways that followed the Platte River. Promotional literature explains that the monument pays "tribute to the perseverance of the pioneer and the ingenuity that developed our wonderfully diverse culture and dynamic American heritage." In other words, the gigantic log arch is intended to get some of the millions of people zooming down Interstate 80 to stop and spend some time and money. Visitors lured off the superslab, or those who venture down from the old road, are greeted in the parking lot by loudspeakers pouring out "Shenandoah" and other stirring songs.

Inside the cavernous building, a cheerful greeter— dressed in cowboy garb and assisted by ladies in pioneer bonnets—welcomes travelers with a warm, "Howdy!" He then explains the interactive adventure they are about to experience. The changing narration from headsets explains the series of multimedia displays and dioramas that vividly depict the evolution of transportation and communication—ranging from pioneer trails and the Pony Express to the Lincoln Highway and fiberoptics. Included in the tour are twenty-four life-size figures representing different periods of history, an abandoned covered wagon, a Pony Express station, vintage automobiles, and a re-created roadside cafe just like some still operating on the old route. To reach the exhibits, visitors take the longest escalator in Nebraska to the second level, just as Jack Nicholson did in the 2002 film *About Schmidt*, based on a novel by Louis Begley.

Filmed at several locations in Nebraska, the motion picture was directed by Nebraska native Alexander Payne and starred Nicholson as Warren Schmidt, a sixty-six-year-old whose wife suddenly drops dead soon after he retires from Woodmen of the World Insurance Society (a firm that still exists in Omaha). Desperate to find some meaning to his life, Schmidt fires up his Winnebago and makes a journey of self-discovery that takes him across Nebraska to his daughter's wedding in Colorado. One of the more memorable scenes during the highway odyssey occurs when Schmidt visits the Archway Monument. Nicholson, who won one of his three Oscars for the 1983 hit *Terms of Endearment*, also filmed in Nebraska, earned yet another Academy Award nomination for *About Schmidt* and was given a plaque making him an honorary Woodmen member.

In 1915, a Seedling Mile opened west of Kearney, only three days after Nebraska's first Seedling Mile was completed at Grand Island. The fifteen-foot-wide, eight-inch-thick Portland Cement pavement outside Kearney was flanked by rows of shade trees planted by H. D. Watson, Nebraska's "Father of Alfalfa"—an early advocate of alfalfa as a cash crop. A little more than four miles west of Kearney, travelers on U.S. 30 pass what once was Watson's 8,000-acre spread, the 1733 Ranch. For many years, travelers stopped to take photos of a sign posted on the road reading, "1733 miles to San Francisco, 1733 miles to Boston." In addition to his agricultural pursuits, Watson operated a campground with a swimming pool for Lincoln Highway motorists.

LEFT *Lincoln Highway exhibit inside the Great Platte River Road Archway Monument, Kearney, NE.*

LOWER LEFT *The Seedling Mile west of Kearney, NE, which opened in 1915. It was fifteen feet wide and paved with eight-inch-thick cement.*

Even after he sold the property and broke up the ranch into small farms, the sign remained. Those farms are gone now, and so is the sign. In the 1990s, the land was cleared and the old Watson place was turned into a residential subdivision. The developers named it "1733 Estates."

Some places deserve a visit even when their time has passed. One such place is the Covered Wagon, just beyond the site of the 1733 Ranch. At one time, the owners advertised that their shop was "a must for tourists, where they can relax, and obtain worthwhile souvenirs at reasonable prices." Folks found it hard to resist the concrete-and-plaster team of oxen pulling the covered-wagon–shaped gift shop, which was attached to a small building that held still more souvenirs. Today the souvenirs are gone, and no one flips over a plate to see if it's genuine Fiesta ware. The wagon and the pair of oxen are crumbling, and chunks of plaster fall on the yucca and weeds. The attached store is locked. Field mice and cobwebs have taken over. A Doberman barks in the distance, urging travelers to go back to the road.

For westbound travelers on U.S. 30, it soon becomes noticeable that the Platte River is changing its course and bending northwestward. The railroad and the Lincoln Highway follow suit. The old route heads through Odessa, Elm Creek, and Overton, where, just east of town, a concrete bridge built about 1919 sits on a forsaken remnant of the original route, adjacent to U.S. 30 and the Union Pacific tracks. A red, white, and blue Lincoln Highway logo painted on an outside wing wall in 2005 by a local Boy Scout troop reminds passersby that the old alignment has not been forgotten.

When the highway approaches Lexington, travelers know they are definitely on old frontier land. Tumbleweeds roll across the road and the Lexington newspaper runs stories about how cattlemen can control pesky prairie dogs burrowing in the ranchlands. Pony Express riders and Oregon Trail pioneers came this way too. Historic markers tell of the coming of the Union Pacific in the late 1860s. Cheyenne and Sioux raiders, upset by the intrusion, attacked construction gangs, scalping workers and their families. In 1867, a band of Southern Cheyenne led by Turkey Leg managed to derail a westbound Union Pacific freight train. Those not killed in the wreck were scalped alive, and the train was looted. Stories are still told of the triumphant Cheyenne galloping away with bolts of bright-colored calico tied to their ponies' tails. The Dawson County Museum in Lexington preserves much of the history of the area and displays a pair of 1928 concrete Lincoln Highway markers.

Farther up the highway, travelers reach Cozad, founded in 1873 on the 100th meridian by John Joseph Cozad, a gambler and real estate developer. He also was the father of Robert Henry Cozad, who left town, dropped his surname, and became the acclaimed artist Robert Henri (pronounced "Hen-rye"). The Robert Henri Museum is in the renovated Hendee Hotel, his boyhood home on 8th Street. Nearby are the restored Rialto Theatre and the 100th Meridian Museum, established in 1994 and filled with historical loot, including the touring stagecoach used by the rotund President William Howard Taft and his family when they toured Yellowstone National Park in 1907.

After Cozad comes Willow Island, with its custom cattle-feeding operation, and then Gothenburg, home of the Sod House Museum. Gothenburg is the self-proclaimed Pony Express Capital of Nebraska, although it seems the log building in a city park was never a relay station of the short-lived mail service. Several miles up the highway, in the small town of Brady, a gray-stucco filling station is pressed against the pavement. Behind the station, the tourist cabins covered in the same kind of stucco have not seen renters for ages. The neon is broken and tattered curtains blow in shattered windows. On the ground are a big rotting pumpkin and a freshly eviscerated pigeon snatched off the grain silo by a hawk. The gas station, however, looks as though it might still be active. A fish is painted on a window with just the word *Tackle*. The door is locked, but inside are cigarettes, candy, and a pop machine. Tires, fan belts, and other accessories are in plain view.

A local man leaves his comfortable stool in a bar across the highway to see what strangers in town are up to when they stop at his pal's gas station. He tells travelers that Bill Thanel owns the place, but he only opens it if one of his regulars is desperate for some gas. Thanel, like his father before him, has made his living here for a long time, but when gasoline prices skyrocketed in the early 2000s, Thanel closed his station. "Bill told

us that he wouldn't charge his customers those kind of prices," explains the man. "He said he may open full time when and if the prices go back down to a reasonable level." The local man returns to his glass of beer and the travelers leave Brady without having had a chance to shake the hand of the most principled guy in town.

Angus cattle graze west of the town of Maxwell, resembling ink spots in fields as yellow as butter. Long strings of train cars headed eastward out of Wyoming are heaped with coal, while the trains going west return empty. In 1863, as the Civil War raged, Fort McPherson was established near here on the Oregon Trail, south of the Platte, to protect white travelers from the Cheyenne. In 1871, the army post was the staging point for a buffalo-hunting party that included Grand Duke Alexis of Russia, Generals George Armstrong Custer and Phil Sheridan, and "Buffalo Bill" Cody. Three miles northwest of North Platte, "Buffalo Bill's" home at Scout's Rest Ranch is open to the public as a State Historic Site. The showman moved his family to North Platte and in 1886 built the impressive two-story Victorian residence at a cost of $3,900. For more than thirty years, Cody was the town's most prominent resident.

North Platte, established in 1866 as a Union Pacific construction camp on the narrow delta at the fork of the North and South Platte Rivers, is the seat of Lincoln County, a substantial trading center, and still a solid railroad and highway town. North Platte is the location of the famed Bailey Yard, the world's largest railroad classification yard, named for former Union Pacific president Ed Bailey. Eight miles long and covering 2,850 acres, the yard employs 2,600 workers and handles at least 10,000 railroad cars every day. In 1995, the yard was listed in the *Guinness Book of World Records.*

Like other frontier railroad and cowboy towns, North Platte acquired a rough-and-tumble reputation. An early chronicler reported that by 1868, "North Platte was invested with reckless desperadoes, brothels, gambling dens, and unlicensed saloons that ran wide open all days of the week and hours of the night. Most men went armed and few law-abiding citizens ventured out alone after dark." Although periodic attempts were made to clean up the town, not much had changed by the time the Lincoln Highway reached the city limits. "Our reputation from Cheyenne to Omaha has placed us on the black list and we will stagnate until we clean up," lamented mayoral candidate A. F. Streitz in the North Platte *Evening Telegraph* of March 26, 1919. "If I am elected mayor, I will do my utmost to suppress bootlegging, social vice, gambling, and to promote everything progressive and clean." Against all odds, Streitz was elected, and that August—clutching a symbolic city key fashioned from flowers—he greeted the Transcontinental Motor Convoy's cavalcade of military vehicles as they arrived in North Platte. It is unknown whether or not any of the soldiers—sick of enduring days of Nebraska mud that reminded them of Iowa gumbo—slipped away from their camp at the city park to visit the many sporting houses of North Platte. It is fairly certain that if any did so, Dwight Eisenhower did not join them. Ike's wife, Mamie, and her

father, John Doud, left Denver that morning and drove for thirteen hours in dusters and goggles, arriving just in time to meet the convoy pulling into North Platte.

Throughout the 1920s, North Platte continued as a wide-open haven for gambling, prostitution, and bootlegging; it was known up and down the Lincoln Highway as "Little Chicago." So-called rooming houses, with such names as Lotus, Rex, Star, Como, Oxford, and Glendale, stayed busy at all hours entertaining railroaders, cowboys, farmers, doctors, lawyers, and clergymen. Supposedly, a local jeweler always brought gifts from his store for the soiled doves he visited.

During World War II, six million servicemen riding the rails stopped at the North Platte Canteen, which opened in the Union Pacific Depot on Christmas Day 1941, just three weeks after Pearl Harbor was bombed. For the next five years, the canteen was a gathering place where cigarettes, food, books, and even birthday cakes were free to anyone in uniform. Many of those uniforms were removed briefly at one of the brothels that prospered during the war. By the early 1950s, North Platte had cleaned up its act and most of the "rooming houses" had disappeared— much to the chagrin of some of the old-timers.

Travelers motoring through the city still find much of the character that always made North Platte a worthwhile stop. The handsome McCabe Hotel and the eight-story Pawnee Hotel, converted into a retirement residence, still grace the downtown. The Fox Theater, built of terra-cotta and brick in 1929, is on the National

Register of Historic Places and operates as the Neville Center for the Performing Arts, home of the North Platte Community Playhouse. At both ends of the route through town are several vintage motels and restaurants. Near the Interstate 80 exit, the Fort Cody Trading Post sells loads of trinkets and road kitsch, just as it did in the 1950s, when the business operated as the Buffalo Bill Trading Post on U.S. 30. The "Tourist Trap," a large steel bear trap hanging near the entrance, rates a smile and maybe a photo.

Headed west, the route points toward Hershey and Sutherland. Every spring, the largest gathering of cranes in the world takes place between these two towns; half a million migrating sandhill cranes stop over along the North and South Platte Rivers. Westbound travelers—even those who miss the season for watching cranes or eagles—earn a reward when they pass this way en route to Wyoming. Without knowing it, they move from the central to the mountain zone and receive the gift of time.

In Paxton, the ideal spot to celebrate that extra hour of daylight or a glorious sunset is "Nebraska's Most Famous Waterin' Hole": Ole's Big Game Steakhouse & Lounge, established on Main Street in 1933 by Rosser "Ole" Herstedt.

Born in Paxton in 1904, Ole opened a grocery store with his brother in 1926, but the store folded when bad times decimated the nation. Ole hit the road, doing what he could to make some money. Road lore has it that during the 1930s, Ole was promised fifty bucks by a ball team in Julesburg, Colorado, if he pitched a baseball game against their rivals and won. Ole did just that, but when the winning team couldn't come up with the cash, he was paid off with a gleaming

RIGHT *Alice "Sam" McConnell, waitress at Ole's Big Game Steakhouse & Lounge, Paxton, NE.*

LOWER RIGHT *Photos cover the walls at Ole's Big Game Steakhouse & Lounge, Paxton, NE.*

walnut bar (and bar back) that had been made for the Plains Hotel on the Lincoln Highway in Cheyenne, Wyoming. Ole hauled the bar back to Paxton, where his timing was just right. National Prohibition was about to end and Ole was ready. At one minute after midnight on August 9, 1933, the town whistle blew and Ole opened his bar.

Over the years the bar became an institution as Ole, an avid big-game hunter, filled the establishment with mounted animal trophies, photographs, and memorabilia collected from his world travels. In 1988, Ole decided to hang up his bar apron and call it quits. Unable to find a buyer, he prepared to close the business and sell his vast animal collection to longtime friends in South Carolina. Then Tim Holzfaster, a Paxton native, intervened. Just twenty-eight years old at the time, Holzfaster did not want his hometown to lose part of its heritage, so he purchased the bar and every one of the stuffed animals and mounted heads. Ole was pleased. Even after he moved to Ogallala, he continued to visit his old haunt—until his death in 1996. Although Ole is gone, his bar—now expanded to a full-service restaurant—is still a favorite stop for travelers, hunters, and Nebraska football fans commuting to "away" games. "We have the best steaks in the country," says waitress Alice McConnell (who prefers her nickname, "Sam"). "We get them right across the street from Mark Hehnke, and before him we got them from his father, Hugo—local grocers who ship prime rib and steaks all over the world."

Beyond Paxton, the Lincoln Highway moves closer to the South Platte River and then streaks by Roscoe and into Ogallala, named for a Sioux tribe and a true cowboy town once known as "The Gomorrah of the Cattle Trail." Life and whiskey were cheap here in the 1870s and 1880s, when Texas drovers arrived with huge herds of longhorns to be shipped east on the Union Pacific. The town has capitalized on its "Wild West" heritage by marketing the Boot Hill graveyard and Front Street, featuring shops and attractions that most tourists find appealing. West of Ogallala, the town of Brule, also named for a Sioux tribe, honors the Lincoln Highway. In 1995, the residents took it upon themselves to mark the route by painting the utility poles with red, white, and blue circles—much as the original Lincoln Highway Association did long ago. Four miles west of Brule on U.S. 30, a historical marker at the foot of California Hill explains that this route was traversed by thousands of gold seekers and emigrants in wagon trains headed west from 1841 through 1860.

Ruts left by the endless procession of wagon wheels still remain visible for travelers who know how to find them.

Just above the Colorado border sits the town of Big Springs, first known as Lone Tree Station because of a big cottonwood tree that became a landmark for wagon trains, army patrols, Pony Express riders, and railroaders passing through the area. In 1867, the town's name was changed to acknowledge the nearby natural spring used to fill steam locomotives. Some townspeople still can recite the basic facts of the first and largest robbery of a Union Pacific train, which took place in Big Springs. On a moonlit night in 1877, Sam Bass, a lawman-turned-brigand, and five companions swept down on the eastbound train stopped to pick up mail. The outlaws made off with $60,000 in shiny twenty-dollar gold coins newly minted in San Francisco, and they took another $1,300 plus several gold watches and rings from the passengers. The robbers cooked supper and divided the loot beneath the Lone Tree, a towering cottonwood. Less than a year after the robbery, Texas Rangers killed Bass on his twenty-seventh birthday. A monument in Big Springs recounts the story of the robbery.

Over time, some folks called the Lone Tree "The Robbers' Roost." Rumor had it that the outlaws had buried some of their gold coins near the tree, but none were ever found. Generations of initials and lovers' words were carved into the cottonwood's thick bark, and hunters built fires in the hollow of the tree to smoke out raccoons. It was struck by lightning at least three times. Although the tree finally died, it stood like a stubborn

ghost for many more years. In 1933, the skeleton was chopped down and used for stove wood. The last remains of the trunk were washed away by Platte River floods.

There is more to the history of Big Springs than tales of outlaws, buried gold, and old trees. Big Springs will never forget June 4, 1965—the day that Duane Earl Pope came to town. One of eight children from a Kansas farm family, Pope had just graduated with a degree in education from McPherson College, where he also had played football. No one really knows what was on Pope's mind that day when he walked into the Farmers State Bank in Big Springs. In minutes, the twenty-two-year-old shot and killed three bank employees and left a fourth employee for dead. All had been shot once in the back and once in the neck. Pope returned to his car and drove away with $1,598.

"Western Nebraska's Finest"

HOKES CAFE INC.

HOUSE OF GOOD FOOD
Souvenirs
Ogallala, Nebraska

• STEAKS • CHICKEN
• SEA FOODS

This was no romantic tale of brigands on horseback riding off with sacks of gold double eagles. This was cold-blooded murder in a small town, and it conjured up images of the not-too-distant past, when Nebraska and the nation had been stunned by the killing spree of Charles Starkweather. Over a span of several months in 1957 and 1958, the nineteen-year-old Starkweather and his thirteen-year-old lover, Caril Fugate, murdered eleven men, women, and children in Nebraska and Wyoming, including Fugate's mother, stepfather, and two-year-old sister. National Guard troops were called out to hunt for the murderous pair and, for the first time that anyone could remember, Nebraskans locked their doors. Starkweather and Fugate finally were arrested by a Wyoming state trooper and returned to Nebraska for trial. Starkweather was convicted and electrocuted in the Nebraska State Penitentiary in 1959; Fugate was sentenced to life in prison but was paroled in 1976.

Starkweather had a major impact on American culture, eventually inspiring such motion pictures as Terrence Malick's *Badlands* and Oliver Stone's *Natural Born Killers*. When he was a boy in Maine, author Stephen King assembled a scrapbook about the gruesome crimes and later incorporated Starkweather into some of his writing. Starkweather inspired Bruce Springsteen's song "Nebraska," and the killer's name is heard in "We Didn't Start the Fire," one of Billy Joel's hit songs.

The 1965 Big Springs killings stirred uneasy memories and led to coverage in *Life* magazine and reports in the *New York Times.* Fortunately, the killings stopped when Pope turned himself in to authorities. He was convicted of robbery and murder in federal court and sentenced to death. After the Supreme Court later vacated that sentence, he received three life sentences and was sent to the federal prison at El Reno, Oklahoma, on old Route 66.

The lone Big Springs survivor was Frank Kjeldgaard,
just twenty-five at the time of the shooting. One of
the three victims was his seventy-seven-year-old
grandfather, Andreas Kjeldgaard, the bank president.
The shooting left the younger Kjeldgaard's legs
paralyzed, and he was wheelchair-bound for life.
He eventually became president of the bank, which
moved into a new handicapped-accessible building.
The old bank building was not torn down; it now
serves a useful purpose as the town's library.

Across the street is the Phelps Hotel, built in 1885
and named after a train engineer. The first church
services in the area were held in the hotel lobby, and
many of the railroaders who stayed there toted guns
to ward off robbers. Sometimes called "The House
of Three Chimneys," the hotel has been completely

renovated, is listed on the National Register of Historic
Places, and is open for tours by appointment.

Big Springs is important in Lincoln Highway history
because it was the town where travelers could take the
controversial and short-lived Colorado Loop. This route
exited Nebraska southwest of Big Springs and then
followed the South Platte River toward Denver through
a slew of Colorado locales, such as Julesburg, Proctor,
Sterling, Fort Morgan, and Aurora. At Denver, the
loop turned north along the front range of the Rocky
Mountains and passed through Lakewood, Broomfield,
Lafayette, Longmont, Loveland, Fort Collins, and
Wellington before entering Wyoming west of Cheyenne.

Actually, the Colorado Loop was an alternative
when the Lincoln Highway boosters decided that
routing the highway across the mountainous state
was totally impractical. Disgruntled, but anxious
to get at least part of the new highway, Colorado
officials mounted a campaign to ensure that the
compromise dogleg would win approval. In the end,
even the Colorado Loop plan failed. Henry Joy, the
man charged with making the final decision, was
bitterly opposed to it. He and the powerful Detroit
automotive interests backing the highway preferred
the more direct route from Nebraska into Wyoming.

The Colorado forces were outraged when the Lincoln
Highway Association dropped the Colorado Loop from
the official highway map. In late 1914, when the Colorado
proponents erected a large billboard near Big Springs,
instructing travelers that the Lincoln Highway turned

LEFT *The Phelps Hotel, Big Springs, NE.*

south at this point and led to Denver, a billboard war ensued. Angry Cheyenne boosters quickly erected their own billboard next to the Colorado sign, urging motorists to turn right and continue due west to Wyoming.

Starting with the first official guidebook published in 1915, the Lincoln Highway Association made it a point not to acknowledge that Colorado ever was considered for the route. In fact, subsequent guidebooks urged travelers to avoid what they termed "misleading signs" erected by the Colorado interests. The 1924 official guidebook went straight for Colorado's jugular:

*Tourists wishing to follow the Lincoln Highway west to
Cheyenne, Wyoming, should not be diverted by markers
or signs indicating that the road turns south through
the village of Big Springs and then by way of Sterling
and Fort Morgan, Colorado to Denver. Numerous
red, white, and blue markers have been placed at
this point to mislead the tourists. The route from Big
Springs to Cheyenne will be found largely good gravel.
The Lincoln Highway does not enter Colorado.*

Travelers continuing on the true route of the Lincoln
Highway take the historic path out of Big Springs and
return to U.S. 30 to make the twenty-mile journey west
to Chappell. The road moves through sagebrush country
to Lodgepole, named for Lodgepole Creek, along which
Indians cut pine poles for their lodges, or tepees. The
Lodgepole Opera House remains on the second floor of a
garage built in 1911. Finch's Drug and Sundries Store on
McCall Street still looks like a place where couples sip a
cherry Coke with two straws, just as they did in the 1950s.
Those wanting something stronger can pop in at the
Junkyard Bar, where a sign warns, "We Won't Bite Hard,"
or they can join the crowd at the Linger Longer Bar.
West of Lodgepole, Sunol has nothing but some deserted
buildings, including the remains of a 1929 tourist court.
The town of Sidney is ten miles farther down U.S. 30.

Travelers can check into the U-shaped El Palomino Motel, a 1950 classic with glass-block windows and a terrific neon sign. Cocktails, dinner, and conversation await at Dude's Steak House and the attached Brandin' Iron Bar & Lounge. Dude's has been around since 1952, when Harry Truman was still president. For starters, waitresses bring out baskets of plump Rocky Mountain oysters, breaded corn fritters, and slices of deep-fried fire known as "jalapeño bottle caps." Before leaving, travelers can cruise Sidney's downtown, where scores of buildings are listed on the National Register of Historic Places.

Sixteen miles west of Sidney, the town of Potter was incorporated as a village in 1912. Prairie cathedrals stuffed with wheat still mark the trail westward on U.S. 30 to the towns of Dix and Kimball, site of the Wheat Growers Hotel. The 1919 Transcontinental Motor Convoy stopped for the night in Kimball, where dusty soldiers washed up in an irrigation ditch. That evening, a big dance was held in their honor at the hotel. Although its windows are now boarded up, the hotel name is clearly spelled out in white bricks along the second-story roofline. Chances are good that the hotel—listed on the National Register of Historic Places—will be saved.

As the highway approaches Bushnell, travelers might glimpse a series of concrete culverts along the original alignment of the old Lincoln north of the railroad tracks. On the west side of town are two large tubes that carried the first generation of the Lincoln Highway beneath the Union Pacific tracks.

Bushnell is the last town on the Lincoln Highway in Nebraska. There is very little to see or do here anymore. A starfish, brittle and broken, was left behind in an old secondhand store. At least a dozen tumbleweeds crowd the locked door. Behind a dirty window sits a baby doll, her blue eyes locked in a perpetual stare, gazing at the road. Back on the highway, travelers push on to Wyoming, eight miles ahead. As they cross Lodgepole Creek, a westbound Union Pacific train appears and stays close the rest of the way.

LEFT *The Brandin' Iron Bar & Lounge, Sidney, NE.*

Chapter Ten

WYOMING

State Line Truck Stop—sprawled across the imaginary border separating Nebraska and Wyoming on the Lincoln Highway—has become nothing more than a decomposing corpse. Once a prominent roadside oasis, the gas station and

cafe complex is beyond resuscitation. Just to the south, the killer is in plain sight— Interstate 80.

Travelers remember earlier trips when all eighteen gas pumps at State Line were busy day and night. Truckers with wallets chained to their belts smoked a butt or two, stretched their legs, and kibitzed about road conditions and any state trooper who might be lurking ahead.

Motorists chatted with the attendants pumping gas, checking oil and tire pressure, and scraping squashed bugs off the windshield. Kids guzzled cold pop while Mom walked the family pooch in a patch of grass.

The gas station straddled both states, but the cafe was far enough west of the border to leave no doubt it was in Wyoming. Manufactured in Kansas, this Valentine diner

LEFT

Hillsdale, WY.

was a place of refuge year-round. When blizzards howled and high drifts shut down the highway, holiday travelers and truckers snuggled into booths over steamy bowls of stew and soup. In the summer, when it seemed as though the entire world was on vacation, the cafe came alive with tourists going to and fro across the American West.

All of that changed when the interstate highway came along in the 1960s and slowly strangled the life out of any business or town not on its path. That included the thriving State Line Truck Stop on the south side of U.S. 30, the old Lincoln Highway. Although the complex hung on for many more years, there simply were not enough customers using the old route.

BELOW *Remains of Smitty's Truck Stop, Pine Bluffs, WY.*

In 1977, Interstate 80, now completely paved, ran across the entire state. By the early 1990s, the complex—by then known as Smitty's Truck Stop and Smitty's State Line Cafe—was a goner, and the tall steel tower bearing the words *State Line* toppled in 1995. Now only coyotes frequent the site, scrounging for pack rats and mice in the abandoned buildings.

Between the diner and the gas station, derelict cars and trucks have been thoroughly cannibalized, stripped of any worthwhile parts. Tumbleweeds are everywhere, a few even wedged inside a wide-open safe in one of the abandoned structures. In another building lie empty wooden rabbit hutches and piles of debris. Yellowed papers swirl outside among the weeds—customer receipts for cafe food and Phillips 66 gas from the early 1990s. There are even old statements and canceled checks—for everything from diesel fuel and fan belts to tires, sugar, and potato chips—from a bank in the nearby town of Pine Bluffs, Wyoming.

There also are payroll checks, weekly time tickets, and employee work records scribbled on index cards. The notes about those who worked at the diner and the gas station make them human. Travelers can picture the waitresses, cooks, and guys pumping gas and wonder what happened to them. What did they look like? Where did they go? A souvenir stuffed doll that never found a home and the papers and handwritten notes are the DNA of the highway. They are reminders that what took place at State Line is a prime example of death by interstate.

A "Welcome to Wyoming" sign, with the black silhouette of a cowboy on a bucking bronco, has been peppered with buckshot—an irony of sorts, since a short distance to the west and south of the Lincoln is the forty-foot Our Lady of Peace Shrine, said to be the tallest statue of the Virgin Mary in the United States. Created of white cast stone over the course of twenty-two months by Cheyenne artist Robert Fida, this monumental work was unveiled in 1999. Smaller statues encircle the shrine, including the Stations of the Cross and various renditions of the Virgin, such as Our Lady of Guadalupe draped with rosaries and a plastic floral garland. There are two kneelers for the faithful. Our Lady of Peace presides between Interstate 80 and the Lincoln Highway, with access from both roads. Some reverentially take photographs. Others offer prayers or find a stick and scratch their initials in the sandy dirt.

At one time, there were 427 miles of the Lincoln Highway in Wyoming. Just as in Nebraska, a large portion of the Lincoln in Wyoming followed the path of the railroad and other pioneer trails. In the 1924 official guidebook, Lincoln Highway Association officials pointed out: "The Lincoln Highway in Wyoming traverses regions of the utmost scenic beauty and only those who have followed the rutted old trail of 1914 and 1915 across that state can appreciate the accomplishments that have been made in the recent past, while driving mile after mile of what are practically boulevards, in open range country, seemingly utterly unpopulated."

Today the journey involves a combination of Interstate 80, as well as U.S. 30 and other generations of the Lincoln. The best bet, however, is to forsake I-80 as much as possible and spend time in these old Highway towns—from Pine Bluffs in the east through some of the most magnificent country on the entire route to Evanston, two miles from the Utah line.

The eastern border town of Pine Bluffs—known as Rock Ranch before the arrival of the Union Pacific in 1868—has always been a crossroads. There was plenty of water, and the surrounding pine hills yielded firewood, small game, and medicinal plants. Early tribal people—including the ancestors of the Cheyenne, Arapaho, and

ABOVE *Period photograph at the Nebraska and Wyoming border.*

Lakota—have been linked to this area. Cattle drovers, sodbusters, and railroaders also passed this way. Visitors at the Texas Trail Museum and Monument, located in the town's original 1915 power plant, learn about the wild times in the 1870s when the settlement was a major cattle shipping point on the Texas Trail. Another popular stop is the town's High Plains Archaeology Museum and a nearby excavation complex and interpretive center, displaying prehistoric artifacts as well as some from the early 1900s, when the site was the town dump.

West of Pine Bluffs, the Lincoln Highway originally meandered through the small towns of Egbert, Burns, and Hillsdale—all established as rail sidings by the Union Pacific. Before the use of block signals, such sidings were developed so trains could be sidetracked and await the passage of higher-priority rail traffic. Every siding was given a name, and whenever a town evolved, it often simply took the name of the siding. The name *Egbert* came from Augustus Egbert, who started as a conductor in 1867 and worked his way up to become a railroad superintendent. Burns was a siding until 1907, when some German immigrants established a town and— being devout Lutherans—tried to name it after Martin Luther. But when a post office was established in 1910, the railroad once again won out. The town took the siding name of Burns—for J. J. Burns, an early telegrapher who ultimately became purchasing agent for the Union Pacific. Hillsdale was named after Lothrop L. Hills, felled by Indians in 1867. From Hillsdale, the original Lincoln turned southwest to Archer, a small settlement with no lodging and little else to recommend it to early travelers. With the advent of U.S. 30 in the late 1920s, these four railroad towns shriveled away when the newer route bypassed them and moved farther to the south.

Today, travelers have the option of seeking out the original route through the old railroad-siding towns or staying with U.S. 30 and I-80. The best way to make the trip is to use all the roads available. Less than twenty miles east of Cheyenne, it is possible to catch early glimpses of the front range of the northern Rocky Mountains rising from the distant plains.

At this point in the long Lincoln Highway journey, the road has found the West that most people visualize. Wyoming is the West of cowboys and Indians, mountains and prairies, pickups and bucking broncs. In fact, the state has more pickup trucks than people and cars combined, and "Old Steamboat," the notorious rodeo bronc that could no longer be ridden in the early 1900s, inspired the distinctive image that appears on the state license plates. When his bucking days ended, Steamboat—so named because a broken bone in his nose caused him to snort like a steamboat—was laid to rest in the middle of the Cheyenne Frontier Days arena.

Wyoming is a state of great contrasts. Within its borders are breathtaking mountains and sweeping grass plains, as well as discarded coal mines and desolate badlands covered with desert scrub. Yellowstone, Old Faithful, and the Tetons draw large numbers of visitors to the state. So does Devils Tower, the rock monolith in the northeast. Declared America's first national monument in 1906, Devils Tower was re-created from mashed potatoes by Richard Dreyfuss in the 1977 movie *Close Encounters of the Third Kind*.

Wyoming is rich in history, legend, and art. It hosted the bloody Johnson County Cattle War; the oilfield-lease shenanigans known as Teapot Dome, which came close to toppling the Harding administration; and such outlaws as Butch Cassidy and "Big Nose" George Manuse. Conversely, it inspired the stunning Western art of Thomas Moran and was the birthplace of the abstract painting genius Jackson Pollock. The state provided the setting for the short story "Brokeback Mountain," written by Annie Proulx, a Connecticut native who now calls Wyoming home. And Neil Diamond lived in Cheyenne for a few years when his father was stationed there with the military during World War II.

Considered politically and socially conservative, Wyoming was nevertheless the first state to give women the right to vote and hold public office. It had the first female justice of the peace and the first female court bailiff, and in 1925 Nellie Tayloe Ross was elected governor, the first woman to hold that office in the United States. Wyoming is nicknamed "The Equality State," and its official seal shows a rancher and a miner standing on either side of a woman who represents the state's motto, "Equal Rights." Despite a heritage of equality, however, the state's past is stained by racial prejudice and acts of violence against indigenous Indian tribes and Chinese immigrants who worked

the mines and helped build the railroads. Wyoming is also where the brutal killing of a college student named Matthew Shepard made national headlines in 1998. Shepard was hung on a fence along the highway by two young men who beat him to death because he was gay.

Although many of the pickups in Wyoming sport gun racks and National Rifle Association decals, the state actually maintains one of the lowest violent-crime rates in the nation. On the other hand, Wyoming has one of the highest rates of domestic violence and ranks near the top in the number of women killed by men. Yet adherence to the law is taken seriously in Wyoming. Big-game hunting is a popular pursuit, but using a firearm to fish is strictly forbidden, and anyone caught drunk in a mine faces at least a year in jail if convicted.

No one is above the law, including Dick Cheney, a Nebraska native who grew up in Casper. Although his scrapes with the law took place long before he entered the political scene, during an eight-month period in the early 1960s the future forty-sixth vice president was twice convicted of drunk driving in Wyoming. He paid the standard fines and briefly had his driver's license suspended. Cheney's "youthful indiscretions," as he later characterized the DWIs, occurred in Cheyenne and Rock Springs, two Lincoln Highway cities—which, along with Laramie and Rawlins, became part of the I-80 corridor along which so many Wyomingites live. More people reside in Denver, however, than in Wyoming, which is the tenth biggest state—larger than Indiana and New England combined—yet is the least populated of all fifty states, with fewer than half a million residents. Keep in mind that there are ten head of cattle or sheep in Wyoming for every human.

When travelers reach the state capital of Cheyenne, the largest city, with a population of approximately 55,000, the old route goes by the name *Lincolnway*. Originally, Lincoln Highway Association officials asked all of the five capital cities located on the historic roadway to use the name *Lincolnway* for the routings through their cities. Cheyenne was the first of the cities to comply. Years later, the city reverted to 16th Street, but the name *Lincolnway* was eventually restored when interest revived in the Lincoln Highway.

Long before the arrival of the nation's first transcontinental highway, Cheyenne was a good place for railroad workers to winter over while the tracks were being laid in the post–Civil War years. By 1867, the army had established Fort D. A. Russell to protect the railroaders from Indians, and once the trains were rolling, the town quickly became a haven for Union Pacific sojourners. All manner of folks arrived in Cheyenne—gamblers, soiled doves, whiskey peddlers, cattlemen, outlaws, and every imaginable opportunist. In the 1870s, large numbers of miners and prospectors used Cheyenne as an outfitting center before they departed for the goldfields in the Black Hills to the north. A stage line ran from Cheyenne to Laramie and on to Deadwood, the tough mining camp in what eventually became the state of South Dakota.

Several hotels and restaurants were built in the city's early years, but the Inter-Ocean Hotel, which opened in 1876 at 16th Street (later Lincolnway) and Capital Avenue, was one of the finest. Owner Barney L. Ford, a runaway slave, was an unlikely hotelier. Born on a plantation in 1822, he had worked his way up from field hand to house servant by the time he was seventeen. He taught himself to read and write, even though it was forbidden, and when his master allowed him to work on a Mississippi riverboat, the young man became proficient at tending bar and cooking. He escaped the boat and became a free man in Chicago, where he got married and learned to be a skilled barber. Ford and his wife, Julia, traveled to Central America, tried the goldfields of California, and went back to Chicago to assist with the Underground Railroad. After the Civil War, they returned to the West and started a hotel in Colorado before moving to Cheyenne in the late 1860s. The first hotel Ford built in Cheyenne burned to the ground in 1870; six years later, Ford opened the Inter-Ocean, said to have been the finest hotel between Omaha and San Francisco.

The Inter-Ocean had plush carpets, red velvet chairs, and a hand-carved mahogany bar. On opening night, guests dined on fresh oysters shipped on ice to Cheyenne and ogled more than fifty different kinds of desserts. Ford made sure a hack was on duty at all times, and the hotel bar became the city's favorite meeting place. In 1883, so-called water closets were installed in some of the hotel rooms. Among the well-known guests who stayed at the Inter-Ocean were

President Theodore Roosevelt and "Buffalo Bill" Cody. After Ford died in 1902, the hotel slowly lost much of its charm. Sadly, the once-grand hotel was destroyed in a 1916 fire.

By then, Cheyenne already had a new favorite hotel—the Plains. Located at the corner of Central Avenue and 16th Street (later Lincolnway), the five-story hotel opened in 1911. By the time the Lincoln Highway arrived a few years later, it had become the lodging of choice for discriminating highway and rail travelers. All of the guest rooms had newfangled telephones and were elegantly furnished, as were the common rooms, lounges, and a mezzanine floor where the Plains Orchestra held forth for gala balls. The dining room featured art-glass windows, a mahogany buffet, and tables with seating for eighty-five. Sunlight

LEFT

Lincoln Theater, Cheyenne, WY.

flooded the lobby through a handsome stained-glass skylight, and the main desk was solid marble.

On October 31, 1913, the date the Lincoln Highway was officially dedicated, several Wyoming towns marked the occasion, including Cheyenne, where celebrants danced around a huge bonfire fueled by sagebrush on the street in front of the Plains. Two years later, Emily Post and two traveling companions checked into The Plains during a motor journey along the Lincoln Highway. A wealthy and socially prominent New York writer, Post would become famous in 1922 as the authority on proper manners with the publication of her best-selling book, *Etiquette.*

Collier's magazine had asked Post to write about her experiences driving the length of the Lincoln Highway from Manhattan to the Panama Pacific International Exposition in San Francisco. Post took the assignment, despite warnings from her high-society friends that such a journey was pure folly because of wretched accommodations, lack of creature comforts, and poor traveling conditions, especially west of the Mississippi. One friend told her that once she reached the western states along the Lincoln, she would encounter ". . . the most terrible people, outlaws and bad men who would think nothing of killing you if they were drunk and felt like it." The undaunted Post recruited her cousin Alice Beadleston to keep her company. She also pulled her son Ned out of Harvard in order to chauffeur her large touring car hand-built in England with right-side controls.

The trio of intrepid travelers had plenty of automotive and logistical problems along the way. When they finally pulled into Cheyenne, Post expressed some surprise that the Wyoming capital city was not as wild and woolly as she had anticipated. "If you think Cheyenne is a Buffalo Bill Wild West town, as we did, you will be much disappointed, though it may be well not to show the progressive citizens of that up-to-date city that you hoped they were still galloping along wooden sidewalks howling like coyotes," wrote Post. She went on to explain that Ned and Alice were "distinctly grieved at the sight of smooth laid asphalt, wide-paved sidewalks, imposing capitol and modern buildings" that they found in Cheyenne. "Even the brand new Plains Hotel was accepted by both of them in much the same spirit that a child who thought it was going to the circus and found itself in a museum of art would accept the compensation of a nice hot supper instead of peanuts and red lemonade."

While at the Plains, Post decided not to take a chance on the grueling desert drive that awaited them in Utah and Nevada. Instead, they departed the Lincoln Highway at Cheyenne and continued the journey via an alternative route, looping through the Southwest. The Post party drove south beyond Denver to follow a section of the old Santa Fe Trail, some of which would become U.S. Route 66 in 1926. From there, they moved westward through New Mexico and Arizona into California and Los Angeles. Weary of driving, Post had the touring car loaded on a rail flatcar and the threesome proceeded by train up the coast to San Francisco, their ultimate destination.

In early August 1919, when the Army's Trans-continental Motor Convoy struggled down the Lincoln Highway, state and local officials, along with an entourage of citizen motorists, greeted them east of Cheyenne. Once the parade reached the city limits, the Fifteenth Cavalry mounted band escorted the convoy though the city to Frontier Park. That evening, Henry Ostermann, field secretary for the Lincoln Highway Association, and the members of his party slept like princes beneath cool sheets at The Plains.

Not every visitor during the heyday of the Lincoln Highway was as thrilled with Wyoming as Emily Post was. Among the critics was James Montgomery Flagg, the famous illustrator best remembered as the creator of the Uncle Sam recruiting poster used in World Wars I and II. Flagg and his new bride stayed at the Plains during their 1925 honeymoon trip across the continent. "The roads are getting worse again," wrote Flagg, "and I hate to look at them, even when visible. We went thro [sic] Laramie to Cheyenne. The street around the Plains Hotel was entirely torn up. And the shabbiness, the dust, and the hard day's ride all combined to make me laugh sardonically at the seriousness with which Cheyenne took itself." Yet even the outspoken Flagg—at the time the highest-paid magazine illustrator in the country—found something good to say about Cheyenne. "I bought a couple of silk bandanas [sic] in a haberdashery, and the proprietor, when I told him I wanted to get some fried chicken to take to the M.Q. ["Motor Queen," a nickname for his bride], who was then sleeping exhaustedly

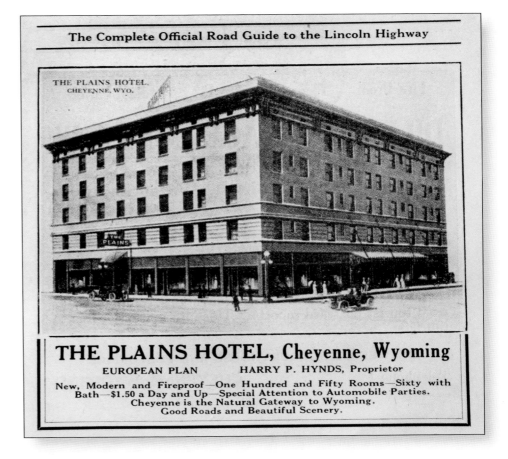

THE PLAINS HOTEL, CHEYENNE, WYO.

THE PLAINS

THE PLAINS HOTEL, Cheyenne, Wyoming
EUROPEAN PLAN   HARRY P. HYNDS, Proprietor
New, Modern and Fireproof—One Hundred and Fifty Rooms—Sixty with Bath—$1.50 a Day and Up—Special Attention to Automobile Parties. Cheyenne is the Natural Gateway to Wyoming. Good Roads and Beautiful Scenery.

at the hotel, at once left his store flat and, without his hat, escorted me to several cafes to help find the chicken. That impulsive friendliness made me forget the mood I arrived in and think kindly of Cheyenne."

There still is much to "think kindly of" in Cheyenne. The Plains Hotel remains the place to stay, especially after a 2003 multimillion-dollar renovation that added many new conveniences without disturbing the hotel's

ABOVE

Road guide ad for the Plains Hotel, Cheyenne, WY.

historical integrity. The 131 spruced-up guest rooms and suites are appointed with "Western high-style décor," and the Capitol Grille offers the freshest Wyoming beef, rack of lamb, and pheasant breast stuffed with cornbread. The Trail Coffee Shop, just off the elegant lobby, serves freshly baked pastries, light lunches, and plenty of Arbuckles coffee, the longtime drink of choice for most range riders. Through all the refurbishing, even the legendary ghosts have stuck around and make occasional appearances, just as they have since the early years of the hotel's operation. Guests and staff claim they catch glimpses of the unhappy spirits—a bride who caught her groom cheating with another woman and in a jealous rage killed both of them with her husband's gun before retreating to the honeymoon suite and turning the weapon on herself.

Both living guests and restless spirits gaze at the Downtown Historic District, highlighted by the Union Pacific Depot, one block south of Lincolnway on Capitol Avenue. Built of multicolored sandstone blocks in 1886, the depot was beautifully

restored to its original grandeur in 2004, two years before being listed on the National Register of Historic Places. The old depot, with its Romanesque clock tower, looks straight up Capitol Avenue and faces off with the state Capitol building, with its twenty-four-carat gold-leaf dome.

Near the Union Pacific Depot, on the corner of Lincolnway and Capitol just across from the Plains Hotel, is the historic Wrangler Building, originally named the Phoenix Block when it went up in 1882. The Wrangler—the Western-wear business for which the old building is named—is considered by many the best store around for cowboy apparel. Since 1943, both real and wannabe cowboys and cowgirls have showed up at the Wrangler to buy shirts, jeans, boots, and belt buckles the size of saucers. Business spikes just before Cheyenne Frontier Days, an annual event since 1897 and the world's largest and oldest outdoor rodeo. Known as "The Daddy of 'em All," the big celebration is staged every July at Frontier Park.

On the sidewalk alongside the Wrangler Building, travelers on a walking tour pass an elderly gentleman with neatly trimmed whiskers and a fine bowler. He stops them with a smile: "Are you having a good day?" When the travelers acknowledge that they are, the old-timer lets them know they have made a wise decision by visiting Cheyenne. "I am from New York and I moved here long ago because this is the best place to live in all of Wyoming. I used to stay at the Plains. Started staying there in 1937. I liked it. They had one-day laundry service and I'd come to my room and there on the bed they would have laid out my starched shirts. Those days are long gone, but I'm still here and so is that hotel and this city." Touching two fingers to the brim of his bowler, the man bows slightly and takes his leave. No wonder Cheyenne once was voted one of the friendliest cities in the nation.

Cheyenne's Downtown Historic District was placed on the National Register in 1974; it is one of four such districts in the city representing more than 1,400 homes and businesses. On Lincolnway in the downtown district is Dinneen Motors, housed in an art deco beauty with hexagonal turrets and terra-cotta trim built in 1927. Over the decades, it accommodated a variety of car makes, including Studebaker, Lincoln, Hudson, Essex, Reo, Edsel, and DeSoto. On West Lincolnway, the Tivoli Building—an eclectic 1892 Victorian edifice that once was a classy speakeasy and brothel—has become the home for the Greater Cheyenne Chamber of Commerce. The nearby Atlas

Theatre, built in 1887, has been rehabilitated through the years and continues to host dramatic productions.

On both the eastern and western ends of Lincolnway in Cheyenne, several vintage motels with distinct signage and architecture continue to operate. One of the favorites is the Lincoln Motor Court, built around 1935 ten blocks from downtown. Known as the site of Wyoming's first outdoor swimming pool, the Lincoln was rebuilt many years later but retained its striking neon sign. Only a few blocks east of downtown, train-buff travelers often stop at Holliday Park to inspect "Big Boy." Old Number 4004 was the world's largest steam locomotive, with a powerful coal-fired engine designed to pull a 3,600-ton train over steep grades without any helper engines. The Union Pacific retired "Big Boy" from active service in 1956. Besides having the gigantic train engine, Holliday Park is where Steve McQueen in 1973 wed Ali MacGraw, his co-star in the 1972 hit movie *The Getaway*.

No visit to Cheyenne would be complete without stopping at the Lakeview Cemetery, the oldest burial ground in the city. An examination of the gravestones and the cemetery records going back to the early 1870s, for example, reveals that almost forty percent of those buried prior to 1900 were under the age of ten—an indication of the poor sanitation and frequent epidemics of that era. Some of the burial "firsts" recorded at Lakeview include: first murder, 1876; first suicide, 1876; first hanging by a mob, 1882; first automobile death, 1915; and first death on the cemetery grounds, 1942. Among the many causes of death are railroad accidents, gunshots, flu epidemics, morphine overdoses, and venereal disease. Frances Pershing, the wife of General John J. Pershing, was buried here in 1915 after she perished in a fire in San Francisco. An 1887 death was the result of drinking ice water and a 1902 cause of death was given as flypaper poisoning.

Cheyenne has always been one of the best stops on the Lincoln Highway, but travelers discover that much more of interest lies ahead. In the early days, the dirt road westward from Cheyenne was in poor shape, with culverts and bridges in constant disrepair. Soon after World War I, however, an effort was made to improve road conditions both on the Lincoln and on the Yellowstone Highway, running from Cheyenne directly to Yellowstone National Park in Wyoming's northwest corner. The 1924 Lincoln Highway guidebook heaped glowing praise on the Wyoming State Highway Department for completing a new road between Cheyenne and Laramie during 1919 and 1920. According to the guide, this new alignment succeeded in "eliminating many of the difficult and dangerous grades on the old route."

Much of the original Lincoln Highway in Wyoming has been covered by interstate or lies abandoned. Nowadays, most motorists make the fifty-two-mile drive from Cheyenne to Laramie on I-80 and U.S. 30. Varicose sections of old road to the west are visible from the interstate highway near Granite Canyon. About one mile south of I-80 is the 3,800-acre Remount Ranch, originally called Lone Tree Ranch. This pioneer cattle and horse ranch was homesteaded in the 1880s and supplied fresh horses (or remounts) for the army. Remount Ranch is best known for inspiring *My Friend Flicka*, published in 1941. While living at the ranch from 1938 to 1968, author Mary O'Hara (the nom de plume of Mary Sture-Vasa) wrote her beloved novel and other classics about the rangelands of Wyoming. In 1990, the ranch was added to the National Register of Historic Places.

At this point, the route reaches a formation known as "The Gangplank." This geological oddity consists of thick layers of sedimentary rock that gradually rise, forming a natural ramp for both railroad and highway travelers climbing the Sherman Mountains, the eroded crest of the eastern flank of the Laramie range. In 1869, a correspondent for the *New York Tribune* described ascending "The Gangplank" to the summit of Sherman Hill:

All around are bare mountain tops. The ashen herbage is brightened by blue lungwort and yellow Arkansas wall flowers in clusters as large as the palm of a hand, or the crown of a hat. Granite boulders of gray and brown, spotted with yellow moss, are scattered here and there. One near the summit is fifty feet high, and shelters the cattle of a ranchman, who has fenced in a little space beside it.

The scene remains unchanged except for a busy interstate highway and speeding motorists who have little time to look at wildflowers.

A few miles to the west, there is not much left of Buford, a small settlement that even during the late

RIGHT *Tree Rock,*
"The famed
landmark of
Wyoming,"
Sherman Hill, WY.

1880s had little more than a railroad station, trading post, schoolhouse, and a few residences. According to local lore, President Ulysses Grant stretched his legs here during a train journey in 1869, and supposedly Butch Cassidy robbed the old Buford Trading Post, but details of the crime are as sparse as the surrounding landscape. In the 1924 Lincoln Highway guidebook, Buford's population was listed as eighty—a number that steadily decreased over the years. In 2003, a fire destroyed the trading post. Almost immediately, a fourth version of the original building quickly took its place. By then, there were only two residents—a father and son who sold tourists an array of souvenir coffee mugs, T-shirts, key chains, and whistles made from animal horns. The population later dropped by fifty percent when the son moved away.

Back on I-80, west of Buford, appears what many people claim is the symbol of the Lincoln Highway in Wyoming—Tree Rock. Teams of Union Pacific surveyors in the late 1860s visited this pine tree growing out of a crevice in a billion-year-old boulder of pink Sherman granite. For many years, locomotive firemen supposedly "gave the tree a drink" from their water buckets during dry spells. In 1902, after the railroad's original grade was moved to the south in order to avoid the steep grade of Sherman Hill, the abandoned grade was used as a wagon road. After the old railbed was incorporated into the route of the Lincoln Highway in 1913, Tree Rock remained a popular resting place and, as always, a photo opportunity. Later travelers on U.S.

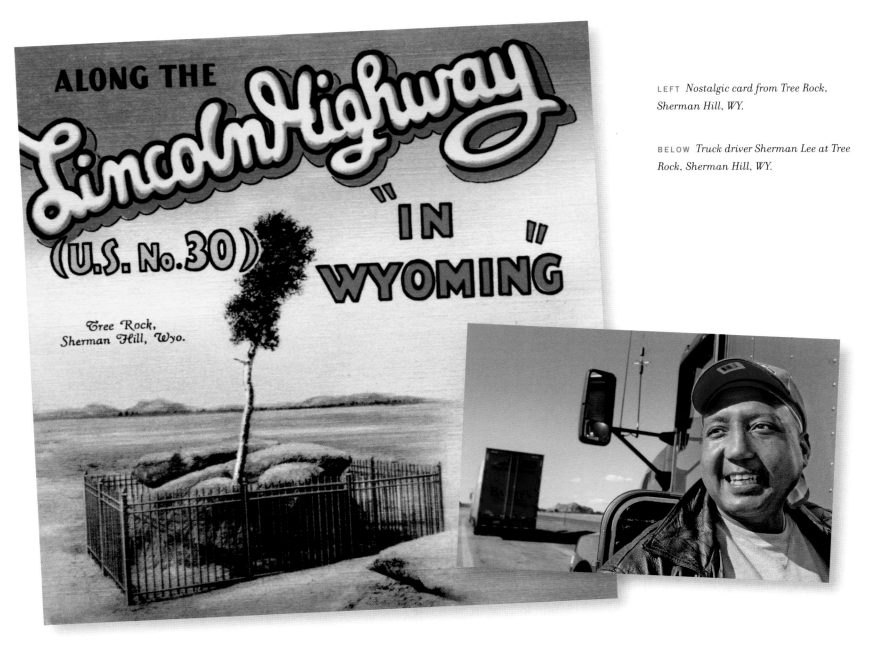

30 followed suit, and today the tree still pulls motorists into the highway-median rest stop on Interstate 80.

The tree is a limber pine, a name that comes from the fact that the tree's branches are flexible and can be bent back completely without breaking. "Limber pines have a way of growing in dramatic places, taking picturesque attitudes, and getting themselves photographed, written about, and cared for, even becoming the core of a legend," wrote noted botanist and author Donald Culross Peattie in 1950. "This pine so constantly occurs in the historically significant passes of the Rockies that it was destined to link up with human history."

The lone pine thrives on the wind. Old-timers joke that snow never melts in Wyoming—it just blows around until it gets tired out. They also claim that a Wyoming wind gauge is a blacksmith's anvil on a length of chain. Railroad and highway surveyors were constantly plagued by winds so strong they could not steady their tripods. Journals of early pioneers tell of people going insane from the relentless wind.

Bursts of road music muffle the howling wind for those motoring down I-80, scanning for faint reminders of the old Lincoln, much of which lies beneath the lanes of the superslab. West of Tree Rock and just south of the original Lincoln Highway alignment, near the summit of Sherman Hill, is a spot where travelers can briefly deviate from the course to see the Ames Monument—a monolithic, sixty-foot-high pyramid standing in the middle of nowhere. Completed in 1882 and designed by the distinguished architect Henry Hobson Richardson,

the monument was commissioned by the Union Pacific Railroad as a memorial to U.S. Congressman Oakes Ames and his brother Oliver Ames, the third president of Union Pacific. Erecting a giant pyramid was the least the Union Pacific board of directors could do to honor the Massachusetts brothers whose financial backing and political shenanigans were key to the building of the nation's first coast-to-coast railroad.

The Ames Monument was constructed of native granite quarried less than a mile away and skidded by horse and derrick to the highest elevation of the original transcontinental railroad route so it could be seen by the trains' passengers. In 1901, however, the rails were shifted a few miles to the south to follow a more desirable grade. The Lincoln Highway took over that old railbed in 1913, and travelers on the gravel road were able to ogle the pyramid until the highway was rerouted in 1920, and again in 1930. The monument remains a forlorn tribute to a time long passed. Unfortunately, the Augustus Saint-Gaudens bas-relief medallions of the Ames brothers, mounted on the pyramid, also caught the eye of sagebrush marksmen, who have shot away both men's noses.

Only stone foundations and a graveyard near the Ames Monument remain from the town of Sherman—at 8,835 feet, the highest point ever on the Lincoln Highway. This ghost town at one time supported hotels, railroad machine shops, a newspaper, and a Wells Fargo express office. "As you approach Sherman, you will see the balanced rocks, and to the right of the station, about one-quarter of a mile, is a rugged peak, near which are graves of some who are quietly sleeping so near heaven, and a solitary pine tree, like a sentinel keeping guard over them," wrote Henry Williams in his 1877 book, *The Pacific Tourist*.

Today travelers on Interstate 80 cross the Sherman Hill summit about half a mile east of the old route. Although the newer crossing reaches a lower elevation of 8,640 feet, it remains the highest spot on I-80. Two significant Lincoln Highway monuments have been relocated to the new summit—a giant bust of Abraham Lincoln and the Henry B. Joy Monument. The bronze head of Lincoln—designed and created in 1959 by Robert I. Russin—is the world's largest and most controversial depiction of the former president. Russin said that he wanted to show a "contemplative Lincoln in the last years of his life, his great heart sorrowing over the rent of his nation." Critics of the work, however, believe the brooding, deep-set eyes and angry scowl give Lincoln the appearance of a madman. Some have dubbed it "The Crazy Lincoln." Artistic merit aside, the 12.5-foot-high, 3.5-ton bust was moved to its present site atop a thirty-five-foot granite base in 1969, when I-80 opened.

The Henry B. Joy Monument—honoring the first president of the Lincoln Highway Association and the president of the Packard Motor Car Company—was moved to the rest area from a remote site on the Continental Divide, about a hundred miles to the west. That original site in the Great Divide Basin, west of Rawlins, was said to have been one of Joy's favorite camping spots along the highway. It was there, in 1915, that Joy witnessed a glorious sunset that convinced him to select the location for his final resting place. Joy, however, did not get his wish when he passed away in 1936. Instead, his widow, Helen, dedicated the stone monument to the man whom many regard as the father of the nation's modern highway system. Surrounded by an iron fence and marked with eight Lincoln Highway Association concrete posts dating from 1928, the granite marker was relocated in 2001 to Sherman Hill to protect it from vandals.

The descent from the summit winds through spectacular red-rock canyons into the Laramie Basin, surrounded by mountain ranges under a vast stretch

BELOW

Both the Henry B. Joy Monument (right) and the Lincoln Monument share space at the Summit Rest Area just west of Cheyenne, WY.

One favorite lodging for kids as well as adults is the Gas Lite Motel, with its hodgepodge of Old West kitsch festooned on the façade. The motel's swimming pool is called a "Wyoming Water Hole," and cardboard figures of John Wayne and a fierce *bandito* stand guard at the office entrance. Inspired by the motel's western décor, guests can head out for one of the most popular attractions in Laramie—the old Wyoming Territorial Prison, built in 1872 and "dedicated to evil doers of all classes and kinds."

True to its mission, the prison housed some of the toughest desperadoes in Wyoming Territory. It was the only penal institution in the country that could claim Butch Cassidy as a resident. Born as Robert Leroy Parker, the notorious outlaw acquired the nickname "Butch" while briefly working as a butcher in Rock Springs, Wyoming, a future Lincoln Highway town. He took his alias surname Cassidy in honor of an early mentor—Mike Cassidy, a savvy horse thief and cattle rustler. In 1894, four years after Wyoming became a state, Butch Cassidy was convicted of stealing horses and was sent to the Wyoming State Prison. After serving eighteen months of his two-year sentence, Cassidy was released when he vowed to the governor that he would sin no more in Wyoming.

Alas, Butch failed to hold up his end of the bargain. A few years after being released from prison, he recruited Harry Alonzo Longabaugh—"The Sundance Kid"—into his Wild Bunch gang. They proceeded to rob trains and banks not only in Wyoming but also in Utah, New Mexico, and Montana before trying their luck in South

of unending sky. Ten miles west of the Sherman Hill rest stop is Laramie, the third largest city in the state and home of the University of Wyoming, the state's only four-year institution of higher learning. Founded in 1886, four years before statehood, the university has earned a reputation as a major research center, with 180 programs of study. Exerting a tremendous influence on the community, it acts as Laramie's cultural hub. Students joke that they attend the "coolest summer school" in the nation, thanks to a combination of constant wind and the 7,200-foot elevation. Temperatures rarely reach the ninety-degree mark.

America, where they faded into the mists of legend. By the early 1900s, Butch's old cell-block home in Laramie was no longer a prison—the new state penitentiary had been built in Rawlins. The University of Wyoming used the Laramie prison as an experimental farm until 1989, when it was restored to its original form from territorial times. Listed on the National Register of Historic Places, the prison is open to visitors throughout the summer and by appointment during the brisk Wyoming winter.

No matter the time of year—even for brave winter travelers—the trip from Laramie, tracing what remains of the Lincoln Highway across the rest of the state, is unforgettable. The stretch of road between Laramie and Medicine Bow alone has been called the best drive in Wyoming.

At Laramie, the route breaks away from Interstate 80 and follows U.S. 30, and the Union Pacific tracks in a wide arc through what used to be called Bosler, as well as Rock River and Medicine Bow, before rejoining I-80 and turning westward to Rawlins and the other towns strung along the highway as far as the Utah line.

Bosler, twenty miles northwest of Laramie, is yet another place that dried up when Interstate 80 made its appearance far to the south. Rusted car cadavers keep each other company in blond grass beneath a sky as blue as any sky can be. There are a few sheds and an empty corral. The two-story Bosler Consolidated School is as lifeless as the row of small buildings on the other side of the highway. But a big eagle nest atop a telephone pole is proof that life goes on.

Twenty miles later, the highway crosses over Rock Creek and enters the town of Rock River, where about two hundred people live full time. Hostler's General Store—named Red Top Service when it was built along U.S. 30 in the 1950s—is a good place to buy salmon eggs, nightcrawlers, and other fishing bait. When the restaurant, owned by Roy and Betty Hostler, is cooking, folks drive from as far away as Laramie just to enjoy a Longhorn burger and scarf up a couple of slices of four-berry pie. "We sure don't regret coming here," says Roy, a native of Pennsylvania, sitting beneath a shaggy bison head mounted on a store wall. "I worked

oldest house in the world." The Fossil Cabin Museum also was listed on the National Register of Historic Places. Thomas Boylan built the museum in 1933 from the thousands of dinosaur fossils and fragments he dug from a "dinosaur graveyard" discovered in 1877 by Union Pacific workers. Boylan and his family are gone, but for a small fee visitors still come to the museum when it keeps irregular hours during the summer and fall.

At Medicine Bow, seven miles west of Como Bluff, travelers are transported back in time to when the town was on the main highway through Wyoming and the imposing Virginian Hotel was the largest between Denver and Salt Lake City. Built in 1911, the Virginian was a first-class hotel with indoor plumbing, steam heat, and electric lights. These same amenities are still available for anyone who checks into the three-story stone hotel, which was fully restored in 1984 and is listed on the National Register of Historic Places.

The hotel's name comes from Owen Wister's 1902 Western novel *The Virginian*, which the young Philadelphian and Harvard graduate wrote while living in Medicine Bow. In Wister's book, a character called the Virginian and another character named Trampas parley in a Medicine Bow saloon. After Trampas suggested that the Virginian was the son of a bachelor, the Virginian calmly drew his pistol. "And with a voice as gentle as ever, the voice that sounded almost like a caress," he uttered the famous phrase that forever shaped the modern perception of the cowboy—"When you call me that, smile." Following a few Wyoming-style cocktails in

hard for thirty years before moving west for good and now I do just what I want to do." That includes sipping coffee every day with pals, selling bait and world-class pie, and maintaining an old gas pump out front that doesn't work but has the Lincoln Highway name on it and a light that shines bright on a winter's eve.

Less than ten miles farther up U.S. 30 is Como Bluff, on the border of Albany and Carbon Counties. This is the site of a modest structure constructed of 5,796 dinosaur bone fragments weighing 112,000 pounds. It became a popular tourist attraction many years before being featured by "Ripley's Believe It or Not" in 1953 as "the

the hotel's Shiloh Saloon and a calves'-liver supper in the vintage dining room, a good night's sleep in the Owen Wister Suite is in order. At breakfast the next morning, a waitress serving pork chops and eggs with sides of applesauce and sliced tomatoes is likely to inquire if any travelers had visitors during the night. "We do have a couple of ghosts," she explains. "They knock around upstairs, but they're real good spirits and don't really bother anybody."

From Medicine Bow, U.S. 30 bends to the southwest, through countryside littered with commercial archaeology, memories of old coal-supply depots, and fading alignments of the original Lincoln Highway. Old haunts come and go, such as Carbon, Home Ranch, Hanna, and Coyote Spring, near where all three generations of the Lincoln in Wyoming converge. U.S. 30 rejoins Interstate 80 at Walcott Junction, and the two routes stay together through Rawlins, Wamsutter, Rock Springs, Lyman, and Evanston to the Wyoming–Utah border. Near Walcott Junction are the remains of Fort Fred Steele, named for a rather undistinguished Civil War officer. Established on the North Platte River to protect Union Pacific Railroad workers from marauding Ute Indians, the post was active from 1868 to 1886, when the army left, though many soldiers had departed much earlier. The relentless wind may have been a key factor that earned Fort Steele the highest desertion rate of any army post in the West. Once the post closed, fires started by sparks from passing locomotives burned many of the buildings. A few old structures remain, including some that were used as places of business when the Lincoln Highway was routed this way.

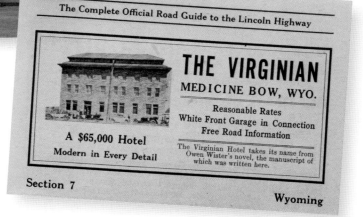

The Complete Official Road Guide to the Lincoln Highway

THE VIRGINIAN
MEDICINE BOW, WYO.

Reasonable Rates
White Front Garage in Connection
Free Road Information

A $65,000 Hotel
Modern in Every Detail

The Virginian Hotel takes its name from Owen Wister's novel, the manuscript of which was written here.

Section 7

Wyoming

About seven miles west of Fort Steele is the planned community of Sinclair, originally named Parco, the acronym for Producers and Refiners Corporation, the Denver-based independent oil company that developed the town and refinery in 1922 for 1,500 employees. During the Depression, the oil company went into receivership when the price of crude oil reached an all-time low of ten cents a barrel. In 1934, Sinclair Oil purchased the refinery and the town. Included in the sale was the Parco Inn, a gracious Spanish Mission–style hotel and the centerpiece of the town's plaza. Many illustrious travelers stayed in the hotel while traveling the Lincoln Highway, including President Franklin Roosevelt and the famed aviatrix Amelia Earhart. In the hotel's elegant Fountain Room, guests dined to the accompaniment of gurgling water spilling from the mouths of wildcat statues into a fountain pool filled with shimmering goldfish. The oil market improved with the demands of World War II, and the town and refinery were officially renamed Sinclair in 1942.

The refinery—noted for its dinosaur logo—now produces more than 60,000 barrels of petroleum products each day; many original buildings, including the hotel, still stand and are listed on the National Register. But changes are evident. Wildcats no longer spout water for the pleasure of patrons seated at tables covered in fine linen cloth. The Baptist Youth Mission came to town and now uses the historic inn as its national headquarters and as a training center for young evangelists. In front of the hotel on Lincoln Avenue, the fountain with a cat motif is dry and has become a place for stray cats to play night games with blowing leaves and discarded sandwich wrappers.

A few miles ahead, Rawlins, another Wyoming railroad town, was founded in 1868, when the tracks were laid. By the 1870s, it was a jumping-off point for hearty souls headed to the goldfields in South Pass. Not long after that, Rawlins became the sheep-ranching center in this part of Wyoming, and it remains so today. Rawlins also was the site of Wyoming's first state prison, which opened for business in 1901, when the first cellhouse was completed. "The Old Pen," as most people refer to the prison, remained active until 1981. Now it is open for guided tours and has a gift shop.

One of the best yarns to come out of Rawlins concerns a local desperado who could have benefited from a little time spent behind the bars at the old state prison. In 1881, George Manuse—widely known as "Big Nose" George Parrot, due to his sizable proboscis—was the most hated man in Rawlins when two hundred vigilante citizens dragged him out of the city jail and strung him up from a telegraph pole at Third and Front Streets. Much of the animosity toward "Big Nose" stemmed from his attempt to rob a payroll train east of Rawlins that left two pursuing possemen dead. To make matters worse, word got back to Rawlins that "Big Nose" was up in Montana having a high old time drinking cheap whiskey and bragging about the Wyoming boys he had killed. All that ended when some Wyoming lawmen went to Montana, took the loudmouthed killer into custody, and brought him home for trial. After he was found guilty and sentenced to hang, "Big Nose" tried to escape but was foiled. Word of the jailbreak attempt prompted his expedited hanging.

After Manuse's body was left hanging for the better part of the day, the undertaker removed it from the makeshift gallows. But because no relatives claimed the corpse, Dr. John Osborne, one of the town's most respected physicians, took possession of it to perform an autopsy and also to study the outlaw's brain in hopes of discovering some abnormality. After making a death mask of Manuse's face, Osborne sawed off the skullcap to examine the brain. Seeing nothing out of the ordinary, the doctor proceeded to skin the corpse. He sent the skin to a Denver tannery with explicit instructions to "make a pair of shoes and leave the nipples on." When the finished shoes arrived, sans nipples, in Rawlins, Osborne was disappointed. But he was so impressed with the shoes that he wore them constantly. He also had a medicine bag made from the chest skin. He gave the skullcap to Dr. Lillian Nelson, the first female physician in Wyoming, who used it for years as an ashtray and a doorstop. The rest of the outlaw's remains were sealed in a whiskey barrel and buried behind Osborne's office.

Dr. Osborne not only practiced medicine but also was at one time the most successful individual sheep owner in Wyoming. In 1892, he was elected as the first Democratic governor of Wyoming—it was said that he proudly wore his "special shoes" to the inaugural ball.

Some years later, Osborne represented Wyoming in the U.S. Congress and then served as first assistant secretary of state under President Woodrow Wilson. He returned to Rawlins to become a banker and died in 1943.

The story of "Big Nose" did not die with Osborne. The outlaw's remains were uncovered in the 1950s by construction workers digging a foundation. The skullcap was retrieved from the elderly Dr. Nelson, and when it was placed on top of the partial skull recovered at the construction site, it was a perfect fit. Today the most popular feature at the Carbon County Museum is the display of the skull and, of course,

ABOVE *Deer being fed at the Drive-In Liquor Lounge, Medicine Bow, WY.*

those fancy two-tone shoes. The whereabouts of Dr. Osborne's unusual medical bag remains a mystery.

Westward on U.S. 30, running alongside the Union Pacific tracks, the route crosses the Continental Divide and enters the Great Divide Basin, from which water flows neither east nor west but simply evaporates into the thin air. This is the glorious landscape that so enthralled Henry B. Joy, the Lincoln Highway guru, and where his monument first stood before it was moved east to Sherman Hill. Out in this red desert, bands of wild horses roam unbranded and unclaimed. They answer only to a dominant stallion that leaves mounds of manure (called "stud piles") to mark the territory and warn any bachelors sniffing out mares to keep their distance.

On this long stretch of road after Creston Junction is Wamsutter, a hardscrabble settlement where pickup trucks are lined up like tethered cow ponies in front of the Broadway Cafe. Next door, the Desert Bar is a black-eyed, split-lip sort of place tailor-made for good ol' boys. Big rigs pulling into Wamsutter snort and belch like rodeo stock. And to the west, three generations of the Lincoln

RIGHT

Former gas station and cafe, Creston, WY.

OPPOSITE

Broadway Cafe, Wamsutter, WY.

Highway intertwine for more than sixty miles out in the sage and sand where jackrabbits as big as lambs race for their lives.

At the Point of Rocks lie the bones of a sandstone stage station built on the south bank of Bitter Creek in 1862 by Ben Holladay—"The Stagecoach King." It is believed that the notorious Jack Slade—an outlaw known to carry the severed ears of his victims in his pocket—held up a stage near Point of Rocks in 1863 and killed seven passengers. The swing station, like others on the Overland Trail, only lasted until the Union Pacific emerged on the scene in the late 1860s and made stagecoach travel obsolete. The graveyard is surrounded by a picket fence that was erected when the site was restored and included on the National Register of Historic Places.

The route just misses the sleepy ghost town of Superior, named Reliance until 1906, when Superior Coal Company took over. Although the town's population dwindled when the last mine closed in the 1960s, Superior did not disappear. Life can be found among the rows

989—The Arch, Rock Springs. Wyoming **HOME OF**

ROCK SPRINGS COAL

WELCOME

ABOVE AND RIGHT

The Arch, Rock Springs, WY, then and now.

of ghostly buildings, the remains of the old union hall, and in dwellings along Horse Thief Creek.

In the city of Rock Springs, Grub's ("Home of the Shamrock") was established "right around St. Patrick's Day in 1946"—hence the name of the signature burger—and still delivers the goods to locals and travelers alike. Founder Nick "Grub" Skorup died in 1996, but a third generation of Nick's family remains at the griddle and behind the cash register. Breakfast and lunch customers vie for one of the twelve stools around a semicircular counter. Most lunch patrons order a Shamrock (that's two beef patties) with fries and ask for "fry sauce," a mixture of mayo and ketchup that is the standard dip with all Grub's french fries.

After a feast of Shamrocks, a good spot to start any tour is the Rock Springs Historical Museum, the former city hall built in 1894 and restored to its original grandeur in 1991. The museum offers displays and information about every aspect of Rock Springs—from railroads and cowboys to labor issues and coal mining. From the museum, a walking tour takes visitors to such historic sites and buildings as the former Western Auto Transit Company, built in 1910 and advertised as "Wyoming's oldest automobile dealer," and the site of the Lincoln Highway Garage, now a parking lot. The tour covers scores of commercial buildings, churches, hotels, markets, and the restored archway announcing, "Home of Rock Springs Coal: Welcome," erected on the Lincoln Highway in 1928 and restored in 1997.

Business Interstate 80 follows the 1926 alignment of the Lincoln Highway through Rock Springs and into Green River, where the wide-open spaces suddenly give way to a series of majestic buttes carved over time by the river. Incorporated in 1868, Green River was the 1869 starting point for noted explorer John Wesley Powell, who explored the Green and Colorado Rivers, and the Grand Canyon. Green River also is where in 1871, just three years after the arrival of the railroad, the Hudson River School painter Thomas Moran came to town and immediately spied Toll Gate Rock and the Palisades, the subjects of his famous "first sketch made in the West." Moran was moved by the rock formations and looming cliffs of the Green River Valley and

ABOVE *An old alignment of the Lincoln Highway in Wyoming.*

painted them over and over again. Moran did his final painting of the cliffs in 1918, at the age of eighty-one.

Five years before Moran made that final painting, travelers through Green River often had to endure long waits at railroad crossings and cross the river on a wagon bridge. It was never a pleasant trek; this was considered Wyoming's worst section of the Lincoln Highway. That changed in 1922, when the state built a new highway bridge and shifted the route.

West of Rock Springs on I-80 is Little America, a self-contained roadside community with its own fire department, zip code, and water department catering to tourists zooming down the interstate. Named for Admiral Richard Byrd's South Pole camp, the original Covey's Little America, down the road at Granger, was a handy stop on U.S. 30 for gas, eats, and a night's sleep in a cozy cabin. In 1949, Little America moved to its present location and has steadily grown into the highway village, offering full auto service and 140 guest rooms. Little America is but one of many hotel and resort properties owned by Earl Holding, the Salt Lake City tycoon who bought Sinclair Oil in the 1970s. The original Little America burned in 1970.

Just beyond Little America, the route bends gently southwestward on its final run in Wyoming. Travelers motor to Lyman—a town founded by Mormons in 1898 that was bypassed by I-80 but has somehow survived—and then reach Fort Bridger, a State Historic Site near Black's Fork on the Green River. Mountain man Jim Bridger built a fort and trading post here in 1834. Early Lincoln Highway travelers liked to stop for chicken dinners at the old Bucking Horse Cafe. There are no chicken dinners available, however, at the tourist curio shop that calls itself the Jim Bridger Trading Post—where, for unknown reasons, a large cutout of Billy the Kid (who never came anywhere near Fort Bridger) stands out front holding a firecracker.

Thirty miles farther is Evanston, the last Lincoln Highway town in Wyoming. Moose antlers and a few Lincoln Highway signs are tacked on an outside

LEFT *Antelope roaming in Wyoming.*

wall at Pete's Rock and Rye Club. In 1920, when the Lincoln was going strong, the city set up a roadside campground. Folks could stay overnight for fifty cents a vehicle. By 1927, the campground had grown to include six small cabins with adjoining carports; a year later, some folks from Rawlins leased the campground from the city and named it Sunset Camp. In later years, the original cabins were replaced with Mission-style buildings. Although Sunset Camp closed long ago, some of the cabins are still there.

The Prairie Inn on Bear River Drive, the old Lincoln route through town, is just the right place to reflect on the majesty of the Wyoming leg of the trip that began at Smitty's Truck Stop, hundreds of miles to the east. In the morning, the journey will continue on to Utah, two miles to the west. Until then, travelers who stop will find it is good to be in Wyoming for one more night of dreams.

Welcome to UTAH

Chapter Eleven

UTAH

The path of the Lincoln Highway in Utah winds through land laid bare to the bone. It is a place where those who came always looked for a shortcut to avoid daunting mountain ranges and scorching desert. Yet the sheer raw beauty of those

same natural barriers has been known to seduce even those who race against time. Sometimes the old Lincoln Highway is difficult to find, yet long stretches—including one of the versions with many miles that were never paved—can be driven from the Wyoming border to the Nevada line.

The original Lincoln Highway was graded dirt when it entered Utah, passing the site of Wyuta (a combination of the two state names) and the border railroad

stop for the Union Pacific. This old alignment of the original Lincoln starts as a north frontage road for I-80 and meanders through sagebrush for a short distance before a fence abruptly blocks the way. On the other side of the fence is Deseret Land & Livestock, a 200,000-acre ranch owned and operated by the Church of Jesus Christ of Latter-day Saints (LDS).

The LDS is one of the largest owners of farm and ranchland in the nation,

LEFT

Wyuta Station, UT.

with vast land holdings in Utah, Nebraska, Florida, and several other states. The Deseret Ranch grazes substantial herds of sheep and cattle, as well as large numbers of mule deer, elk, moose, antelope, and sage grouse for a profitable game-hunting experience. *Deseret* comes from the *Book of Mormon* and means "honeybee"—the buzzing creature that became the state symbol and official insect—and also provided the nickname "Beehive State." Pioneer Mormon prophet Brigham Young named the Promised Land for the honeybee, a symbol of industry and diligence, and the territory of Deseret petitioned for statehood in 1850. Congress rejected the name and instead chose Utah, derived from the Ute word meaning "People of the mountains." Nevertheless, many Utah businesses and organizations continue to use *Deseret* or *Beehive* as part of their name.

The fenced grazing lands of the Deseret Ranch are a good indication that anyone tracking the old road today should return to I-80, often a real beehive of activity itself due to construction or heavy seasonal traffic. Only six miles into Utah, the highway skirts Wahsatch, an abandoned railroad stop and cattle-shipping center. (Named for the nearby Wasatch Mountains, the station for unknown reasons had an extra "H" inserted in its name.) In 1868, hundreds of workers lived at the treeless site as the railroad was built through the rugged countryside. There was a busy boardinghouse, and a roundhouse where locomotives turned around. Now there is nothing left but a sign near the tracks that says Wahsatch.

Long before the Union Pacific laid its railbed, many others passed this way. They blazed a trail deep into a narrow chasm that was named Echo Canyon because laughter, gunfire, hoofbeats, animal bellowing, rushing water, and thunderbolts reverberated throughout the long, stony chamber. This canyon trail has always been an important corridor for beast and man. Great bison herds, bands of Shoshone and Ute Indians, and fur trappers and traders used this natural passage between the lush grasslands of Wyoming and the salt deserts to the west. In later years, more than a few highwaymen also used this route for preying upon mail carriers and travelers. The names of more than 150 trappers, mountain men, and overland travelers—some dating back to 1820—remain on the walls of Cache Cave, a popular rendezvous spot located on private land high above the trail.

The ill-fated members of the Donner-Reed Party passed through Echo Canyon in early August 1846, during their arduous journey to California that ended in disaster three months later when they were trapped by snow in the Sierra Nevada. The following year, the canyon became part of the Mormon Trail, the route by which Brigham Young led the vanguard of his Latter-day Saints to their new home in Great Salt Lake City (the name until 1856, when it became Salt Lake City). Until the coming of the railroad in 1869, tens of thousands of Mormon pilgrims made the journey by wagon and later on foot, using handcarts to haul their possessions to the sanctuary of Deseret. Fascinated by Echo Canyon, many of them recorded their thoughts about the place in journals and trip logs. One such was pioneer William Clayton, who made this entry on July 16, 1847:

There is a very singular echo in this ravine, the rattling of wagons resembles carpenters hammering at boards inside the highest rocks. The report of a rifle resembles the sharp crack of thunder and echoes from rock to rock for some time. The lowing of cattle and braying of mules seems to be answered beyond the mountains. Music, especially brass instruments, have a pleasing effect and resemble a person standing inside the rock imitating every note. The echo, the high rocks on the north, high mountains on the south with the narrow ravine for a road, form a scenery at once romantic and more interesting than I have ever witnessed.

In 1857, when Brigham Young refused to step down as territorial governor, President James Buchanan declared that Utah Territory was in a state of rebellion. U.S. Army troops marched to Utah to secure the territory for the Union and enforce laws prohibiting the widespread Mormon practice of polygamy. As a result, Brigham Young dispatched his Mormon Militia to Echo Canyon, where they dammed the creek with rocks and built fortifications to hold off the soldiers and prevent them from entering Deseret and Salt Lake City. The Mormon warriors cut pine poles and slathered them with stove black so they looked like protruding cannons when observed from the canyon floor. They also dug several deep trenches across the canyon floor to slow the army's advance, allowing sharpshooters hidden above to ambush the soldiers. Provisions and ammunition were cached, and at least five hundred well-armed men were positioned to do battle in rifle pits dug into the rocky soil and behind the boulders.

Ultimately, the defensive breastworks at Echo Canyon were never used. After learning about the fortified canyon, the U.S. troops made an end run around the Mormons and entered Salt Lake City by taking a longer and more circuitous route. Utah was then placed under military occupation. Although he remained at the LDS helm until his death in 1877, Young grudgingly surrendered his title of territorial governor. Following a long struggle, the LDS leadership renounced polygamy in 1890, thus paving the way for Utah Territory finally to become a state in 1896. Yet reminders of the so-called Utah War survive in Echo Canyon, where remnants of the fortifications are listed on the National Register of Historic Places. Some of the old breastworks are visible on the sides of cliffs approximately twenty miles west of the site of Wahsatch Station, and a rock-wall dam built by the Mormon defenders is visible along the canyon road.

Although a battle pitching Mormons against federal troops was avoided, Echo Canyon has been the scene of much bloodshed—some accidental and some intentional. In 1860, a makeshift posse of three men from a westbound emigrant wagon train tracking a horse thief found him napping in Echo Canyon. "We ordered him to give himself up and the horses," one of the men scribbled in his journal. Instead of complying, the thief "showed his teeth and threatened to shoot us. There was no other alternative. We killed him and buried him by the side of the road." When the wagon train passed through Echo Canyon the following day, the men erected a wooden headboard inscribed: "George B. Baker, shot on the 3rd day of July, 1860 for horse-stealing and attempt to murder. We killed him because he would not give up himself to be hung by our train."

Long before Utah's statehood, British author and explorer Sir Richard F. Burton—packing a pair of pistols, a Bowie knife, and a ration of opium—made an overland stage trip to Utah and no doubt passed the wooden marker for the horse thief. Famous for his role in the controversial discovery of the Nile River's source in 1858, Burton was on a mission to meet with Brigham Young and investigate the custom of polygamy for a forthcoming book entitled *The City of the Saints: Among the Mormons and Across the Rocky Mountains to California*, published in 1861. Burton's stagecoach route to Great Salt Lake City through Echo Canyon impressed the colorful adventurer: "An American artist might extract from such scenery as Echo Canyon, a system of architecture as original and as national as Egypt ever borrowed from her sandstone ledges or the North of Europe from the depths of her fir forests."

Gold and silver prospectors and the Overland Stage also took advantage of the Echo Canyon route. Starting in 1860, Pony Express riders carried the mail

down the Mormon Trail through Echo Canyon. For eighteen action-packed months, those slender boys rode fleet ponies through the sagebrush and dodged rocks that fell in their path as they dashed past Cache Cave and the many distinctive rock formations that still fascinate every traveler who sees them. In late 1861, the Pony Express service went out of business with the advent of the transcontinental telegraph. Eight years later, the Union Pacific pushed through the canyon en route to the historic ceremony for the driving of the last spike with the Central Pacific Railroad at Promontory Point, on the north side of Great Salt Lake.

The Echo Canyon route—a timeless path that has carried so much humanity—was an obvious choice when the Lincoln Highway routing was being decided. Still, the going was less than ideal. A 1919 editorial in the *Salt Lake City Tribune* stated that Utah highways had to follow "the lines of least resistance." The problem was that in many instances that meant going through countryside prone to washouts, flooding, and landslides.

In 1919, the U.S. Army's Transcontinental Motor Convoy entered Utah and made the descent into Echo Canyon beneath a gray sky. A light rain fell on the vehicles as they lumbered down the slippery dirt road winding below red and terra-cotta cliffs. This alignment of the highway was still so narrow that the army trucks had difficulty navigating the many twists and turns. It took seven hours for the convoy to make the forty-one-mile trek from the summit of Echo Canyon to the town of Echo at the bottom. Happily for

road travelers, the conditions were much better in the early 1920s, when the Union Pacific made considerable improvements to the route through Echo Canyon.

Today's travelers on Interstate 80 through Echo Canyon can watch for old U.S. 30 on the west side of the canyon as the Lincoln weaves around and sometimes beneath the superslab. Traversing the canyon is much easier than when the road was a narrow dirt trail, but in winter, blizzard conditions can still close I-80 for hours or sometimes days between Echo Junction and the Wyoming border. The route passes the site of Castle Rock, a former Pony Express and stage station named for a sandstone formation. A small community sprang up, and later Castle Rock was a rail stop—with homes, stores, a rooming house, a gas station, and a schoolhouse that opened in 1872 and finally closed in 1937.

Historic sites and markers dot the road through Echo Canyon; near the canyon's mouth is a rest stop and travelers' center off the westbound lanes of I-80. Besides loading up on tourism information, maps, and travel literature, those who stop can hike to

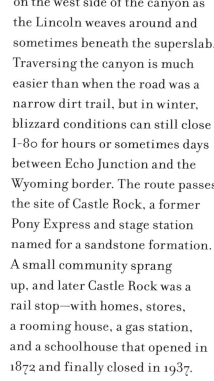

the top of a hill and enjoy views of eastbound trains in the morning and westbound trains in the afternoon.

A white cross overlooking the railroad was erected in memory of William John Antoniewicz, the first state trooper murdered in Utah—December 8, 1974—after stopping a speeding car nine miles east of Echo Junction on I-80. The twenty-seven-year-old rookie trooper was struck in the chest and back when the driver fired two rounds from a .38-caliber revolver. While Antoniewicz lay bleeding on the pavement, the killer got out of his car and kicked him in the face several times before fleeing. Eighteen months later, an informant enticed by the promise of a reward gave up the shooter, and murder charges were filed against Emory Dean Beck. His 1977 trial in Coalville ended in a hung jury, but rather than face a second trial, Beck pleaded guilty to a lesser charge of second-degree murder. He received the maximum sentence—five years to life—and was paroled in 1989, a few days after the slain officer's forty-second birthday.

RIGHT *Devil's Slide, parallel limestone rock formations that extend up the side of Weber Canyon, UT.*

A few miles west of the train-spotting hill, travelers have a choice about which Lincoln route to take at the canyon's mouth, which is sometimes called Main Forks but is better known as Echo Junction. Originally, Utah's Proclamation Route, unveiled in August 1913, called for the route to cross the Wasatch Mountains at Echo Canyon and then bear to the south through a few small towns before descending Parley's Canyon into the Salt Lake Valley. But even before the route could be publicly announced, Utah officials—bowing to pressure from boosters in the city of Ogden—decided the route had to be changed.

The Lincoln Highway Association relented and within a month announced that the official Lincoln route would turn northwestward at Echo Junction and proceed through Weber Canyon to Ogden. The route would then head due south out of Ogden, skirting the eastern edge of Great Salt Lake to reach the capital city named for the body of water. The Ogden leg only lasted two years before LHA officials decided to revert to the more direct route to Salt Lake City that had been laid out in 1913.

Most of today's Lincoln Highway travelers avoid taking the short-lived route to Ogden and instead go south from Echo Junction on the 1915 version, the first route selected. Even so, it is never a bad idea to deviate slightly and drive the short distance to Echo, the first town on the Ogden route. This settlement, named for the nearby canyon, started as a stagecoach stop in 1854 and added a Pony Express station in 1860. When the railroad came through in 1868, the population boomed. Documents in the Summit County Historical Society report that after the railroad moved on, seven human skeletons were discovered beneath a saloon that was torn down. During the demolition of the stage station, a pair of gold-rimmed spectacles, a five-dollar gold piece, and a love letter to a Pony Express rider were found concealed in the walls.

By the time of the Depression, many citizens had moved away from Echo to find employment. A church built in 1876, a schoolhouse from 1914, and a few other buildings

RIGHT *1914*
Lincoln Highway
bridge, Lamb's
Canyon, UT.

FAR RIGHT
Lincoln Highway
bridge, circa 1915,
Lamb's Canyon,
UT.

OPPOSITE
Salt Lake City, UT.

still stand. According to locals, the ghost of a former owner, identified only as "Fat," lingers at the Kozy Cafe. Occasionally he makes his presence known, especially if some of his favorite Johnny Cash tunes are playing on the jukebox and the volume suddenly increases. There also are tales of empty stools squeaking as if being turned, and the sound of shuffling boots.

Those who don't wish to continue on the Ogden route need only backtrack half a mile from the town of Echo to the canyon junction, where they can pass under Interstate 80 and take Echo Dam Road, formerly a stretch of the Lincoln Highway. In this area, the 1915 Lincoln and the Union Pacific tracks were relocated by 1930, after the Bureau of Reclamation spent three years constructing an earth-fill dam on the Weber River. A small Lincoln Highway bridge on the east

shore of the huge Echo Reservoir, created by the 155-foot-high dam, serves as a reminder of the old route.

Echo Reservoir attracts water skiers and anglers, including ice fishermen in the winter bundled up like mountain men come from afar. They dangle jigging spools tipped with grubs through holes in the ice to catch a mess of trout and perch. Anglers huddled on stools sometimes high-five each other and toast with thermos coffee after a fish is successfully pulled from the icy waters.

Not far south of the reservoir, the town of Coalville, seat of Summit County, has changed much over the years, but community pride remains important. That is evident at the fully restored 1904 native-stone courthouse, the Sagebrush Grill, and the Summit Mercantile Company. There a sign boasts: "We carry

everything in merchandise of highest quality." Elk antlers hang on the walls and employees in spotless white aprons shuttle bags of groceries to customers' cars.

The route continues to Hoytsville, a town on the Weber River first settled in 1859 and known for its impressive brick and stone homes. The three-story Hoyt Mansion, with nine fireplaces, is considered one of Utah's most elegant nineteenth-century residences. Travelers who stop for a bite at the Spring Chicken Inn in Wanship, settled in 1857, find that the original route of the Lincoln, winding its way through Silver Creek Canyon to Parley's Summit, lies buried beneath Interstate 80.

Soon after beginning the final approach to Salt Lake City, the route passes Kimball's Hotel, located in the Snyderville Basin between the Kimball and Silver Creek Junctions on the north side of I-80. Built in 1862 by William Kimball, whose father served as a counselor to Brigham Young, the stone building was a station on the Overland Stage route. Some of the more famous travelers who spent the night in one of the hotel's eleven rooms included Mark Twain, Walt Whitman, and Horace Greeley. At this point during his 1861 journey to Nevada, Mark Twain was awestruck when he first beheld the Salt Lake Valley: "All the world was glorified with the setting sun and the most stupendous panorama of mountain peaks yet encountered burst on our sight. We looked out upon this sublime spectacle from under the arch of a brilliant rainbow."

By the 1890s, after noticing that more non-Mormons were passing through the area, the Kimball family

To the south is Park City, once a busy mining center that was almost a ghost town in the 1960s before becoming the most popular resort town in the Wasatch Range. Besides ski areas, chic shops, and luxury homes, the winter playground has more than a hundred sites listed on the National Register of Historic Places. Host of some of the 2002 Olympic Winter Games events, Park City is also known for the annual Sundance Film Festival, started in 1978 and propelled into international prominence by Robert Redford.

Only a few miles farther is Parley's Summit, named for Parley Parker Pratt, a pioneer Mormon leader whose name was also given to Parley's Canyon and Parley's Park, the original name of Park City. Pratt led an early caravan down the Mormon Trail and in the late 1840s built the Big Kanyon Road—a toll road that descended into Salt Lake City. In 1857, the disgruntled former husband of a woman whom the polygamist Pratt had taken as one of his many wives murdered the religious leader during a preaching mission in Arkansas. Pratt is still held in high esteem by the LDS; a Salt Lake City monument erected in 1998 honors him. Travelers can exit I-80 on Foothill Boulevard and find a section of the old Lincoln Highway now named Parley's Way. At Parley Plaza is the heroic statue of Pratt, with his surveying equipment and toolbox.

While in Salt Lake City, visitors can cruise to Capitol Hill, overlooking the downtown and the site of the state Capitol, with walls of native granite framed by twenty-four Corinthian columns and topped by a gleaming copper dome. A fine example of

wisely established a saloon in the hotel. They also dammed the creek and cut blocks of ice that were wrapped in sawdust and stored in nearby caves before being transported to Salt Lake City. At the time the Lincoln Highway was established and routed past the front of the sandstone hotel, rooms were being rented and the Kimball Ranch was still working. In 1960, as plans were being implemented for the construction of Interstate 80, the hotel was no longer in use. Fortunately, preservation-minded citizens were able to spare the old building from demolition by persuading the highway engineers to slightly alter the path of the superhighway.

RIGHT *Magna, UT.*

Renaissance Revival style, the building was completed in 1916 and patterned after the nation's Capitol. On the western slope of Capitol Hill lies the Marmalade District, an architecturally diverse neighborhood that includes many pioneer-era homes lining streets named for the imported fruit trees planted there.

Surrounded by high white walls in the heart of downtown Salt Lake City, Temple Square is the symbolic world center of Mormonism. This sprawling site is, without question, the most popular tourist attraction in Utah, easily outdrawing the many natural wonders, including three national parks—Zion, Bryce Canyon, and Arches. Within Temple Square is the Mormon Tabernacle—home of the renowned choir and pipe organ. To demonstrate the Tabernacle's remarkable acoustics, visitors sit at the rear of the building while a tour guide drops a straight pin near the podium at the opposite end. Although the Tabernacle with its domed roof is open to the public, the nearby Mormon Temple is accessible only to practicing Mormons during religious ceremonies. Construction of the Temple began in 1853 and ended forty years later, after countless wagonloads of enormous granite blocks had been hauled to the site from a quarry in Little Cottonwood Canyon, twenty miles away. A statue of the angel and prophet Moroni (pronounced "Mah-*roh*-ny"), an iconic figure from the *Book of Mormon*, tops the tallest of the Temple's six spires. Moroni—in flowing robes and with a long trumpet pressed to his lips—is made of hammered copper and covered with a thick overlay of gold leaf.

Westbound travelers following the Lincoln Highway face several routing options as they head out of Salt Lake City toward Nevada. They can take an original version of the Lincoln that circles south of the Great Salt Lake Desert. This improved dirt route passes old Pony Express stations, remote working ranches, and small settlements, such as Fish Springs and Callao, all the way to Ibapah, only six miles east of the Nevada border. From that point, travelers drive to Ely, Nevada, and then either swing south to Los Angeles or continue westward to San Francisco.

Over the years, the Lincoln Highway Association made upgrades to this route, including construction of shortcuts through mountain passes. State officials, however, wanted to change the route substantially in order to keep motorists in Utah longer, thus putting more money into state and private coffers. Utah officials wanted the route to divide closer to Salt Lake City; Northern California interests were in full agreement. They were vehemently opposed to motorists taking the old route to Ely, where they would have the option to go to Southern California instead of to San Francisco and points north. After an often-contentious struggle with Utah officials, the Lincoln Highway Association ultimately had no choice but to reroute the highway at the end of 1927. The state sank its money into a new and very costly road linking Salt Lake and Wendover, which ran due west across many miles of salt flats to the Nevada border. Instead of being used for paving the original southern route of the Lincoln, the funds went into the Wendover Road. It was designated as part of the Victory Highway, established in 1921 to honor Americans killed in World War I. Later, U.S. 40 followed this same path. In the late 1960s, Interstate 80 replaced both highways. Nowadays, motorists on I-80 to Wendover find themselves driving down what feels like a never-ending airport runway.

On the other hand, travelers taking the original alignment face no such monotony on their desert treks. Instead, they have an opportunity to go back in time, much as they did when traversing Echo Canyon, where layers of history stick like desert varnish to the steep rock cliffs.

Turning south and then west out of Salt Lake, the route crosses the Jordan River and passes through the town of Magna and past the old copper mills at Arthur and Garfield. At Magna—where travelers can find tasty burgers and ice cream at the Grub Box—a 1928 concrete Lincoln Highway marker was salvaged in 1999 and erected in a city park. Magna and the surrounding area started as a farming community, but that quickly changed in the early 1900s with the rise of the copper industry. As prospectors and miners set up tents and shanties, the settlement first was called Ragtown, but it became Pleasant Green when three hundred tidy cottages were erected. It's theorized that the name was changed to Magna either after a nearby mine, or from the Latin word *magna*, used by the Masonic Order in the phrase *Magna est veritas, et praevalebit* ("Great is truth, and it will prevail").

BELOW *Stuck in the mud, Garfield, UT, circa 1916.*

West of Magna, near what once was the town of Garfield, are several remnants of old Lincoln Highway that were paved in concrete in the early 1920s. Garfield was eliminated in the 1950s to make room for plant expansion. The old site, as well as the pieces of surviving Lincoln, are owned by Kennecott Utah Copper Corporation, headquartered in Magna and operator of the world's largest open-pit copper mine (in Bingham Canyon). While forging a working relationship with the Utah chapter of the revitalized Lincoln Highway Association, the mining giant preserved and restored several sections of the concrete highway, including a stone retaining wall.

Kennecott owns most of the property between Magna and the shores of Great Salt Lake, the largest saltwater lake in the Western Hemisphere and a draw for travelers throughout the heyday of the Lincoln Highway. Black Rock, a natural landmark on the southern shore, marks the route's entrance into Tooele County. Commercial saltworks began operating near here in the mid-1800s. To the east of Black Rock were several public beaches, including Garfield Beach, a popular spot to picnic and swim until Saltair, a huge resort and entertainment center, opened in 1893. Over the years, a combination of three devastating fires and receding lake waters took a heavy toll on the resort, yet a version of Saltair lingers on the shore and struggles to survive by hosting concerts and special events.

Although Great Salt Lake is often referred to as "America's Dead Sea," its marshes provide important habitat and a staging area for millions of migratory waterfowl and shorebirds. For many years, starting in the late 1980s, the lake also became the winter quarters for a solitary pink Chilean flamingo, a species of bird not even remotely near its native home. The bird soon was dubbed "Pink Floyd" by the many birders and curiosity seekers who flocked to the south shore. "Pink Floyd" had been a resident of the Tracy Aviary in Salt Lake City, but when someone neglected to clip its pretty wings, the big bird checked out. It returned that winter and every subsequent winter for a number of years, hanging out with gulls and swans and dining on the brine shrimp that give flamingo feathers their color.

The lake and its denizens became a memory when the old road turned south at Lake Point and headed into the Tooele Valley toward Adobe Rock, named for an adobe cabin that once provided shelter for those who stopped for water at a fresh spring. This landmark was familiar to the Donner-Reed Party, Mormon settlers,

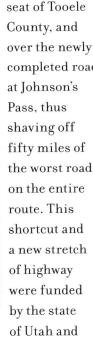

and Lincoln Highway travelers, and it's still prominent for those making the journey today. From this point, the original 1913 route turned west and went to the town of Grantsville, some forty miles west of Salt Lake, and then turned south into the Skull Valley.

In 1919, the route was changed to go south to Tooele, seat of Tooele County, and over the newly completed road at Johnson's Pass, thus shaving off fifty miles of the worst road on the entire route. This shortcut and a new stretch of highway were funded by the state of Utah and pledges that then totaled $150,000 from F. A. Seiberling, president of the Lincoln Highway Association and the Goodyear Tire and Rubber Company; John Willys, of the Willys-Overland Motor Company; and Carl Fisher, "The Father of the Lincoln Highway." At the same time, the new rock-and-dirt road was built across eighteen miles of mudflats west of Dugway. Since this part of

OPPOSITE *The old Gem Theater, Magna, UT.*

LEFT *The Grub Box, Magna, UT.*

the project was funded by $75,000 from Seiberling, the road was named the Goodyear Cutoff. When state officials realized that it would take at least another $100,000 to complete the ambitious project, this route was never completed. It was a moot point by 1927, when the Lincoln Highway routing dramatically shifted with the completion of the road going straight west across the Great Salt Lake Desert to Wendover and then into Nevada.

Travelers sticking to the 1919 routing pass Benson Grist Mill, a restored mill that still operated during the early years of the Lincoln, and then Grantsville before heading southeast to Tooele, at the western base of the Oquirrh Mountains. Incorporated in 1853, Tooele was a quiet farming and mining center until the town was completely transformed by the outbreak of World War

II. By 1942, the U.S. government had purchased 25,000 acres just south of town and constructed an ordnance depot that became the Army's largest supply center in the West. The ordnance depot—primarily a repository for stockpiles of chemical and biological weapons— quickly became the largest employer in the region.

Continuing on Utah 36, the route moves through the town of Stockton and turns westward on Utah 199, passing what was once a small settlement named Clover on the east side of the Stansbury Mountains and Johnson's Pass. Goshute Indians drew water from the springs on Clover Creek long before the coming of surveying crews and white settlers. When the Goodyear Cutoff was under construction, the convict laborers who carried out much of the work were housed on the other side of the mountain pass. By the mid-1930s, the old campground on Clover Creek was home to more than 130 young men of the Civilian Conservation Corps. Now, mule deer show up to water at the creek, and crows black as shiny licorice snack on fresh road kill.

At the summit of Johnson's Pass, it is only a short distance to Willow Springs and then a southerly run to the path of the old Pony Express and Stage Route, leading to Nevada. But before travelers motor on, a mandatory stop is Orr's Ranch in Skull Valley, just south of where Utah 199 and 193 meet. Between 1913 and 1927, when the Wendover Road that now follows Interstate 80 was adopted, this ranch was one of the most popular resting places for travelers on the Lincoln Highway. Remarkably, it still is.

A Lincoln Highway sign hangs on the ranch gate, and if travelers bouncing down the road leading to the headquarters roll down the dust-covered windows, they might hear the song of red-winged blackbirds. "Historic Orr's Ranch" is carved into a big slab of cottonwood on the side of the road.

The story of the ranch starts with Matthew Orr, a native of Scotland who came to the United States with his family in 1853. They settled in Salt Lake City, where Matthew and his father, a skilled stonemason, hired on when construction of the Mormon Temple began. By 1875, Matthew struck out southward and moved to Skull Valley. Attracted by some natural springs, Matthew in 1890 homesteaded the land that became Orr's Ranch. When he died in 1891, his widow, Mary Ann, and their trio of sons—William,

RIGHT *Orr's Ranch, Skull Valley, UT.*

LOWER RIGHT *Dennis Andrus inside the log cabin where Dwight Eisenhower stayed the night at Orr's Ranch, Skull Valley, UT.*

Hamilton, and Daniel—decided to stay on. For the next five years, they made improvements to the land—as required by law in order to "prove up" their claim to the homestead and take legal possession of the land.

William, born in 1868 and the oldest of the three Orr sons, married Pearl Kauffman in 1914, just after the original routing of the Lincoln Highway became official in their part of the country. They lived on the ranch and raised five daughters—Shirley, Doris, Lorraine, Charlotte, and Geraldine.

Word soon got around that motorists on the Lincoln Highway in Utah had best take advantage of a stop at Orr's Ranch for scarcities such as fuel and food. Mary Ann and Pearl were well known for serving fine turkey dinners with all the trimmings that only set a traveler back seventy-five cents. The spring water was plentiful—and so cold it froze the drinker's throat. The Orr boys also worked on the ranch. Dan Orr maintained a workshop, and gasoline was hauled from Tooele in fifty-five-gallon steel barrels to refill the tanks of parched cars that sputtered into the ranch. The old log cabin in which Matthew and Mary Ann had first lived was converted to a kitchen and a guest room that rented for a dollar a night. Some travelers camped in a pasture. Many who stopped for food or gasoline paid with silver dollars, which Pearl stashed away in a sack.

Turkey dinners and campsites are no longer available for travelers who manage to find their way to Orr's Ranch, but strangers who still show up are greeted warmly by William and Pearl Orr's daughter

LEFT *Top of a gasoline barrel, "MAN'F'D MAR 1913," at Orr's Ranch, Skull Valley, UT.*

Shirley and her husband, Dennis Andrus. With the help of a large family that includes three sons and many grandchildren, Shirley and Dennis operate the ranch and maintain many of the original buildings and artifacts. "I was raised here with the cattle and fields of hay and we rode on wild horse chases across the land," says Shirley, who has safely tucked away her mother's deerskin riding skirt and gauntlets.

"Our ranch has always been a gathering place," says Shirley. "You have to remember that we were the last stop around these parts, so everyone stopped here." That included Lincoln Highway champion Henry Joy in 1915; Henry Ostermann, the Lincoln Highway Association's field secretary; Orville and Wilbur Wright; ace aviator Eddie Rickenbacker; and a dashing young army officer named Dwight Eisenhower and his Transcontinental Motor Convoy in 1919.

when the cabin was built. A Lincoln Highway sign is nailed on an outside wall and Dan Orr's two gasoline barrels are still out back, where he always kept them.

A seventy-mile stretch of unpaved but fairly decent road runs from Orr's Ranch to the Nevada line. But everything changed around these parts, including the routing of the Lincoln Highway, in 1941 when World War II broke out and the U.S. Army established the Dugway Proving Ground, a major range and testing facility for chemical and biological weaponry. The top-secret site is about the size of Rhode Island, encompassing more than a million acres of desert surrounded on three sides by mountains. Operational by 1942, Dugway was used during the war to test toxic agents, flamethrowers, chemical spray systems, biological weapons, and protective clothing. The base remained active during the Korean War, and by the late 1950s it became the home of the U.S. Army Chemical, Biological, and Radiological Weapons School. Dugway Proving Ground not only is one of the most secretive military installations in the country but also is one of the most controversial because of the type of testing carried out there. Public awareness of the testing at Dugway was greatly heightened in March 1968, when more than 6,400 sheep were found dead in Skull Valley outside the Dugway boundaries. In spite of open-air tests conducted at Dugway, including one that took place the day before the incident, the Army would not admit any fault or liability but paid the ranchers for their losses.

"In western Utah, on the Salt Lake Desert, the road became almost inaccessible to heavy vehicles," Eisenhower later wrote in an official report about the arduous sixty-two-day journey. "From Orr's Ranch, Utah, to Carson City, Nevada, the road is a succession of dust, ruts, pits, and holes. This stretch was not improved in any way, and consisted only of a track across the desert."

The log cabin where Eisenhower bedded down for the night during his journey still survives. "My mother and grandmother cooked up a big meal and fed him and the other officers in that old cabin," says Shirley. Nearby is a stand of poplars that were planted back

ABOVE *Kearney's Ranch Hotel, Callao, UT.*

Once the army acquired the huge mass of land for the Dugway site, fences were erected and roads cut off, including the original route of the Lincoln Highway and the Goodyear Cutoff, built in 1919 but never paved. No public access is allowed within the Dugway perimeter, but it is easy enough to skirt the entire site and cut south on a rock-and-dirt road that follows the high fence posted with warning signs:

RESTRICTED AREA
USE OF DEADLY FORCE AUTHORIZED

The blunt message on the sign has no effect on large herds of pronghorn antelope that quietly graze on the other side of the fence. On either side of the dusty road, there is nothing but desert and occasionally more pronghorns and herds of sheep. Traveling the rugged Pony Express and Stage Route between Dugway and Fish Springs often is referred to as "riding the Pony"—not a particularly pleasant experience.

The road passes Simpson Springs, a popular watering stop for Indians and explorers such as Captain J. H. Simpson, whose name is attached to the site. Simpson paused at the watering hole in 1858 while searching for an overland mail route between Salt Lake City and California. Besides becoming a mail station, Simpson Springs served as a station for both the Pony Express and the Overland Express. From the 1890s—when gold mining started at nearby Gold Hill—until the 1920s, it was an

oasis for freighters and miners. In the 1930s, young men from a nearby Civilian Conservation Corps camp came to the springs for water. A stone building has been restored here, and there are a few remnants of foundations.

The road continues to amble through the sagebrush-scented desert. Sometimes falcons glide by, riding the

LEFT *Bonneville Salt Flats, UT. The huge steel sculpture, built by artist Karl Momen in the 1980s, is called* Metaphor: The Tree of Life.

hot wind, and dust devils twist far away. At another Pony Express monument, bullet holes mark the medallion. At Fish Springs, back in the days when the Lincoln Highway was riding high, a rancher posted a sign on the salt flats that read: "If in Need of Tow, Light Fire." The fellow knew well that inexperienced drivers who ran out of gas or became bogged down in the sand, mud, or snow could easily perish. Stranded travelers would gather sagebrush and anything combustible and make a bonfire. After what probably seemed like an eternity, along would come the rancher with his team of draft horses. During negotiations, the rancher quoted a price; if there was any balking, he kept raising his fee until all agreed.

In 1959, the Fish Springs National Wildlife Refuge was established. Visitors come to the 17,992-acre refuge—much of which is marshland fed by natural springs—to observe more than 275 species of birds, including swans, Canada geese, many varieties of ducks, snowy egrets, and great blue herons. Mosquitoes and gnats can be pesky at times. Except for restrooms

RIGHT *Muffler Man, Wendover, UT.*

and cold drinking water at the refuge headquarters, there is no lodging or food—and it is forty-two miles to the nearest gasoline and grocery store. The burned wreck of an old upside-down bus—looking rather like the remains of a landlocked whale—lies beyond the refuge to the west. Nearby, an abandoned mine shaft offers cool shade. In the 1890s and early 1900s, this mine and others in the area yielded lead and silver ores.

To the west are visible the peaks of the Deep Creek Range. The road leads to what was Boyd's Station, named for Bid Boyd, the station keeper. After the short-lived Pony Express went out of business, Boyd still lived in the rock building for more than fifty years. The old trail keeps going west to present-day Callao, once known briefly as Willow Springs Station. During his journey on the trail that became the Lincoln Highway, the English adventurer Sir Richard Burton made note of his visit to this Pony Express station: "The express rider was a handsome young Mormon, who wore in his felt hat the effigy of a sword. . . . The station-keeper was an Irishman, one of the few met amongst the Saints. Nothing could be fouler than the log hut, the flies soon drove us out of doors: hospitality, however, was not wanting and we sat down to salt beef and bacon for which we were not allowed to pay."

After passing the ghostly sites of the Pony Express, the trail leads to Ibapah, the last town on the route in Utah. Located in a valley next to the Deep Creek Range, Ibapah was settled in 1859. The trading post—used by many Lincoln Highway travelers—sits across from the old Sheridan Hotel. Two gas pumps remain active outside the trading post; inside on winter days, a fire burns constantly in the stove. Booted customers clomp across the plank floor, shopping for work gloves, canned goods, and other essentials. Back on the road, the residents of Ibapah erected a historical marker in 1997. Four plaques honor the history of the Lincoln Highway, the Pony Express, early settlers, and the Goshute tribe, whose members have lived in this area for centuries. Their reservation encompasses 108,000 acres across Utah and into Nevada. These days, tribal elders worry constantly about their culture vanishing as more young people leave the area.

The old route has run its course in Utah. Cattle sometimes wander across the road, and creatures make their moves in the shadowy twilight. A jackrabbit breaks from the brush and vanishes. Then a pronghorn appears just off the road in the sage—and then another and another. Soon a band of pronghorns is in flight and the race is on. There are no road signs, no notice of borders crossed—just the land and the last of the sun dropping behind the mountains.

Chapter Twelve

NEVADA

The Lincoln Highway entering Nevada was an unimproved dirt road in 1913 and nothing has changed. What does change is the time zone. Travelers enter the Pacific time zone, the fourth and last on the Lincoln Highway. But time and

borderlines are meaningless in these parts, where the only true boundaries are eternal mountains stacked row after row and a sky with no horizons.

After twenty miles of driving across the Goshute Indian Reservation and through wide valleys covered by tufts of bunch grass and sagebrush, a scattering of buildings and corrals comes into view—the Tippett Ranch. This once-thriving ranch was named for John Tippett, an enterprising Englishman who immigrated to the United States after the Civil War. Attracted by the lure of mineral riches in Nevada, Tippett and his partner, Frank Bassett, parlayed their early gold-prospecting success in White Pine County into ownership of the Glencoe Mine in Antelope Valley, on the west side of the Kern Mountains. Before the gold strike played out in the late 1800s, Tippett married Bassett's sister Alice, and together they established the ranch.

Besides running herds of sheep and cattle, the Tippetts and Bassett used some of their mining profits to form the

LEFT

Ely, NV.

Christmas [1902] when I was driving the mail we were at Tippett's Ranch and they had a dance there. There were only four women, so they could make a set for a quadrille. I played the harmonica and an old Scotsman played the harmonica also, and we traded off and danced all night."

Larson returned to the ranch the following year: "That Christmas we went back to Tippett's to a dance and this time there were only three women there, so I was the slimmest man. We drew presents under the Christmas tree, and I drew a Mother Hubbard dress and some corsets, so I put them on and danced with the men."

John Tippett died on a bitterly cold January day in 1906 and was laid to rest after gravediggers used black powder to blast open the frozen ground. His widow, Alice, married Gus Sellas, a hardworking Greek immigrant who pitched right in and helped run the ranch and mercantile store.

Early Lincoln Highway travelers pulled in at the Tippett Ranch to get a meal, precious fuel for their vehicles, radiator water, and often a drink of something stronger than tea brewed from sagebrush. For many years, in fact, the stretch of Lincoln Highway running from the bone-dry Utah border to Tippett Ranch was called Whiskey Road. Miners, ranchers, and passersby knew they could quench their thirst at the ranch. Goshute Indians from the reservation— where federal regulations prohibited the sale of whiskey—also came to buy beer, liquor, and wine.

Not only did the Tippett Ranch survive throughout the first part of the twentieth century, it also prospered

Tippett Mercantile Company. The ranch store soon became a popular supply center for locals and travelers, and between 1896 and the 1920s, it served off and on as a post office for the region.

When he was eighty-one in 1963, Raymond Larson recalled carrying the mail across the rangelands of Nevada and Utah in an open buggy or on horseback: "At during World War II and for years afterward, when farming and ranch operations boomed and business stayed brisk at the store. William Sellas, a younger brother of Alice Tippett's second husband, Gus Sellas, became the owner of the entire operation after Alice died in the 1920s. Sellas never married and became known for his generous spirit and work ethic. It was always said that no one was ever turned away from the

LEFT *Tippett Ranch, NV.*

Tippett Ranch, where some of the tastiest meals in Nevada were cooked on a woodstove. Over the years, family and trusted employees either died or moved away. In 1969, Bill Sellas—many miles and years away from the Greek village where he was born—breathed his last. The following spring, when a new crop of lambs and wildflowers appeared, the ranch and store were sold. Livestock continue to graze on the land, but the store is long closed and everything else is deserted. The old wooden sign listing the services offered has been replaced with one that says, "NO TRESPASSING." A corral surrounded by a fence of slender pine poles is empty. The large grain house with its thick plank floor, the chicken coop, and the blacksmith shop—all built in the 1890s of stacked stones with no mortar—are as stout as they were when the ranch was alive.

RIGHT *Moose sculpture, Ely, NV.*

OPPOSITE *Hotel Nevada, Ely, NV.*

Tippett Ranch is now a phantom place, but it is worth a visit. It is deathly still, with only the occasional sound of rusty corrugated tin rattling in the wind—except when the big cottonwoods are in leaf and the foliage creates a liquid whisper. The name *Tippett* stands out in raised letters over the door of the vacant ranch house. The aroma of sagebrush has replaced the smells of ranch life. Ducks splash on a stock pond, and in the soft mud are the tracks of deer and antelope. At the water's edge is a stump with a branch shaped like the thumb of a hitchhiker who will never get a ride.

Back on the road, majestic Wheeler Peak—sixty miles to the south and wearing a cap of snow—soars more than 13,000 feet into the heavens. The old route—only 675 miles to go before reaching San Francisco—winds past more ranchland and steadily climbs the road that the 1916 edition of the Lincoln Highway guidebook generously described as "90 percent excellent and 10 percent fair." The road here offers a stunning view of the Steptoe Valley as it crosses Schellbourne Pass at 7,650 feet, just south of Cherry Creek. Both a stage stop and a Pony Express relay station were near the pass, and later the Schellbourne Ranch acted as a highway stopover for motorists. Just beyond the pass, the original highway joins U.S. 93 coming south from the 1928 Wendover routing of the Lincoln.

Back on paved road, the route heads south to McGill, founded in the early 1900s and site of one of the busiest copper smelters in the nation. The ore was hauled by rail from the vast open-pit mines to the massive smelter. The operation shut down in 1983, after which residents began leaving McGill. Most of the smelter has been torn down, including the large smokestacks. The McGill Drug Store, a popular rendezvous for townspeople since it opened in 1908, closed in the mid-1980s, but the building still has a working soda fountain and all the fixtures. Listed on the National Register of Historic Places, it serves as a free public museum where visitors can get a glimpse of the past and top it off with an ice-cream soda.

Twelve miles south of McGill, the glow of lights beckons night ramblers to Ely, where there are plenty of places to take a hot shower, wrestle with a steak, and test one's luck at games of chance. One of the preferred spots for these pursuits is the historic Hotel Nevada and Gambling Hall, in the heart of downtown. When completed in 1929, the six-story hotel was not only the tallest building in the state but also the first one to be fireproof. For many years, the Nevada was a popular stopover for the Hollywood crowd en route to the slopes of Sun Valley. Over the years, the guest list has included Ingrid Bergman, Gary Cooper, Jimmy Stewart, Lyndon Johnson, Mickey Rooney, Ray Milland, and Evel Knievel. It is rumored that Frank Sinatra—without his "Rat Pack"—quietly checked in once or twice for some rest and recuperation from the hubbub of Las Vegas. Just like the rest of Ely—once home to several mining companies—the hotel has had to endure the boom-and-bust cycles of the copper industry. In the mid-1990s, the Nevada was completely restored, and the comfortable guest rooms are named for some of the many luminaries who once stayed there. Guests find a

pair of suckers on their pillows at night, a reference—in good fun—to the name for the vast majority of gamblers.

Across Aultman Street from the Hotel Nevada—on the site of the city's first hoosegow—stands the Jailhouse Motel and Casino, where customers can dine in their own cell. The neighboring Liberty Club, established in 1933 and serving since Prohibition, boasts that it's "Ely's Oldest Bar in Ely's Oldest Building." At the Liberty, patrons drink ice-cold beer while playing the slots, darts, pool, and shuffleboard. A vintage Lincoln Highway sign hangs on a wall; outside, another old sign suggests that everyone "Chew Copenhagen Snuff."

One of the many miners who toiled in the copper mines near Ely was William Ryan, a tough Irishman whose daughter Thelma Catherine Ryan was born March 16, 1912. Although his wife, Kate, was a native of Germany, Ryan nicknamed their baby girl "Pat" and called her his "St. Patrick babe in the morn." The Ryans soon moved to California, where Pat grew up to become a high-school teacher in Whittier. There in 1940, she met and married a young lawyer named Richard Nixon, the future president of the United States and her husband for forty-three years. When the Nixons visited Ely during a campaign junket, they waved from a convertible in a parade held in honor of one of the nation's most controversial political figures and his faithful wife, who started her life in Ely and became First Lady.

Another facet of the old mining town's heritage remains on the west end of High Street, in an area once known as "Bronc Alley." Starting in the 1880s, this red-light district filled three blocks on both sides of the street and supported numerous brothels, saloons, and dance halls. Like gambling, prostitution is legal in licensed brothels in most of Nevada, including Ely, where the world's oldest profession is practiced in the oldest bordello in town—the Big 4 Ranch.

Called Rainey's when it first opened in 1880, this establishment had many owners and names until the 1930s, when it became the Big 4—after the four prominent businessmen who bought and managed the brothel. Although it has changed hands several times since, the name has stuck, and the Big 4 Ranch has kept its doors open. Nevada's strict health regulations are followed and physicians periodically test women working at the Big 4. Customers must comply with the state's mandatory condom law. Novelty souvenir gifts are available, such as windproof cigarette lighters in erotic shapes and Big 4 casino chips that say, "Never Teasing, Always Pleasing."

In the late 1990s, when a city councilman started a campaign to ban legal prostitution in Ely, a crowd of more than four hundred citizens showed up at a public meeting to discuss the issue. It was estimated that only about thirty of those were opposed to brothels operating in the city limits. People from all walks of life spoke on behalf of the brothels, including a physician who tended to the employees' health issues. An elderly man recalled that when he was a boy, some of the "painted ladies" fed and clothed him and his younger sister while their widowed father toiled long hours in the mines. Business owners insisted that the women were never out of line and made good neighbors. Despite the uproar, the brothels remained open, and a slice of the town's history continues.

Capitalizing on history is one of the keys to Ely's success today, and, even though shopping malls and fast-food franchises have proliferated, Ely has retained much of its colorful past. Visitors can tour the Nevada Northern Railway Museum and then board a train pulled by a restored 1910 steam locomotive, for an excursion through old mining operations. Ely also is only an hour's drive from Great Basin National Park, Nevada's only national park, established in 1986. Within the park's more than 77,000 acres are limestone caves, groves of ancient bristlecone pines, alpine lakes, mountain streams and meadows, a glacier, and a plethora of hiking trails, which explains why a perennial best-selling book in Ely has been a birding guide.

After all bets have been placed and birds spotted, there is time for elk burgers at the Silver State Restaurant, followed by milk-shake chasers at Economy Drug, before bidding Ely farewell. To the west, the path of the Lincoln Highway becomes U.S. 50 across the

center of Nevada. This byway always came out second best to Interstate 80, the popular northern route that enters the state at Wendover on the Utah line. In the July 1986 issue of *Life* magazine, the 287-mile stretch of U.S. 50 between Ely and Fernley was described as "The Loneliest Road in America." The article went on to quote an unnamed Automobile Association of America adviser who was highly critical of the highway: "It's totally empty. We don't recommend it. We warn all motorists not to drive there unless they're confident of their survival skills."

When the "Loneliest Road" moniker stuck, the Nevada Commission on Tourism turned what was intended to be a negative into a positive. It marketed the once-disparaging phrase and developed a tongue-in-cheek promotional campaign encouraging travelers to use their "survival skills" to drive the maligned ribbon of road. The state legislature then officially designated this portion of U.S. 50 as "The Loneliest Road in America" and posted special signs along the route. Chambers of commerce, shops, and visitor centers, in fact, hand out "Highway 50 Survival Kits," which include a guide,

The Perfect Road Across Nevada
U. S. 50, THE LINCOLN HIGHWAY
THE COOLEST AND MOST SCENIC ROUTE THROUGH NEVADA
NEVADA U.S. 50   FASTEST, SAFEST, EAST-WEST ROUTE
Historical and Interesting
Parallels Old Pony Express and Overland Stage Route
Summer Temperature Maximum 90°, Minimum 45°   NEVADA U.S. 50

LEFT

Soda fountain at Economy Drug, Ely, NV.

LOWER LEFT

Vintage ad for "The Perfect Road Across Nevada, U.S. 50, The Lincoln Highway."

Survivors also may revel in the knowledge that by taking U.S. 50, they had a much more interesting trip than did those who chose the conventional interstate highway route far to the north. U.S. 50 roughly parallels the trail blazed by the brave Pony Express riders that became the Lincoln Highway. It passes through desert valleys and encounters switchbacks, numerous mountain passes, sagebrush flats, old mining camps, and ranchland. The road climbs snow-mantled mountain ranges, several with summits more than 7,000 feet. At times there is so little traffic that critters lie on the pavement to warm themselves. There are few towns and not many people along the way, but the rare stopping places are memorable.

West of Ely, the highway climbs up through Robinson Canyon near the old mining digs at Ruth, once headquarters for several famous open-pit copper mines, including the Liberty Pit, the state's largest. The road moves through Robinson Pass, at 7,607 feet; continues past Illipah, formerly known as Moorman's Ranch; and runs near Rosevear's Ranch, where only some stones and timbers remain. The roughly seventy-seven-mile stretch of highway between Ely and Eureka, the next town to the west, provides some of the best high-desert scenery in Nevada. Much of the original route is gone, but pieces show up here and there—along with old bypasses, dirt ranch roads, and trails that once led to active lead and silver mines. As the road moves over Little Antelope Summit and then Pancake Summit, with the Diamond

maps, and information about attractions and services. At several designated stops in four communities along the way, travelers can get their U.S. 50 travel passport stamped and then send the documentation to the state tourism office in Carson City. In return, the travelers receive an official "I Survived Highway 50" certificate signed by the governor and welcoming them to "a select group of hardy explorers, who have completed the journey across Highway 50 in Nevada." The certificate goes on to say that the recipient "may now revel in the knowledge that you have shown uncommon fortitude and courage by facing the unknown without flinching."

Mountains rising ahead, tall poles are used as markers on the edges of the road to guide snowplows in winter.

Beyond Pinto Summit, the highway turns northwest. Nestled in the cleavage of the mountains between two passes is Eureka, county seat and the only city in Eureka County. Once known as "The Pittsburgh of the West," Eureka was one of the largest towns in Nevada during the late 1800s, when sixteen smelters churned out great clouds of smoke and soot while producing silver that yielded a return second only to the legendary Comstock Lode. The riches produced at Eureka came with a steep price, however, in terms of human lives lost due to the lead fumes and lethal smoke of the smelter blast furnaces. For years, the sky was stained black and soot covered everything and everyone in the town. The air pollution was so terrible that most pregnant women left Eureka for at least eighteen months to ensure the health of their infants.

Winters were so brutal here that a system of brick-lined tunnels was used to get deliveries to the scores of saloons and also provide passage for children going to school. Winters are still long and fierce, but most of the tunnels have collapsed and almost no one walks to school. Through all the adversities, the stalwart citizens have remained hopeful, and Eureka boasts of being "The Friendliest Town on the Loneliest Road in America."

The city's focal point is the brick Eureka County Courthouse, built in 1879 and still open to the public, even though county offices have been moved to an annex. Near the courthouse are a 1928 concrete Lincoln Highway marker and a plaque commemorating the twenty-two-mile section of the Highway built near Eureka in 1919 with funding from General Motors. Other architectural highlights include a museum in the restored *Eureka Sentinel* newspaper offices and the Eureka Opera House, built in 1880 on the site of the burned-down Odd Fellows Hall. Travelers on the Lincoln Highway enjoyed coming to this theater as early as 1915, when the first silent movie was shown. Later, the building was restored and received a National Trust for Historic Preservation Honor Award in 1994.

At the Owl Club Bar and Steak House, travelers find that Eureka deserves its reputation for friendliness. Owner Lola Alanis—born in 1957 in Mexico City— creates daily menus reflecting her heritage as well as

LEFT *Rosevear's Ranch, NV.*

the culinary tastes of her adopted home. That means breakfast regulars and drop-ins can order huevos rancheros and fresh chorizo or ask for chicken fried steak with eggs. Although she has worked in large Mexican resorts, Lola has no regrets about downsizing to a remote Nevada community—especially one that has always welcomed newcomers. In the late 1800s,when the mining was at its height, more than seventy-five percent of Eureka's population was foreign-born. "I really found myself here," says Lola. "It is peaceful and when I lived in big cities, there was no time to even think. Now I walk with my dog up into the hills and I can think and pray. It is silent and serene. Up there I am closer to God."

Back on U.S. 50, the route encounters more mountain ranges and steep summits as it passes just north of Antelope Summit, rising to 10,220 feet. Forty-five miles west of Eureka is Hickison Summit—site of Indian petroglyphs dating as far back as 10,000 B.C. The ancient pictures and symbols—carved in sandstone in a gully north of the highway—are part of the Hickison Petroglyph Recreation Area, operated by the U.S. Bureau of Land Management. At a scenic overlook, mountain ranges tower in the distance; in the winter, cougar, deer, and rabbit tracks show up in the snow on a walking trail flanked by piñons and boulders covered with the mysterious glyphs. Near this place, an early generation of the Lincoln Highway once ran.

Travelers stopped at the summit and broke out tins of meat and fruit while their car radiators cooled. Piles of rusted litter and broken glass (varicolored from the desert sun) serve as a reminder of times past.

Twenty-five miles ahead, after climbing the 7,484-foot Austin Summit, travelers find the ramshackle town of Austin huddled on the north slope of the Toiyabe Mountains. Junkyard dogs yap and howl at the entrance to this old mining town that, like Eureka, at one time boasted a population of close to 10,000. That number has shrunk over the years to about 250 full-time residents, who see to it that their town retains much of its gritty historic patina. At least eleven buildings—churches and places of business—are listed on the National Register of Historic Places, including the International Hotel, built in Virginia City in 1859 and moved to Austin in 1863. The Gridley Store, built in 1863, was operated by Reuel C. Gridley, a man best remembered for losing an election bet in 1864 and having to carry a bag of flour down Main Street from one end of town to the other. Gridley did not stop there but went on with his famous sack to Virginia City, Sacramento, San Francisco, and several other cities, raising more than $275,000 to fund the Sanitary Commission, a relief agency for Union soldiers.

A mile west of town, Stokes Castle is a major local attraction. The three-story stone tower was built in 1897 for Anson Phelps Stokes, an East Coast financier with an eccentric streak and substantial mining interests in the Austin area. Intended as a summer home for the

Stokes family, the castle was an exact replica of an ancient watchtower near Rome. It was constructed of eight hundred tons of hand-hewn native granite. Stokes, his family, and a few friends traveled west in June 1897 and spent a month at the castle. They returned for a few days later that year and again in the summer of 1898, when Stokes sold out of the mining business. Once those ties were severed, however, the Stokes family never stayed another night in the castle. Over the next half-century, the property went through a series of owners and fell into disrepair. In the 1950s, a promoter attempted to purchase the structure and move it to the Las Vegas strip. To halt any more such schemes and make sure the castle stayed in the family, a Stokes relative bought the property in 1966. Now surrounded by a chain-link fence to prevent vandalism, the tower provides spectacular vistas over the picturesque Reese River Valley.

LEFT *Left behind by the Lincoln Highway's "Tin Can Tourists," Hickison Summit, NV.*

According to local lore, the Shoe Tree was started by a honeymooning couple camped by the tree who started squabbling. When the angry bride said she was going to take off down the highway, her groom replied that if she did, she would be barefoot. He tied her shoestrings together and pitched her shoes into the tree, where they dangled from a branch. Then the man jumped in the car and drove to a saloon in nearby Middlegate, where, after a beer or two, the bartender convinced him to return to his wife. The next year, the happy couple returned and tossed their new baby's first pair of shoes into the tree. From then on, legions of passersby have followed suit. Tennis shoes, running shoes, cowboy boots, ballet slippers, high-heeled shoes, sandals, and every other imaginable kind of footwear hang from the tree.

A couple of miles west of the Shoe Tree, the folks at Old Middlegate Station continue to dispense cold beer, hospitality, and a steady stream of road wisdom. This oasis, operated by Russ and Fredda Stevenson, includes a bar, cafe, small grocery, RV campground, and a few rental cabins. The entire ceiling over the bar and restaurant is covered with folding money of every denomination, placed there over the years by customers from around the world. "It was said that this all started in the old mining days, when a bartender served as a banker," says Russ Stevenson. "He'd write the miners' names on the bills and pin the money to the ceiling for safekeeping. The ceiling became their bank, and when they needed some money, the bartender would get it for them." Stevenson figures there are several thousand

After Austin, the next town of any size is Fallon, a hundred miles to the west. This stretch of road is one of the most isolated on the old Lincoln route, as it snakes through New Pass Canyon, Alpine, and Cold Springs to Eastgate. At this point, the original route and a 1925 loop to the south that traversed Carroll Summit meet up and become one. About a mile west of the junction is the Shoe Tree, a giant cottonwood festooned with hundreds of pairs of shoes. For many of those who stop to toss a pair of shoes into the boughs, the tree is living art.

LEFT AND LOWER RIGHT *Austin, NV.*

LOWER LEFT *"The Loneliest Road in America," Austin, NV.*

American dollars sticking to his ceiling, as well as money from Russia, China, Switzerland, Japan, and many other foreign nations. One section of the ceiling is reserved for the many U.S. Navy flyers stationed at nearby Fallon who come to Middlegate for rations of beer.

On quiet evenings, when only the coyotes are singing, the Stevensons and their regulars still talk about the mysterious man wearing a pea coat and thick eyeglasses who camped outside in his Ford Econoline van for two weeks in 1991. It turned out to be author Stephen King, on a cross-country research trip. "He'd always come in here to eat and he'd sit at the bar and write on a legal pad," says Fredda. "It was kind of creepy." King must have been inspired. A few years later, *Desperation*, a horror novel about several people traveling the desolate U.S. 50 in Nevada, was published and eventually made into a television movie.

After pinning a dollar to the ceiling, travelers push west to Fallon. The route cruises by Frenchman's Station

and Sand Springs, and then near Rawhide Ranch, a legendary nudist colony. It also passes a solar-powered public telephone known as "The Loneliest Phone on the Loneliest Road in America." At Salt Wells, the lights of Fallon are visible at night; often during the day, sonic booms resonate as jets from the Naval Air Station at Fallon (where "Top Gun" pilots train) streak through the sky.

The Overland Hotel and Saloon on East Center Street in Fallon remains a reliable haunt for road warriors of the Lincoln Highway. Built in 1908, the hotel had a sterling reputation by the time it found itself on the original Lincoln Highway route through town. The hotel paid special attention to travelers and provided a free bus to meet all trains. Since the day its doors opened, the Overland has never closed. George Machado, a retired trucker, bought the property in 1996 and maintains the same standard of service that made the Overland one of the Lincoln Highway's

RIGHT *Remains of the Carroll Summit Station, Summit, NV.*

LOWER RIGHT

Carroll Summit, NV, 1950s.

CARROLL SUMMIT

most desirable stopovers. Keeping in mind Nevada's heritage of Basque settlers and sheepherders, Machado offers diners a selection of Basque lamb dishes, as well as beef tongue, trout, and Rocky Mountain oysters. "Many of the people who come here to eat or drink in the saloon or rent one of our guest rooms are fans of the Lincoln Highway," says Machado. "We are very aware of the road's importance to Fallon and to this business."

About ten miles west of Fallon, the Lincoln Highway route split. The main route continued west to Reno and then crossed into California at Donner Pass. A longer route, called the Pioneer Branch, turned southwest and took travelers through Nevada's capital of Carson City and around the southern end of picturesque Lake Tahoe. Years later, the Pioneer Branch became U.S. 50 and the northern route became alternate U.S. 50 to Fernley and from there U.S. 40 (today's Interstate 80) to Reno. At Fernley, where I-80 and alternate U.S. 50 meet en route to Reno and beyond, Mary & Moe's Wigwam Restaurant, Casino, and Indian Museum is a gathering place just as it was when Mary and Moe Royels opened it as the Dainty Cone in 1961. No longer simply a drive-in for ice cream and burgers, the Wigwam survived I-80's bypassing of Fernley in the mid-1960s and even expanded, thanks to hard work and a loyal customer base.

Reno—"The Biggest Little City in the World"—is only thirty miles west of Fernley. The state's legalization of casino gambling in 1931, and the passage of liberal divorce laws, put Reno on most radar screens. Even though the quickie-divorce business died as more

LEFT *Carpet Genie, Reno, NV.*

states passed laws easing divorce requirements, the gambling industry has grown ever larger. Ironically, so has the quickie-wedding business, as a result of relaxed marriage regulations. The Chapel of the Bells, open since 1962, was Reno's first drive-through wedding chapel. Lovebirds in a hurry can be married in the comfort of their car just by pressing a button for quick service at

the drive-up window. The chapel accepts all major credit cards. For those wishing to go through a more formal ceremony indoors, there is no lack of conveniences—from a wheelchair ramp to such services and extras as wedding photos, video recordings, bridal bouquets, champagne goblets, wedding gowns, and honeymoon lingerie. The basic cost for the paperwork and the filing fee is twenty dollars, with a $12.50 surcharge if the couple needs a witness.

Heading out of glitzy Reno, with its many vintage motel signs and blinking neon, the route moves on to Mogul, where a distinctive bridge from 1914 spells out "Lincoln" and "Highway" on the two opposing rails. It was saved from destruction and relocated to a safe pull-off on I-80.

Only the town of Verdi remains before the road reaches the California state line. Founded as a mill and railroad town in 1867, Verdi of course was named for the famed Italian opera composer Giuseppe Verdi. In 1870, one of the first train robberies in the West occurred near Verdi when a Sunday school superintendent named John Chapman and some confederates boarded the Central Pacific Overland Express and commandeered the train. They made off with $41,000 in gold coins but were later captured and convicted.

This northern route of the Lincoln Highway was the path taken by the Donner-Reed Party. The only natural landmark those overland pioneers would recognize today is the Sierra Nevada, the range that doomed their long trek. Winter travelers snug inside their heated vehicles with snow-chained tires cross the Truckee River over the reinforced-concrete Truckee River Arch Bridge, just east of California's border. Their only worry is which restaurant to choose when they stop for lunch in the land of milk and honey.

Chapter Thirteen

CALIFORNIA

When the Lincoln Highway reaches California, the western terminus of the historic route is less than two hundred miles away. The end of the road is so near, in fact, that travelers could make dinner reservations at a San Francisco restaurant.

Committed open-roaders, however, will pace themselves and savor the last leg of the trip. No need to hurry.

In previous eras, drivers felt exhilarated just knowing they were almost there. The difficult part of their trek was behind them and, once the Sierra Nevada were crossed, the rest of the highway to the Golden Gate was mostly concrete and downhill.

Alice Ramsey—a twenty-two-year-old from New Jersey who made highway history in 1909 when she became the first woman to drive an automobile from coast to coast—was ecstatic when she and her three female companions reached the California border. More than fifty years after their journey, she wrote:

Victory was in sight. We had passed the worst of our road problems, and the heat too. All around us were mountain peaks and each time we stopped the views became more extensive and more gorgeous. Trees were plentiful and greener than we had seen for a long time. It was incredible that so soon after

LEFT

The Highway Garage, built in 1915, Livermore, CA.

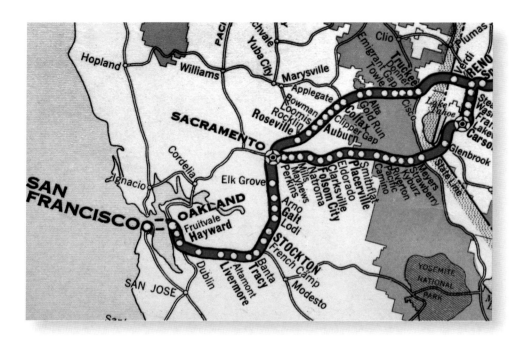

leaving that arid, barren desert we could be refreshed in the cool shade of towering evergreens. . . . Majestic sugar pines, Douglas firs and redwoods lined our road on both sides. What a land! What mountains! What blue skies and clear, sparkling water! We almost chirped as we exclaimed over the grandeur that surrounded us on both sides.

The Ramsey party took what became the southern route, or Pioneer Branch, of the Lincoln Highway (west from Carson City and around the southern shore of Lake Tahoe). This route crossed the Sierra via Echo Pass at 7,394 feet, a mile west of Meyers, an old Pony Express stop originally known as Yank's Station.

Travelers taking that path today stick to the Pony Express Trail, now U.S. 50, through Little Norway, Phillips, Strawberry, and Kyburz into Placerville. From there, it is not far to Sacramento, where the Pioneer Branch rejoins the northern route of the Lincoln, running from the California line through Truckee, past Donner Lake and over the Donner Pass, more or less following today's Interstate 80.

It is difficult to comprehend what miseries the eighty-seven members of the Donner-Reed Party endured that infamous winter of 1846–47 when they were trapped by storms that buried the upper elevations of the Sierra Nevada in deep snow. Their plight might even stir feelings of guilt in some road-weary travelers soaking in a clawfoot tub at the Truckee Hotel, originally opened as the American House in 1873, twenty-six years after the forty-six Donner-Reed Party survivors were rescued. The guilt intensifies after a meal of deep-fried chicken with applesauce and peanut butter cookies still hot to the touch at Smart's Wagon Train Coffee Shop, a reliable stop since 1947.

Truckee, a corrupted version of a Paiute Indian chief's name, was a rough-and-tumble railroad and lumbering town in the late 1800s. Saloons, bawdyhouses, and gambling dens lined Front Street, where a "lively scrimmage" often erupted among the overflow of rowdy lumberjacks, cowpunchers, Chinese laborers, and railroaders. Most of the shenanigans and violence were blamed on a combination of liquor and the incredible winter storms that paralyzed the town and gave folks a good case of cabin fever.

Rich oral history abounds in this region. Residents still tell stories of the most unforgettable storms, such as the brutal winter of early 1889, when by January sixth more than twenty-four feet of snow had fallen in Truckee and the temperature plummeted to thirty-five degrees below zero. Twenty-foot snowdrifts in the winter of 1907 snapped power lines in Donner Pass and plunged a large portion of California and Nevada into darkness. By the time spring arrived, a record 884 inches of snow had fallen in the Sierra. There are tales of the mammoth snows of 1911 and 1916, and of the "Friday the Thirteenth Storm" in November 1931, when fifty-four inches of snow fell in just five days and bootleggers had a difficult time making their deliveries. Still, most old-timers agree that the blizzard of 1952 was "The Mother of All Storms." For one week, starting on January 10, a single snowstorm covered Donner Pass with 154 inches of snow, while eighty mph winds created snowdrifts more than forty-four feet high. Mail was carried by sleigh. Small houses were buried and residents of larger houses used their second-story windows as front doors.

These epic snowfalls also enabled Truckee to evolve into a resort city. As early as 1913, the first California ski club was organized in Truckee. Townspeople realized the potential impact of the new road on the entire region and the nation. "The great importance of the proposed highway to the entire country is indicated by the rivalry between all of the cities through the middle of the West and on the Pacific Coast to have the highway pass through them," reported the September 21, 1913, edition of the *San Francisco Examiner*.

Between 1913 and 1928, many skiers crossed the Sierra on the Lincoln Highway at Donner Pass. They continue to come in large numbers on I-80, as do vacationers drawn by Lake Tahoe, just to the south. Tourism drives the economy, and the area has become a major destination for year-round recreation.

Heading west past Truckee beneath Interstate 80, the Lincoln stays south of the interstate on Donner Pass Road. Southeast of picturesque Donner Lake in Donner Memorial State Park, the human and natural history of

BELOW *Cave Rock, Lake Tahoe, CA.*

the region is on display at the Emigrant Trail Museum. The Pioneer Monument, dedicated in 1918 and located near the museum and one of the Donner campsites, honors all who made the perilous journey across the Great Plains and mountain ranges to reach California.

It is often believed—in fact, it has become part of American legend—that some of the Donner-Reed Party, in order to stave off starvation, resorted to eating from the corpses of those who had died. In 2006, however, at a Donner-Reed Party symposium during a national conference hosted by the Society for Historical Archaeology, new data were released casting doubt on whether any of the survivors resorted to cannibalism. Based on archaeological research conducted at the Donner encampments, scientists identified bones of deer, dogs, horses, oxen, and rodents but could not conclusively prove that any of the fragments were human. While they could not claim for certain that the snowbound survivors of the 1846 expedition *did not* resort to cannibalism, the findings questioned the long-held belief. "The Donner Party's experience was bad, but it wasn't as bad as everybody's been told," said University of Oregon anthropologist Julie Schablitsky, after completing a three-year study.

In winter, the snow often closes the road in the area, precluding travelers from reaching the reinforced-concrete Donner Summit Rainbow Bridge erected just east of the pass in 1926 and restored in 1995. Several roads were built to mount the Donner Summit, including wagon trails, the dirt Lincoln of 1913, U.S. 40, and finally Interstate 80 in 1962, about two miles north of the original mountain pass. In compliance with state law and to ensure a safe journey through the steep granite walls of the 7,239-foot Donner Pass, drivers strap chains on their vehicle's tires in winter.

After travelers negotiate the pass, the payoff comes soon enough. The westward route passes Soda Springs, Big Bend, Cisco Grove, using I-80 through Emigrant Gap—the boundary between the High Sierra and the foothills—and

VIRILE TO RISK AND FIND; KINDLY WITHAL AND A READY HELP. FACING THE BRUNT OF FATE INDOMITABLE—UNAFRAID.

OPPOSITE *Donner Summit Bridge, Donner Lake, CA.*

LEFT *Donner Party Memorial, near Truckee, CA.*

ABOVE *Vintage ad for Raffles Hotel, Placerville, CA.*

UPPER RIGHT *Ranger Phil Sexton in Big Bend, Tahoe National Forest, CA, on an alignment of the original Lincoln Highway.*

RIGHT *Panning for gold, Auburn, CA. The sculpture is by local dentist Dr. Kenneth Fox.*

then, flanked by cedars and pines, continues on to Baxter, Gold Run, Colfax, and Applegate. Remnants of the Lincoln combine with I-80 moving through this countryside and into towns that reinforce the stereotypical image of California—manicured flower beds, luscious fruit trees, athletic-looking people, and neighborhoods as neat as grandma's underwear drawer.

Auburn, the seat of Placer County and once a gold-mining camp in the foothills, is straight out of central casting, with a remarkable Old Town section. Vintage downtown businesses line Lincoln Way, now transformed into a promenade of shops and offices and the Auburn Hotel. Patrons at the Auburn Country Grill peruse a menu listing daily specials, steaks, ribs, and other "awesome vittles." Another dining choice up the street is the Club Car Restaurant & Lounge, also open seven days a week and featuring live entertainment. The Auburn Drug Company, which has been around since 1896, has retained its marble soda fountain so that customers waiting for prescriptions can enjoy a creamy treat. Lee Photo has developed the town's snapshots since 1945, while down the block are an honest-to-goodness barbershop, a chocolate shop, a jewelry shop, and three independent shoe stores. A middle-aged man locking up his store for the evening nods at passing travelers who exclaim that they have not seen one chain store in the entire downtown. "And you won't ever see one," remarks the man as he turns the key.

The western route out of Auburn to Newcastle, Penryn, Loomis, and Rocklin includes some remnants of the original Lincoln. After passing through Roseville, the highway enters the suburbs of Sacramento, the state capital founded in 1848 by John Sutter. Historically associated with roads and trails, Sacramento is where the forty-niners came to seek their fortunes. Depending on their destination, Pony Express riders ended or started their daring rides from Sacramento, as did Wells Fargo coaches. Railroads, steamboats, and highways—including the Lincoln—made Sacramento a major commercial center.

As in Auburn, the older part of Sacramento is called Old Town and takes in several blocks of restored Gold Rush—era buildings lining cobblestone streets. A large bronze statue of a Pony Express rider stands frozen in time beneath the elevated lanes of the freeway on the edge of the district. Visitors to the California State Railroad Museum and the Towe Auto Museum learn how travelers over the years have literally been drawn to the historic city. Sacramento—called Sac, Sactown,

or Sacto by hip locals—has had its share of interesting personalities. Noted author Joan Didion, for example, was born in Sacramento; Theodore "Ted" Kaczynski, the "Unabomber," reportedly resided for a time in the Hotel Berry; and in 1975, Lynette "Squeaky" Fromme, one of Charles Manson's devotees, was pinched for trying to shoot President Gerald Ford at Capitol Park. In 1960, hometown boy Russ Solomon—a pop music icon—opened the first Tower Records store in his father's pharmacy in the Tower Building at 16th and Broadway.

Early Lincoln Highway travelers generally felt as though their journey was almost over when they reached Sacramento. And for all practical purposes, it was. Drivers making the journey today have to decide which of the two Lincoln routings to follow from Sacramento to San Francisco. The original 1913 Lincoln left Sacramento to the south and proceeded through the Central Valley to Elk Grove, Galt, Lodi, and Stockton, seat of San Joaquin County. From Stockton,

the highway turned slightly southwest to French Camp, Banta, Tracy, and Altamont—where, at a speedway in 1969, a free Rolling Stones concert turned into what became known as the Altamont Death Festival. As the Stones sang "Sympathy for the Devil," a posse of Hells Angels, hired as security guards for five hundred dollars' worth of beer, clubbed bystanders with pool cues and stabbed and kicked to death a young man who dared approach the stage. After the Altamont Pass, the original Lincoln came to Livermore and through Dublin Canyon to Hayward, followed by Oakland and then a ferry ride across the bay to San Francisco.

In 1928, the Lincoln Highway was rerouted to a new alignment that roughly follows Interstate 80 westward across the Sacramento River via the art deco Tower Bridge to West Sacramento, where several low-budget motels cling to the roadside amid a hodgepodge of debris-laden vacant lots and weather-beaten produce stands. The route then crosses marshlands studded with bulrushes on the Yolo Bypass, a three-mile causeway.

On the other side of the wetlands is Davis, home of a branch of the University of California as well as the famous Redrum Burger, an enormous one-pound hamburger that has been a Davis tradition since 1986. Originally called the Murder Burger, this new name—*murder* spelled backward—was selected by owner Jim Edlund following a naming contest after locals complained about the original name.

This routing then moves on to Dixon and then Vacaville, towns that became famous for orchards of

almonds, walnuts, figs, peaches, and apricots. Vacaville maintains a historic downtown and has created a Lincoln Highway interpretive site at the restored Ulatis Creek Bridge. From this point, the pull of San Francisco Bay grows stronger as the road proceeds toward Fairfield—with a 1928 concrete highway marker in front of the Solano County Courthouse—and then merges through the maze of freeways into Cordelia and Vallejo on San Pablo Bay. The route winds past the old port towns of Rodeo, Pinole, San Pablo, and the deepwater harbor of Richmond, where the air fills with salt water and industrial smells as travelers push on to El Cerrito.

Ahead are Berkeley, Oakland, and Emeryville, edging the bay waters across from San Francisco, the final city on the highway. The 1928 route of the Lincoln came into downtown Berkeley near the water. Home of the renowned state university, Berkeley has long been a place where drifters and outcasts find themselves. Dharma bums such as Jack Kerouac and Gary Snyder lived within a stone's throw of the Lincoln Highway's route on San Pablo Avenue, and a historic punk music club sits on Gilman Avenue, a few blocks up from the thundering freeway. Residents of this notoriously progressive town still meet sometimes at the Berkeley Pier and march up to campus for a demonstration, or merely to have a parade.

The pier itself at one point stretched nearly three miles into the bay toward San Francisco. It was built

to be a deepwater dock for an auto ferry, but it fell into disrepair after the Bay Bridge opened in 1931. Now there is only a trail of decaying pylons for much of that span. Currently, the pier extends a more modest 3,000 feet into the waves and is covered with birds and fisherman.

Providing a fitting symmetry, the Lincoln Highway starts and finishes its transcontinental journey by crossing water—the Hudson River back east and San Francisco Bay at the terminus. Drivers take Interstate 80 over the San Francisco–Oakland Bay Bridge.

When the Lincoln Highway first opened, a major draw for early travelers was the 1915 Panama-Pacific International Exposition in San Francisco. The world's fair was supposed to celebrate the discovery of the Pacific Ocean and the completion of the Panama Canal, but most San Franciscans saw it as an opportunity to showcase their city's remarkable recovery after the devastating 1906 earthquake. The fair grounds were constructed on 635 acres of swampy land reclaimed from the bay in a part of the Presidio now known as the Marina District.

The fair opened on February 20, 1915, as throngs of people rushed into the grounds. From opening day until midnight of December 4, when a bugler blew "Taps" from the Tower of Jewels, more than eighteen million people passed through the entrance gate. Among the celebrity fairgoers that year were former presidents Theodore Roosevelt and William Howard Taft, future president Franklin D. Roosevelt, "Buffalo Bill" Cody, Thomas Edison, Henry Ford, and such silent-film sensations as

Charlie Chaplin, Mabel Normand, and Fatty Arbuckle. A quiet youngster named Ansel Adams, destined to become one of the world's most acclaimed nature photographers, was a frequent visitor.

Undoubtedly everyone's favorite building at the fair was the magnificent Palace of Fine Arts, designed by Bernard Maybeck and inspired by ancient Greek and Roman architecture. The central dome, buff-colored Corinthian colonnades, and towering walkways were reflected in a lagoon. Maybeck's intent was for the palace to resemble a Roman ruin in order to show, in his words, "the mortality of grandeur and the vanity of human wishes."

In a twist of irony, the palace is the only building remaining from the 1915 exposition. Everything else was torn down soon after the gates closed, but the palace was so popular that San Franciscans could not bear to have it dismantled. Yet, over the years, the building meant to look like a ruin ironically became one. It was not properly maintained, and vandals had their way with it. After World War II, the newly created United Nations, which first convened in San Francisco on April 25, 1945, used the palace for a limousine motor pool. Eventually declared unsafe, the building was slated for demolition. Determined efforts to save the remarkable piece of architecture—including one in which Maybeck took part in 1957, at the age of ninety-five—proved effective, and building restoration started in the early 1960s. Today the palace continues to attract visitors.

Francisco Peninsula above the Presidio—the old garrison with its ancient eucalyptus trees—and the enormous Golden Gate Bridge. The road leads to Lincoln Park, along the headland of Point Lobos. This land originally was a cemetery, mostly for paupers and Chinese immigrants, until 1901, when officials banned all burials within the city limits. In 1909, it became a park and some graves were removed, but many of the deceased still lie beneath the rolling sod. In 1923, the park was chosen as the site of the Palace of the Legion of Honor, a replica of the French pavilion from the 1915 exposition. Surrounded by pines and cypress trees, the museum was dedicated on Armistice Day in 1924 in honor of the 3,600 Californians who died during World War I. It holds a large collection of paintings, sculpture, and decorative arts, including more than a hundred sculptures by Auguste Rodin.

In late afternoon, the light reflects off the lagoon and a pair of swans glide through water fringed with great Monterey cypress trees. From this special place, travelers continue the last few miles of their long journey to the San

The original Lincoln Highway markers in Lincoln Park vanished long ago. In 2002, however, a replica terminus marker was erected on the edge of the parking lot, near a bus stop overlooking a golf course. On the marker, adorned with the Abraham Lincoln medallion and the distinctive "L" are the words, "WESTERN TERMINUS OF THE LINCOLN HIGHWAY." When an old man waiting to board a bus notices people looking at the marker, he says aloud, to no one in particular, "I traveled that road. Is it still there?"

For some travelers, the trip cannot end in this park, no matter how beautiful. The journey continues to the edge of the Pacific below the steep cliffs of Sutro Heights and the ruins of the Sutro Baths, named for Prussian-born Adolph Sutro, the generous man of wealth who loved his city and the sea that embraces it. The Cliff House, a place of refreshment and comfort that has endured fires and remodeling through numerous incarnations since 1863, welcomes travelers. This is Land's End.

Below the Cliff House on Ocean Beach, tides sweep away the morning's sand castles. No surfers are in sight, and only a few people venture out on the beach. All that remain are broken shells and sand dollars and a few vanishing footprints, as well as the memories of past times on these same sands—times in the 1960s when the country's young men and women spent unforgettable days prowling the city's back streets and frenzied boulevards while protests raged. And the rich recollections of evenings spent on the beach, sipping sweet wine, counting the Pacific stars, and feeding driftwood and dreams into a fire that everyone thought would never burn out.

Inside cars parked along the seawall are all sorts of people. One man pulls a tripod and camera equipment from the back of a battered van with a surfboard strapped on the roof. Born in Bogotá, Colombia, in 1944, Luis Pinillos moved to California twenty years later. He has never left. He comes to Ocean Beach every afternoon, no matter whether it is raining or foggy. He sets up his video camera and records the sights and sounds of the beach at sunset. On the sound tracks of his videos are the cries of gulls, howling wind, crashing surf, and the songs of whales and dolphins. "This is my playground," says Luis. "I feel so alive here. It is very cold, but that is the price of magic." Squawking gulls and a few crows hover above him and sweep down to grab pieces of bread he tosses into the wind. When the sun disappears into the ocean and all the bread is gone, Luis packs up his gear and leaves. As he pulls away, he is smiling, just as he was when he first arrived.

In New York, where the old road starts, life is going a mile a minute, just as it should. And along the road of Mister Lincoln—across the land in villages, farmhouses, and cities—the lights are turning off one by one. Another day has finished on the Lincoln Highway. The journey has come to an end.

WESTERN
TERMINUS
OF THE
LINCOLN
HIGHWAY

Acknowledgments

I AM A SON OF THE OPEN ROAD. I seek out those remaining ribbons of varicose concrete and asphalt paths that remind all of us of a time before America was generic. In so doing, I sometimes think of John Steinbeck and his writing about highways and those who travel them. I consider Steinbeck on the morning of October 26, 1938. On that day, while fighting flu and facing all the demons that writers have to battle daily, he completed writing *The Grapes of Wrath*. The last sentence of his diary entry for that date reads: "Finished this day—and I hope to God it's good."

Indeed it was good and will remain so forever. Steinbeck's classic book deserves to be read and reread for the lessons it teaches. It is a book worthy of a standing ovation.

In accepting the 1962 Nobel Prize for Literature, Steinbeck said: "The ancient commission of the writer has not changed. He is charged with exposing our many grievous faults and failures, with dredging up to the light our dark and dangerous dreams for the purpose of improvement."

Early in my life I was fortunate to figure out that I wanted to be a writer. I had no notion it would be such an interesting journey. Through my writing I am leaving enough of the past—including my own past—to help others know where they are going by looking back to see where we have been. Yet it is important not to dwell in the past, but instead to learn the lessons the past teaches. As the proverb puts it:

Live not in the past, look instead towards the future,
But in order to know where we are going
It is well to look back to see where we have been.

In writing this book about the Lincoln Highway, I was most fortunate to encounter many people who were willing to share their time and wisdom with me so that I could better understand this historic roadway's past, present, and future. To every man, woman, and child I have met in the thirteen states the Lincoln Highway traverses, I offer my sincere thanks. That goes for every waitress, mechanic, service-station attendant, fry cook, cop, farmhand, salesperson, and shopkeeper along the way. Every one of them has earned my respect and my everlasting gratitude.

I am so honored and pleased to have worked as a creative partner with Michael Williamson, one of the most brilliant and committed photographers I have ever known. Michael's poignant images allow all those who pick up our book to see inside the heart and soul of a highway that bridges America and acts as a mirror reflecting the nation it has served for so long. Michael, my friend, you are a maestro with your camera. It was a pleasure to travel the road with you and be part of this memorable experience. Muchas gracias.

An extra special helping of praise has to go to Anne Garrett and Jim Fitzgerald of the James Fitzgerald Agency. Not only are Jim and Anne my talented literary agents but, more important, two of my truest friends. Simply put, without their help this book would not have been published. And that would have been a damned shame. Jim served with valor on the home front while Anne accompanied Michael Williamson and me on one of the definitive road journeys down the Lincoln Highway. From Times Square to the Golden Gate, she put up with the hardships and savored the pleasures of open-road travel. She endured the good, the bad, and sometimes the ugly on a lengthy trek with two veteran road warriors who like nothing more than telling stories, consuming road chow, and seeking out the unpredictable. And that, dear Anne, is why this book is dedicated to you.

At W. W. Norton, my longtime editor and friend, Robert Weil, helped keep the book and me on track. For that I am grateful. Robert has edited many of my previous works, and his wisdom, diligence, and devotion have been invaluable. Thanks, my good friend—as usual, you went above and beyond. I look forward to following more roads with you in the future. Bob's gifted assistant, Tom Mayer, not only helped tremendously in the evolution of the book but also provided me with some insight into the Bay Area communities around the western terminus of the Lincoln Highway.

Without the love, understanding, and support of Suzanne Fitzgerald Wallis, my own true love and life partner, this journey would not have been possible. Suzanne resides in my psyche and soul and makes every day a masterpiece. And both of us recognize the importance of our feline muse, Cosmo, at one time a no-name cat prowling the Osage Prairie and now the ruler of our hearts.

My appreciation also goes to all my family and friends for their continued encouragement and support. You are the best.

—MICHAEL WALLIS

IT WAS A WARM EVENING in late summer of 1965 when Grandpa Beatty interrupted my firefly-catching experiment. I was a crazed eight-year-old staying with him for the summer at his Springfield, Illinois, home hoping to catch enough of the blinking bugs to fill a mason jar and light up a room. I was at least five hundred bugs short when he gave me one of those "good news, bad news" speeches. The bad news: It was time to get packing as we would be leaving the next morning so that I could get back to my home in Los Angeles in time for the new school year, due to start the following week.

The good news was that we'd be driving the entire 2,400 miles on Route 66 in Grandpa's huge, black 1959 Lincoln Continental Mark IV. The car had an unusual feature in that its flat rear window was electric and rolled down into the back seat. I lost my rights to roll it down after he eyed me in the rear view mirror launching spitballs with my slingshot at cars I thought were following us too close.

Because he was a diabetic, Grandpa had to stop often on the five-day trip both to rest and to take his insulin shots. While he napped, I had the run of various truck stops, curio shops, tourist traps, and roadside attractions. I made a complete nuisance of myself by constantly begging truckers to sound their air horns, mooching ice water at the diners, and asking inane questions of motorcycle riders such as, "Can you ride with no hands on the handlebars?" Of course I volunteered that *I* could do it on my Schwinn Sting-Ray bicycle.

It was on this trip and many others that followed where I learned the real secret that makes traveling America by car such a rich experience. It's the people. I've driven well over one million miles on various roads in this country and have collected a good number of stories, anecdotes, and sometimes wild experiences. But the tales are never about concrete and asphalt. They are about the characters and fellow travelers who live and roam these great ribbons of pavement.

My coconspirator on this book, Michael Wallis, understands this more than any other modern American writer. He completed the seminal volume on Route 66 in the late 1980s just about the time I'd started regularly driving the Lincoln Highway. As cross-county roads go, the Lincoln has the edge in some ways over Route 66 because it's older and is a true coast-to-coast highway. But Route 66 is an embedded part of our culture, resulting from the 1960s television show and a hit song.

So, it was only fitting that two true geniuses, editor Robert Weil and literary agent Jim Fitzgerald, hatched the idea to put Michael and I on the road together for this project. It is my hope that you will use this guide like a jar of fireflies to illuminate your way across this great country while you experience the fascinating people and places on America's "Father Road."

I'd like to offer a deep-felt thanks to some of the folks that made this book possible: Mitch Dakelman and the late Doug Pappas in New Jersey; Olga Herbert, Carol Duppstadt, Carleen and Ronald Farabaugh, and Bernie and Ester Queneau in Pennsylvania; Bob Lichty, Rosemary Rubin, Frank C. Dawson, and Belinda Dawson Dunlap in Ohio; Bob Owens, Kathy Dirks, Joel Franken, Luis Navar, Nathan Mahrt, and Ron Preston in Iowa; Bob Stubblefield, Klint Schlake, and Riley and Patsy Sermeno in Nebraska; Lyn Asp in Franklin Grove and the kind folks at the Ronald Reagan Boyhood Home in Dixon, Illinois. Also hats off to Dr. Peter Kesling and John and Billie Pappas in La Porte, Indiana; Colleen Neilson in Nevada; and Jan Haag, Richard Schmidt, and Phil Sexton in California.

In Washington, DC, at the Library of Congress, much thanks goes to Constance Carter, Jennifer Harbster, and Chris Baer. And a special thank-you to the "Angel of the Lincoln Highway," Craig Harmon. Also to Joe Elbert, my editor at the *Washington Post*, big-time thanks for being so flexible with my schedule.

On a personal note, my intense respect goes out to Robert Weil, Tom Mayer, and Jim Fitzgerald, whose patience was much needed and appreciated. To my daughters, Sophia and Valerie and Dale Maharidge, three people who logged tens of thousands of miles with me and never once complained about my driving or said, "Are we there, yet?"

And to Michael Wallis and Anne Garrett— I'll always have room in my car to take a road trip with you guys. Your wonderful companionship made me never want to travel alone again.

—MICHAEL S. WILLIAMSON

Lincoln Highway Resources

Lincoln Highway Association (LHA), 136 Elm Street, P.O. Box 308, Franklin Grove, IL 61031-0308, tel. 815-456-3030; www.lincolnhighwayassoc.org. *Note:* There are links to all state Lincoln Highway chapters at this site.

Lincoln Highway Association Collection, University of Michigan, Special Collections, 7th floor, Harlan Hatcher Graduate Library, Ann Arbor, MI 48109, tel. 734-764-9377; www.lib.umich.edu/spec-coll

Lincoln Highway Heritage Corridor (LHHC), P.O. Box 582, Ligonier, PA 15658, tel. 724-238-9030; www.lhhc.org

Ohio Lincoln Highway Historic Byway, P.O. Box 20509, Canton, OH 44701, fax 330-456-8310; www.historicbyway.com

Lincoln Highway Trading Post, P.O. Box 6088, Canton, OH 44706, tel. 800-454-8319; www.LHTP.com

Dwight D. Eisenhower Presidential Library and Museum, 200 Southeast Fourth Street, Abilene, KS 67410, tel. 785-263-6700; www.eisenhower.archives.gov

Society for Commercial Archeology, P.O. Box 45828, Madison, WI 53744-5828; www.sca-roadside.org

National Register of Historic Places, National Park Service, 1201 Eye Street NW, 8th floor (MS2280), Washington, DC 20005, tel. 202-354-2213; www.cr.nps.gov/nr/

Northern Indiana Center for History, 808 W. Washington Street, South Bend, IN 46601, tel. 574-235-9664; www.centerforhistory.org

PERIODICALS AND BOOKS

American Road magazine, P.O. Box 46519, Mt. Clemens, MI 48046, tel. 877-285-5434; www.americanroadmagazine .com

Family Motor Coach Association magazine, Family Motor Coach Association, Inc., 8291 Clough Pike, Cincinnati, OH 45244; www.fmca.com

Lincoln Highway Special Resource Study, National Park Service, Midwest Regional Office, 1709 Jackson Street, Omaha, NE 68102, tel. 402-661-1846; www.nps.gov/ mwro/LincolnHighway

Lincoln Highway Journal, Lincoln Highway Heritage Corridor, 114 S. Market Street, P.O. Box 582, Ligonier, PA 15658, tel. 724-238-9310; www.lhhc.org

A.L.A. Automobile Green Book, Road Reference and Tourists' Guide: Eastern States Edition. Boston: Scarborough Motor Guide Company, 1933.

Anderson, Warren H. *Vanishing Roadside America*. Tucson: University of Arizona Press, 1981.

Ansaldi, Richard. *Gas, Food and Lodging: A Postcard Odyssey Through the Great American Roadside*. New York: Congdon & Weed, 1984.

Belasco, Warren James. *Americans on the Road: From the Autocamp to Motel, 1910–1945*. Boston: MIT Press, 1979.

Berger, Kevin, and Todd Berger. *Where the Road and the Sky Collide*. New York: Henry Holt and Company, 1993.

Bianco, Anthony. *Ghosts of 42nd Street*. New York: William Morrow, 2004.

Bryson, Bill. *The Lost Continent: Travels in Small-Town America*. New York: Viking, 2003.

Buettner, Michael Gene. *A History and Road Guide of the Lincoln Highway in Ohio*, 5th ed. Lima, OH: privately printed, 1999.

Butko, Brian. *Greetings from the Lincoln Highway: America's First Coast-to-Coast Road*. Mechanicsburg, PA: Stackpole Books, 2005.

_____. *The Lincoln Highway: Pennsylvania Traveler's Guide*. Mechanicsburg, PA: Stackpole Books, 1996 (2nd ed., 2002).

Butler, John L. *First Highways of America: American Roads and Highways from 1900–1925*. Iola, WI: Krause Publications, 1994.

The Complete Official Road Guide of the Lincoln Highway. Detroit: Lincoln Highway Association, 1915.

Cromie, Alice. *A Tour Guide to the Old West*. Nashville, TN: Rutledge Hill Press, 1990.

Davidson, Janet F., and Michael S. Sweeney. *On The Move: Transportation and the American Story*. Companion book to exhibit at Smithsonian's National Museum of American History. Washington, DC: National Geographic Society, Book Division, 2003.

Davies, Pete. *American Road: The Story of an Epic Transcontinental Journey at the Dawn of the Motor Age*. New York: Henry Holt and Company, 2002.

Duncan, Dayton, and Ken Burns. *Horatio's Drive: America's First Road Trip*. New York: Alfred A. Knopf, 2003.

Flagg, James Montgomery. *Boulevards All the Way—Maybe!* New York: George H. Doran Company, 1925.

Franzwa, Gregory M. *Iowa*, Vol. 1 of *The Lincoln Highway*. Tucson, AZ: Patrice Press, 1995.

_____. *Nebraska*, Vol. 2 of *The Lincoln Highway*. Tucson, AZ: Patrice Press, 1996.

_____. *Wyoming*, Vol. 3 of *The Lincoln Highway*. Tucson, AZ: Patrice Press, 1999.

Franzwa, Gregory M., and Jesse G. Petersen. *Utah*, Vol.

4 of *The Lincoln Highway*. Tucson, AZ: Patrice Press, 2003.

_____. *Nevada*, Vol. 5 of *The Lincoln Highway*. Tucson, AZ: Patrice Press, 2004.

Gladding, Effie. *Across the Continent by the Lincoln Highway*. New York: Brentano's, 1915.

Gray, Pamela Lee. *Ohio Valley Pottery Towns*. Images of America Series. Chicago: Arcadia Publishing, 2002.

Hokanson, Drake. *The Lincoln Highway: Main Street across America*. Iowa City: University of Iowa Press, 1988.

Hurley, Andrew. *Diners, Bowling Alleys, and Trailer Parks: Chasing the American Dream in the Postwar Consumer Culture*. New York: Basic Books, 2001.

Jakle, John A., and Keith A. Sculle. *The Gas Station in America*. Baltimore: The Johns Hopkins University Press, 1994.

Kaszynski, William. *The American Highway: The History and Culture of Roads in the United States*. Jefferson, NC: McFarland & Company, Inc., 2000.

Lane, David R. (uncredited writer), and Gael S. Hoag. (biography section). *The Lincoln Highway: The Story of a*

Crusade That Made Transportation History. New York: Dodd, Mead & Company, 1935.

Lee, Nancy, ed. *The Century in Times Square*. New York: Bishop Books, Inc. 1999.

Lewis, Tom. *Divided Highways: Building the Interstate Highways, Transforming American Life*. New York: Penguin Books, 1999.

Lichty, Bob, and Rosemary Rubin, eds. *The Lincoln Highway Anniversary Cross Country Tour Guidebook*. Canton, OH: privately printed, 2003.

Liebs, Chester. *Main Street to Miracle Mile: American Roadside Architecture*. Boston: Little Brown and Company, 1985.

Maharidge, Dale, and Michael Williamson. *Denison, Iowa: Searching for the Soul of America Through the Secrets of a Midwest Town*. New York: Free Press, 2005.

Margolies, John. *The End of the Road: Vanishing Highway Architecture in America*. New York: Penguin Books, 1981.

McNeese, Tim. *From Trails to Turnpikes: Americans on the Move*. New York: Crestwood House, 1993.

Model, Eric. *Beyond the Interstate: Discovering the Hidden America*. New York: John Wiley & Sons, Inc., 1989.

Norfleet, Barbara. *When We Liked Ike: Looking for Postwar America*. New York: W. W. Norton & Company, 2001.

Pappas, Doug. *The Lincoln Highway in New York/New Jersey*. Hartsdale, NY: Northeast Chapter, Lincoln Highway Association, 1997.

Patton, Phil. *Open Road: A Celebration of the American Highway*. New York: Simon & Schuster, 1986.

Polster, Bernd, and Phil Patton. *Highway: America's Endless Dream*. New York: Stewart, Tabori & Chang, 1997.

Post, Emily. *By Motor to the Golden Gate*. New York: D. Appleton and Company, 1916.

Queneau, Bernard. *Personal Diaries from the Summer of 1928*. Reprinted from family scrapbook.

Rae, John B. *The American Automobile: A Brief History*. Chicago: University of Chicago Press, 1965.

Ramsey, Alice Huyler. *Veil, Duster, and Tire Iron*. Pasadena, CA: Castle Press, 1961.

San Francisco: The Exposition City 1915. Los Angeles: H. H. Tammen Company, 1913.

Shaffer, Marguerite S. *See America First: Tourism*

and National Identity, 1880–1940. Washington, DC: Smithsonian Institution Press, 2001.

Stewart, George Rippey. *U.S. 40: Cross Section of the United States of America*. Boston: Houghton Mifflin Company, 1953.

Thornburg, Billie Snyder. *City and Prairie Bones*. North Platte, NE: The Old 101 Press Publishing Company, 2005.

Traub, James. *The Devil's Playground: A Century of Pleasure and Profit in Times Square*. New York: Random House, 2004.

Trego, F. H. *Hints to Transcontinental Tourists Traveling on the Lincoln Highway*. Detroit: Lincoln Highway Association, 1914.

Trogdon, Wendell. *U.S. 50: The Forgotten Highway*. Mooresville, IN: Backroads Press, 1999.

Walker, Alton P. *Six in a Flivver*. Pittsburgh: Dorrance Publishing Company, 2002.

Welsch, Roger L. *A Treasury of Nebraska Pioneer Folklore*. Lincoln: University of Nebraska Press, 1984.

Wilkins, Mike, Ken Smith, and Doug Kirby. *The New*
Roadside America: The Modern Traveler's Guide to the Wild and Wonderful World of America's Tourist Attractions. New York: Simon & Schuster, 1992.

OTHER WEB SITES

The American Roadside, the latest American roadside news: www.theamericanroadside.com

Diner City, online guide to classic diners and the American roadside: www.dinercity.com

Diner For Sale Dot Com, reliable source of information regarding the purchase and sale of these roadside gems: www.dinerforsale.com

Drive-in Movie.com, the focal point for drive-ins on the Internet: www.driveinmovie.com

Eccentric America, a guide to all that's weird and wacky in the USA: www.eccentricamerica.com

Federal Highway Administration: www.historicroads.org

Federal Highway Administration: www.ruralheritage.org

The Lincoln Highway: An Introduction to America's First Transcontinental Road for the Automobile: www.ugcs.caltech.edu/~jlin/lincoln

Motel Americana, exploring classic roadside architecture since 1995: www.sjsu.edu/faculty/woods/motel

Patrice Press: www.patricepress.com

PreservationDirectory.com, resource for historic preservation, building restoration, and cultural resource management in the United States and Canada: www.preservationdirectory.com

Primarily Petroliana, online community of gas-station antiques collectors: www.oldgas.com

Roadfood.com, guide to the most memorable local eateries along the highways and back roads of America: www.roadfood.com

Roadside, news and views from the back roads and main streets of America: www.roadsideonline.com

RoadsideAmericana.com, a guide to offbeat tourist attractions: www.roadsideamerica.com

Rocky Mountain roads: www.rockymountainroads.com

Two-Lane Roads, links to information on historic roadways, roadside nostalgia, highway preservation, and the RV lifestyle: www.two-lane.com

Credits

All photographs © Michael S. Williamson except those listed below.

iv; 2, above and below; 3; 4; 5 above and left; 7; 8; 9; 10; 11; 12 above, below left, below right; 34 above left and right; 37 below; 46; 66 right and left; 68 above and below; 78 below; 80 above; 82 above; 83 above and below; 84; 96 above; 117; 118 above right; 120 above; 143 right; 144 above; 147; 153 above; 155 left; 159; 163 below, 169; 171 below left and below right; 180 below; 181 below; 189; 203; 204; 209 left; 215 below; 220 left; 231; 235 above; 255 below; 262 below; 272 left; 276.

viii; ix; 6; 18; 38; 74; 88; 104; 122; 140; 166; 194; 224; 248; 266.

1, Lincoln Highway National Museum and Archives; 22, courtesy of Loew's Theatre Corporation; 57 right, courtesy of Bill Griffith © 2001; 62, courtesy of Pennsylvania Lincoln Highway Heritage Corridor; 93 below, courtesy of Sturgis House; 113, Williamson Collection / courtesy of Bernie Heisey; 132, courtesy of Craig Harmon; 137, courtesy of the Jelly Belly Candy Company; 157, courtesy of R. Crumb; 173, courtesy of Ritenour Family; 197, Special Collections Library, University of Michigan; 232 far right, Special Collections Library, University of Michigan; 237, courtesy of Kennecott Utah Copper Corporation; 241 right, Special Collections Library, Michigan; 268, courtesy of Library of Congress; 273 above, courtesy of Placer County Historical Society; 292, Anne Reid Garrett © 2007.

About the Authors

A best-selling author and award-winning reporter, MICHAEL WALLIS is a historian and biographer of the American West who has gained national prominence for a body of work that began in 1988 with his biography of Frank Phillips, entitled *Oil Man*. His other thirteen books include *Route 66: The Mother Road*, credited with sparking the resurgence of interest in the highway; *The Real Wild West: The 101 Ranch and the Creation of the American West; Mankiller: A Chief and Her People; Billy the Kid: The Endless Ride;* and *Pretty Boy: The Life and Times of Charles Arthur Floyd*. His work has appeared in hundreds of national and international magazines and newspapers, including *Time, Life, People, Smithsonian, The New Yorker,* and the *New York Times*. A charismatic speaker who has lectured extensively throughout the United States, Wallis was featured as the voice of the Sheriff in *Cars*, an animated feature film from Pixar Studios.

MICHAEL S. WILLIAMSON, a staff photographer for the *Washington Post*, has won two Pulitzer Prizes, including one for his book *And Their Children After Them: The Legacy of* Let Us Now Praise Famous Men. His work has appeared in *Life, Newsweek, Sports Illustrated, Time*, and other major publications and has won numerous accolades, including the World Press Photo and Nikon World Understanding Through Photography awards. In 1995, the National Press Photographers Association named him Newspaper Photographer of the Year. He has traveled widely on assignment, including trips to Central America, the Philippines, and across the United States.

This book is set in Filosofia, with display
in Trade Gothic and Grand Canyon.

Book design and composition by
Judith Stagnitto Abbate, Abbate Design.